# BLOODY OLD
# BRITAIN

# BLOODY OLD BRITAIN

## O. G. S. CRAWFORD
AND THE
ARCHAEOLOGY
OF MODERN LIFE

## KITTY HAUSER

**Granta Books**
London

Granta Publications, 12 Addison Avenue, London W11 4QR

First published in Great Britain by Granta Books 2008

Copyright © Kitty Hauser, 2008

A CIP catalogue record for this book
is available from the British Library.

1 3 5 7 9 10 8 6 4 2

ISBN 978 1 86207 873 4

Typeset by M Rules
Printed and bound in Great Britain by
Cromwell Press, Trowbridge, Wiltshire

*For Peter, with love*

# CONTENTS

# PREFACE

There were forty-nine box files in the basement of Oxford's Institute of Archaeology, each full of photographs mounted on card. Looking at these images gave me a strange sense of vertigo. It was as if I were looking at the world they depicted from a great and inhuman distance. I had come to see if there were any aerial photographs among the archive amassed by O. G. S. Crawford, field archaeologist and pioneer of aerial archaeology in Britain in the 1920s. But I had not expected this. I did not expect to find image after image of inscriptions, ancient and modern; of signs in the street, graffiti and adverts; of hieroglyphics and swastikas; of wayside pulpits, housing estates, burial mounds, standing stones, trenches, doorways and shop fronts. I did not expect to see the box shown to me by Bob Wilkins, the Institute's long-serving photographer and unofficial guardian of the archive, a box which contained something described as 'Marx-sites' – photographs, taken in the 1930s, of buildings (or the sites of buildings) where Karl Marx had lived, worked or gone drinking when he was in London in the nineteenth century. There was a box with little but photographs of horse-drawn carts taken all around the world, from Cyprus to Moscow, and another one full of images of advertisement hoardings in Southampton. There were boxes, too, of photographs of archaeological sites and finds from all around the world. The source of the vertigo had something to do with the fact that the ancient sites seemed no more distant than the modern ones. It was as if all of human history were equidistant from the photographer, as though all of it were within his reach. With its typologies and its defamiliarizing jolts, the whole archive looked like a conceptual artwork, but it was not; it gave the impression of a deadly serious but obscure purpose.

Individually the photographs – most but not all of which were taken by Crawford himself – were deadpan, clear, beautiful in many cases. There was a loneliness about them. And there was a sense of urgency, too, as if it were imperative that a record be kept of a barn door in Cumberland with four tiny forepaws nailed onto it, or of the stone cairns left by a roadside on the island of Harris, marking the places where coffins rested on their way to interment, or of the graffiti scratched into the wall of the Wool House in Southampton by French prisoners of war. This was clearly a man whose eye was trained to seek out traces: traces of customs, sites of use and settlement, marks left behind. The photographs were a miscellany; but it was a miscellany that seemed to add up to something. A particular sensibility and faith underwrote all of them, invisibly structuring the archive as a whole; the consistency was both conceptual and visual. A sequence of photographs taken in Berlin in 1934 showed Communist graffiti that had been painted over; after these were postcards of Hitler giving a speech, and amidst them, an interloper: an aerial photograph of Worthy Down near Winchester, in which the faint traces of an ancient settlement in the Hampshire fields are still visible after centuries of farming. The juxtaposition was suggestive. The world, it seemed, was irrevocably scarred by history, and the truth about the past would surely emerge, just as the ancient sites on Worthy Down revealed themselves to an aerial observer. Crawford was keeping the record; he was gathering in. But for what?

The archive had itself been scarred by history. Once upon a time these mounted photographs were bound together in albums.

Obliterated pre-Hitler slogan, "Wählt Mälmann"
"Vote for Mälmann"

# HANTS

Worthy Down, near Winchester

Ph. George Allen.

## ADOLF HITLER

Jahrtausende vergehen, so wird man nie von Helde[n]
[sp]r[e]fen, ohne des deutschen Heeres des Weltkrie[ges]
gedenken.

But at some point since they ended up in Oxford the albums were disassembled, their covers discarded, and their contents – a pile, now, of loose folios – hurriedly replaced in the box files in which they are still to be found. That, presumably, was how Worthy Down came to be among the Berlin photographs. But despite (or perhaps because of) this disarray, a powerful and visionary sense of world history emerged from the archive's contents.

Outside, the traffic rumbled slowly past the Institute windows. All of the photographs seemed aerial; they all seemed confident that the world was knowable in its entirety to the camera-wielding observer. I was thinking about the fantasy of total historical knowledge – the surveying eye in the sky – that had something in common with ideas of the Last Day, the day in which that which was covered will be revealed, that which was hidden shall be known. And I was trying to remember something I had heard, by contrast, about a certain kind of Japanese garden in which a number of rocks are deliberately arranged in such a way that they can never all be seen at once by a stationary observer. Such a garden is the embodiment of the conviction that the world always exceeds our capacity – unavoidably human – to observe or understand it.

From what standpoint would the images in Crawford's archive make sense? The archive was anamorphic, like the distended images you get in the Victorian children's game which have to be viewed in a curved mirror in order to see them properly. I had to find the mirror in which the archive and its contents made sense. The mirror was the man. I tried to find him.

As it turned out, this was not straightforward. Crawford had written an autobiography, very descriptive of his childhood and his archaeological career, but curiously reticent about both his personal and his political life; it shed little light on the photographs. He had left his papers to the Bodleian Library, and there were plenty of them from every part of his life except from the key decades of the 1920s and 30s – these, it seemed, had largely been destroyed in the Blitz. He had left instructions for a number of parcels of papers to remain unopened until the year 2000, and this seemed promising. But when they were opened, there was little among them apart from private letters, mainly from before the First World War, and a poem, penned by Crawford, and addressed to me, the reader of 2000. It begins, appropriately enough, with an archaeological metaphor:

> If you are digging up the past, my friend
> > And hunting for a clue you fondly think
> May throw some light upon your victim's life –
> > How often did he fornicate, or overdrink? –
> Or hoping that those broken arcs of ink
> > May be combined into some specious round
> of scandalous import – that down these lines
> > Some hint of what you seek may yet be found;
> Eschew that search within the paper mound . . .
>
> Leave such imaginings alone, and look
> > rather at what he wrote in many a book.

It was a warning: he wanted his published works, his archaeo-logical output – which was considerable – to be his legacy. But I was not looking for scandal. I was looking for the eye that had taken the photographs, the vision behind the archive. I wanted to know what faith had made the vision possible, and what had happened to that faith.

In fact there *were* clues, scattered among Crawford's surviving papers, and in his published – and unpublished – works. There were clues, too, among the photographs. What emerged was that there had indeed been a faith: a faith in evidence, a faith in consequences, a faith that history had a pattern, and a faith in our ability as camera-wielding human observers to make that pattern out. The past was legible and the future was bright, an optimism both heroic and foolish. It was a cosmology as alien to us, almost, as that of the sixteenth-century miller whose world view was reconstructed by the historian Carlo Ginzburg in his book *The Cheese and the Worms*. But after the faith came a fall. It turned out that Crawford's world view – as represented in the photographic archive – was ruined already, well before his albums were taken to pieces and disordered.

Would Crawford recognize himself in these pages? I do not know if I have found him. Nothing I have written is, as far as I know, not true. But this is no assessment of Crawford's role in the history of archaeology, neither is it a full account – if such a thing were possible – of the man's life in all of its parts. The fact is that the story told here is an allegory as much as a biography. It is an allegory of vision and blindness, of faith and its loss.

Facts are but the Play-things of Lawyers, – Tops and Hoops, forever a-spin . . . Alas, the Historian may indulge no such idle Rotating. History is not Chronology, for that is left to Lawyers, – nor is it Remembrance, for Remembrance belongs to the People. History can as little pretend to the Veracity of the one, as claim the Power of the other, – her Practitioners, to survive, must soon learn the arts of the quidnunc, spy, and Taproom Wit, – that there may ever continue more than one life-line back into a Past we risk, each day, losing our forebears in forever, – not a Chain of single Links, for one broken Link could lose us All, – rather, a great disorderly Tangle of Lines, long and short, weak and strong, vanishing into the Mnemonick Deep, with only their Destination in common.

Thomas Pynchon, *Mason & Dixon*

We do not see things as they are, we see them as we are.

Anaïs Nin

# CHAPTER I

Osbert Guy Stanhope Crawford grew up in a house in East Woodhay, near Newbury in Hampshire. From the garden the chalk uplands of the North Hampshire Downs loomed up like a 'great green wall', as it seemed to the child, frowning in some places high above the cornfields and meadows, and smiling in others. The green wall held secrets: submerged flint-strewn terraces, old ways, and earthen mounds, to which nobody paid much attention.

The Grove, as it was called, was a household of women. When his mother died in Bombay a few days after giving birth, the baby Osbert had been sent to England on a P&O liner and delivered into the care of Dorah and Gertrude, two of his father's five unmarried sisters, who were living then in London. It was 1886. His father stayed in India, where he was a High Court judge. 'Dadda is the Queen's servant,' he wrote later to his infant son, 'and has to obey orders.' The boy used to have nightmares about tigers. He'd seen them in Regent's Park Zoo, thought he heard their roar echoing along the Marylebone Road, and he was sure they prowled the coast of Bombay where his father remained until he died, in 1894.

The sisters who brought up the judge's son and comforted him in his night terrors were possessed by a religious fervour which, wrote Crawford many years later, set them quite apart from the modern world. Two other sisters, Eleanor and Edith, were nuns. Eleanor was a Sister Superior in Poona. Edith lived at Spelthorne St Mary, an institution near Feltham in Middlesex, helping recovering drunkards and drug addicts, where she spent her days in prayer, writing devotional poetry and saving the souls of those in her care.

Religion infused Crawford's childhood home, and it ran through the family like a dominant gene. Crawford's father and his sisters had been brought up in the Rectory at Woodmansterne in Surrey; their father was a clergyman of Fife ancestry. The religiosity of these siblings went deep, and took a variety of forms: the ecstasy of Sister Edith, the Low Church devotion of Dorah, the High Church introspection of Gertrude, the philanthropic impulse common to all of the sisters. Out in Bombay their brother produced a steady stream of semi-scholarly disquisitions, diagrams of the evolution of Christianity, and letters to the papers on issues of theological doctrine. The forms of observance may have differed between these siblings. Yet none of them doubted that the world in which they dwelt was just the waiting room for a hereafter whose superior reality must be asserted at every turn, and for which we should all prepare. Historical events and the world of nature were ciphers of a greater truth which in time would be revealed in its entirety to the faithful. In this environment the young Osbert learned to read and write. 'Hull is the mouth of the Humber,' he wrote with unsteady hand. 'Immortality, Immortality, Immortality. London, the metropolis of the world. No untruth escapes punishment.' His aunts read him Cardinal Newman's long visionary poem 'The Dream of Gerontius', and he thrilled to the idea of eternity it summoned up, where a thousand years in the eyes of the Lord are 'but as yesterday: and as a watch of the night which is come and gone'.

After Crawford's father died, his sisters moved, along with their small charge, to East Woodhay. Crawford later described it as 'a land of small grass fields and dairy farms, interspersed with the residences of people with independent means'. He was sent to a prep school in Reading. Here, where the boys wore badges printed with the faces of generals at the Transvaal Front of the Boer War, history was taught as a series of episodes each encoding a moral lesson. Crawford gazed at scenes of African battles in the pages of *The Daily Graphic* and followed, as it came out, H. G. Wells's serial *The War of the Worlds* in pictures. 'He spends a good deal of his time alone,' the headmaster told his aunts. 'I wish I could send him back with unbitten nails.' In 1900 he was sent to board at Marlborough College, which was about 15 miles away from his home, near enough for him to cycle home on Saturday afternoons in summer.

Crawford later described Marlborough as a 'detestable house of torture', with its savage bullying and forced games. Team sports and muscular athleticism took a high priority at this public school in the early twentieth century, and continued to do so until after the First World War, when its pupils included Louis MacNeice, Anthony Blunt and John Betjeman, who didn't enjoy Marlborough much more than Crawford did. Teaching was an intensive regime of Latin, Greek and Ancient History, supplemented by Maths and French. Between lessons Crawford read historical novels, poetry, and the works of Ruskin on aesthetics and sociology, writing enthusiastically and earnestly to his aunt Edith about his passions for architecture and literature. It was at about this time that he started to take photographs; a school trip to Rome in 1904 was an 'almost mystic experience' which Crawford recorded with a camera. 'I dream about Cathedrals now,' he told his aunt, 'sometimes St Alban's (I was, I think, photographing the shrine there by gas-light . . .), sometimes Westminster, and often Canterbury.' The boy had evidently taken Ruskin's *Stones of Venice* to heart; but in an atmosphere which even the headmaster worried was one of 'a sort of hearty, self-satisfied Philistinism', he knew better than to confide his new passions to his fellow pupils. 'There is no one here,' he told Edith, 'to whom I can say so much or so freely.'

On wet and windy days when team sports were cancelled, the boys were sent on long runs over the downs around Marlborough, something remembered later by the First World War poet Charles Sorley in 'The Song of the Ungirt Runners'. Running in this poem is a communion with elemental nature, and a blow for freedom away from the regimentation of team sports: 'We run because we like it,' he wrote, 'through the broad bright land.' Crawford was sent on such runs (known at Marlborough as 'sweats') because he often got 'overlooked or forgotten' when team lists were drawn up. Like Sorley, he enjoyed these runs across the downs, and along the way he would stop to look at church architecture. The running was not intended to be pleasurable (sometimes it was used as a punishment), but it was for both boys a release from the claustrophobic conformity and petty rituals of institutional life. And it gave a particular kind of physical knowledge of the surrounding land, a knowledge – through the feet as well as the eyes – of pathways, contours, distance, junctions and alignments, the opening up of views.

The landscape that Sorley and Crawford ran through was sculptural and ancient. Just north of Marlborough is the Ridgeway, the raised chalk road used for thousands of years to cross right across England from the coast of Dorset to the Wash in Norfolk. All along the Ridgeway there are remnants of prehistoric life: grassy mounds that were burial chambers, uplands scarred with hill forts and encampments, the Uffington horse carved white out of the chalky ground. Not far to the west of the school, a few miles along the old road to Bath, a constellation of prehistoric remains have clustered around the river Kennet for more than 4000 years. The stone circles and avenues of Avebury, the conical mound of Silbury Hill and the chambered tomb at West Kennet had already been there for at least 2500 years when the Romans came to Britain and built their roads across the

Marlborough Downs. They were there when the Romans left; and they remain there as the world has gathered speed around them, restored, protected and labelled, the enigmatic objects of much discussion and the subjects of millions of photographs.

In 1900, when Crawford was at Marlborough, they were not yet the focus of quite so much public attention. Before motor transport it was quite an undertaking to get to these sites by coach, on horseback, or on a bicycle. With the building of the railway in the mid-nineteenth century, the old coaching road from London to Bath that went past Marlborough had become almost deserted, as cross-country travellers abandoned coaches for the trains that ran through Swindon to the north, or through the Vale of Pewsey to the south; and before the coming of the motor car, the downland area around Marlborough felt remote. Antiquarian enthusiasts and local archaeological societies took a keen interest in the mounds, barrows and standing stones that littered this ancient landscape between the railway lines, but they were not yet the tourist attractions that they later became. Undifferentiated, in a sense, from the rest of the countryside, what's more most of these sites and monuments were barely protected by law. Landowners could, if they wished, remove or plough over them; and in an untold number of cases, they surely did. Many ancient sites and monuments – including Avebury – had by this time fallen into a state of ruin; others had been forgotten about or buried under thick layers of turf. The more prominent remains of prehistoric monuments and pathways were, however, familiar enough to locals and to those at the school; they punctuated the landscape and served in their ancient role of landmarks and vantage points for passers-by or schoolboys out on a 'sweat'.

The school's Natural History Society had an Archaeological section, organized by Crawford's house master, F. B. Malim. Malim believed in athleticism and the invigorating benefits of outdoor pursuits; and so instead of visiting museums or arranging lectures, members of the school Archaeological Society went on trips to the West Kennet Long Barrow, Avebury and Stonehenge, on horseback or bicycle. If they went in the evening, they were guided by moonlight falling on the stones; sometimes they lost their way. 'It was a country to be enjoyed on foot or in the saddle,' wrote Malim. 'Every way there was firm, close turf and the open sky and the wind that blows over the Downs.' It was these trips, Crawford wrote many years later in his autobiography, that first got him interested in field archaeology. Malim had been much impressed by a book by Arthur and George Hubbard called *Neolithic Dew-ponds and Cattle Ways*. According to the Hubbard brothers, the circular hollows which dot the uplands of the Sussex, Marlborough and Wiltshire downs were prehistoric man-made ponds designed to collect dew, providing water even on dry days. Unlike most antiquarian books *Neolithic Dew-ponds* did not depend on other written sources or previous theories; there was a rugged but gentlemanly kind of amateurism about it, based on experience in the landscape, on physical evidence and deduction. The rather primitive photographs in the book showed two stiff-postured Edwardian gentlemen in hats (the authors, presumably) 'in the field', standing (for scale) beside embankments, hollows and Neolithic roadways, for all the world as if they were the first men on the moon. Here was a scholarly activity that was very much in tune with Malim's outdoor ethos, and he encouraged his young charges to be like the Hubbards and go out and explore the world on their doorstep, scattered as it was with the traces of pre-historic man.

Crawford didn't need much encouraging. Not only did it get him out of school for a legitimate reason, it also offered an alternative model of knowledge to that offered by schoolwork, with its learning by rote and its inculcation of 'moral values'. Fieldwork meant freedom. He bought a schoolboy's 1-inch Ordnance Survey Map of the Marlborough district, which went as far east as his home in East Woodhay. Gothic letters marked

antiquities, and he set out to see them, on foot or by bicycle. He visited the Iron Age hill fort at Chisbury with its views and the half-ruined medieval flint chapel perched inside the ancient earthworks. Back home at The Grove in school holidays he looked differently at that 'great green wall' that loomed above the garden, the horizon of the village. It was marked on his map 'in queer old-fashioned letters' with the mysterious words 'tumuli' and 'camp' at Inkpen, and with 'hill fort' on Walbury Hill, the highest point for miles around, an Iron Age stronghold and – much later – the hill from which radio masts broadcast news from the races at Newbury. Later he went back to the mounds marked 'tumuli' and dug into them, finding urns and a single bronze razor buried deep beneath the grass and earth.

Crawford left school in 1905 and pleased his aunts by going to Keble College, one of Oxford University's newest foundations, brick-built, and very High Church. He embarked on the next lap of the well-worn Establishment path of a classical education with an idea to enter the Civil Service. He did not, however, distinguish himself academically. After just managing a third-class pass in his second-year exams he began to look around for a way of getting closer to British prehistory. In those days, though, it barely existed as a field, let alone a degree subject. Despite the great volumes of archaeological and anthropological spoils that had accumulated in Oxford's museums in the course of the long nineteenth century, neither subject could be studied at degree level there. The first Professor of Archaeology at Oxford was appointed in 1885; he left after a year in which it became apparent that the post was unsalaried. His successor – whose own interest was in Greek sculpture – spent much of his time trying to get Classical Archaeology onto the Classics syllabus, amidst much opposition from scholars whose literary bias would not allow for even this much of an intrusion of knowledge that did not come from books. Archaeology at Oxford at the beginning of the twentieth century remained, as Crawford wrote later, the 'study of classical sculpture and Greek vases'; and even that was annexed to the more respectable study of ancient authors known as 'Greats'. Not until 1991 did it become possible to take a degree at Oxford University in non-Classical archaeology and anthropology.

It was, though, possible to take a certificate or diploma in a number of more practical subjects, such as Geography, Economics and Rural Economy; and from 1907 these courses, supplemented by papers in Classics, could be taken as part of a less well-regarded 'pass' degree, suitable for those social unfortunates who were planning on entering business, agriculture or surveying. Telling his tutor at Keble in 1908 he was taking up Geography was 'like a son telling his father he had decided to marry a barmaid', wrote Crawford in his autobiography. Geography, after all, was an upstart discipline. Oxford's School of Geography, the first in the country, had only been set up in 1899, very much with the practical needs of the Empire in mind. Lectures were aimed at probationers who were going out to join the Civil Service in India, Egypt or the Sudan; the School also provided facilities for colonial civil servants home on furlough. Vast maps plotted the geology, vegetation and physiography of the world's continents. Explorers like Sven Hedin and Ernest Shackleton, fresh from the Antarctic, came to give talks. Students learned surveying, map-reading and cartographic skills, and were sent out into the Oxfordshire countryside to try them out, practising for the wide open spaces of Africa and Asia. 'I immediately felt at home,' wrote Crawford, 'in the new environment of maps and things of this world.'

Crawford did not at this point have imperial ambitions. He wanted, he thought, to be an archaeologist of the British Isles, which was then a gentlemanly pursuit rather than a paid occupation, and there was no obvious course of training for it. He had been encouraged to take up Geography by a man called Harold Peake, who was just such a gentleman in pursuit of prehistoric Britain. Peake was the honorary curator of the Newbury Museum, a man of private means, big ideas and unconventional methods. He was obsessed by the question of the evolution of civilization: the origins of cultivated grain, of metallurgy, mythology, social class; the development over millennia of agriculture, religion, urban life. Peake did not trust books as a guide to those origins or courses of development. He had his own theories, some of them based on what he had seen amongst the native peoples of British Columbia, others wilder. Harold Peake lived in a place called Boxford, just north of Newbury, not far from Crawford's home. When he heard that a young man down from Oxford for the holidays was digging up the 'tumuli' on the scarp above Inkpen, he sent his friend R. Hippisley Cox to drop in. Hippisley Cox was the managing director of Romano's, the Theatreland restaurant on the Strand, and the author – in 1914 – of *The Green Roads of England*. Hippisley Cox shared with Peake a passion for tracing the course of ancient pathways and trade routes across the southern counties of Britain; when he called in on Crawford's amateur excavation he was doing the Berkshire

Ridgeway in a dog cart. Not long afterwards Crawford cycled over to Boxford to lunch with Peake, who told him that if he wanted to do prehistoric archaeology, he'd be better off studying Geology and Geography than bothering with any of the existing books on the subject. Thus it was that not long after returning to Oxford in 1908, Crawford decided to switch from Greats to Geography.

Westbrook House where Harold Peake lived with his wife Charlotte (known as Carlie) became something of a second home to Crawford over the next few years. The Peakes were the very type of the Edwardian Bohemian intelligentsia: comfortably off, they spurned organized religion, wore sandals and went in for vegetarianism, Japanese art, the resuscitation of folk rituals and the re-organization of mass society. They kept 'open house', and their visitors included the young historian Lewis Bernstein (later Lord Namier), Francis and Geoffrey Toye (who both went on to musical careers), Hippisley Cox, the musical folklorist Mary Neal and the suffragette Emmeline Pethick-Lawrence, who, together with Mrs Neal, had run a London club where working-class girls were encouraged to experiment with drama and traditional dance. Every summer Carlie Peake put on a Masque play in woodland near Boxford Common, with music and dancing arranged by her talented house guests. Over time this became part of a bigger Newbury Folk Festival, with Mrs Peake as its president. A sort of pagan cult – only partly a joke – described obscurely as the 'Kataric Circle' bound the Peakes to their more impressionable house guests, including young Crawford. Harold Peake had the idea that churches dedicated to St Catherine had replaced sites where an earlier deity called Llud (known to the Romans as Nodens) was worshipped. Peake came to this conclusion because Llud – the Celtic god of the Severn estuary, associated with healing – shared St Catherine's symbol of a wheel; the idea was reinforced by the high incidence of chapels dedicated to St Catherine that overlook a harbour or have a good view of the sea, since Llud had many of the characteristics of the

sea god Poseidon. Somehow the Peakes and their visitors honoured this pagan connection by performing ceremonies in which
they walked round in circles lighting fires, looking out for
'Kataric portents', and signing off their letters with a wheel
symbol, 'yours in Kata', and so on.

What was it about, all these resurrections and theatrical re-
inventions of pre-Christian or pagan activities in the fastnesses of
pre-war Berkshire, all this folk dancing, symbol-tracing, song-
reviving, old-road-following, origin-seeking? The Peakes and
their friends certainly weren't the only ones doing it in the early
years of the twentieth century. It was evidently a response to
industrialization and rapid urbanization and their effects. Some
say too it was a sort of nationalist navel-gazing accompanying
anxieties over the British Empire. Britain's humiliations in the
Boer War in particular caused middle-class commentators to fret
about the racial stock of the average British soldier. It was feared
that modern city life, with its promiscuous mixing of nations,
classes and races, together with unhealthy working conditions
and degenerate popular entertainment, was producing etiolated
specimens of humanity who could not be relied upon to defend
the Empire. Eugenics was one solution; folk dancing was another.
Re-introducing the songs and the dances of a pre-industrial
culture would re-invigorate the 'race consciousness' of a once-
proud people, and fill their stunted hearts and bodies with joy.
No one believed this more than Mary Neal, a rival of the better-
known folklorist Cecil Sharp, and a regular visitor at the Peakes'.
Her missionary zeal for the 'healing power' of folk culture
brought her into contact with large numbers of working men and
women through her 'Espérance Guild' of morris dancers, and her
work at Stratford-upon-Avon in connection with Frank Benson's
revivalist Shakespeare festivals. In 1910, for example, she organized factory workers from Hull, children from London and
Warwickshire locals to sing and dance as part of the Summer
Folk Festival at Stratford's Memorial Theatre. Cosmopolitanism

was a mistake, according to Neal. 'In art,' she wrote, 'in high politics, in its true and inner life each nation must carve its own
destiny according to its own distinctive individuality and the special gifts with which it has been entrusted.' For England, that
meant folk songs, Shakespeare and country dancing.

Nationalist myths, as Ernest Gellner has pointed out, claim to
protect folk culture while they effectively prepare a people for
mass society – and for war (little more than a decade separated
the Boer War and the First World War). What seems to look
backwards in time might in fact be attempting to mould the
future. Certainly this was true of the Peakes and their circle,
although the future they were hoping for was rather more
utopian than the carnage of 1914–18. All of their tracings, excavations and re-enactments were about trying to get back to a
point in history before it all started to go wrong, before all the
trouble started; before the alienation, degradation and cultural
desiccation of modern industrial life, before the divisions of social
class and religion. Carlie Peake's Masques and Mary Neal's folk
dancing were part of this attempt. Archaeology had a role to play
in it, too, since that sought-after point might well turn out to be
long long ago, before industrialization, before the impositions of
Christianity, and Roman authority, in the uncharted territory of
prehistory which Harold Peake made his speciality. And if this
point could be re-discovered and celebrated, the stream of history
could perhaps be re-diverted into a different sort of future.
Peake's interest in origins was far from academic; the course of
evolution, properly understood, could provide signposts to possible futures, roads not yet taken.

All of this made a big impression on O. G. S. Crawford; he
loved it at Westbrook House, which he visited often in the years
leading up to the First World War. The Peakes' stance against
Christianity was unusual enough, but for Crawford, brought up
in the oppressive shadow of a faith with which he was gradually
becoming disillusioned, it was liberating. With its in-jokes, its

private rites and nicknames (Crawford was 'Mog', Carlie 'the Missus', Harold 'the Boss'), Westbrook House offered a different kind of belonging, an alternative to the religious other-worldliness of his aunts, the collusive rituals of Marlborough, and the prejudice of the Establishment at Oxford. Here, it seemed, neither standard bourgeois morality nor the austerities he was used to applied. It was an environment – unlike his home, school and university – in which few subjects were off-limits; it was convivial; and they had a very good cook. The Peakes had no children, and Mrs Peake was very kind to Crawford, who was clearly quite a serious – if not depressive – young man. She counselled him on the 'blue devils' of melancholy that affected him during these years, and wrote him long breezy letters addressed to 'the Very Blessed and Really Rather Reverend Mog'. Evidently the pagan horseplay at Westbrook House was not enough to shake a natural propensity for piousness. Crawford later described himself in these years as 'priggish'. But if Crawford's religious upbringing had imprinted itself onto his personality, something of the millenarian outlook inherited from his aunts could transmute fairly comfortably into Harold Peake's evolutionism, with its vast scope of historical and prehistorical time, telescoping into a foreseeable future. Preparation for this future was not a matter of humility, faith and good works, but historical and geographical knowledge, with a spade in one hand and the Ordnance Survey in the other.

Westbrook House showed Crawford that another social world could exist within spitting distance of the one he was more used to. At the same time Boxford was the portal to another world – which was really this world, seen differently – where grassed-over tracks were once the busy thoroughfares of Bronze Age traders, where St Paul's Cathedral was the site of the worship of a Celtic god (the clue is in Ludgate), and where the words of old songs, still sung, contained vestiges of ancient and extraordinarily weird belief systems, all much stranger and more real than anything read about in books. Seen through the eyes of Harold Peake, England was an old but unexplored country, littered with clues to its past that no one has bothered to even notice let alone read properly, but which linked up in intriguing ways. You could start by looking in your own back garden; and there was no point in consulting a guidebook for this old country, because (in Peake's opinion) there wasn't one you could rely on. The map had yet to be drawn. At Boxford the ancient past was to be found outside books, outside language; in this sense it was an effective reversal of the prevailing atmosphere of Oxford, where little was trusted that had not been written down. Peake in fact blithely underestimated the contribution of other workers in the field of British prehistory, which was according to him more or less a *tabula rasa*, ready to receive his own eccentric imprint. But Crawford was excited by this apparent lack of textual authority, brought up as he had been to venerate without question the word of the Bible and the works of classical authors. He was also excited by the other kinds of freedom with which he associated archaeological fieldwork: the freedom of the open air he had experienced at Marlborough; the freedom from social convention he witnessed at the Peakes' house; the freedom from sartorial conventions he enjoyed on excavations. The passions of Crawford's life were rooted in a distinctly social and sensual stratum.

What Crawford picked up from Peake was that the best guide to Britain's misty past was not books but the landscape itself. Partly this was a question of those ancient fragments that had been left behind in it, under ground, down wells, on the beds of rivers or shored up in museum collections. If, for example, Bronze Age artefacts of alluvial gold from the Wicklow Hills in Ireland were found in Wiltshire, on the south coast, and in Cherbourg, it suggested a trade route going from Ireland to those areas. If it were possible to plot a map of all such gold fragments dating from the same period, a picture of manufacture, communication, trade and settlement could begin to be built up, fanning out through the British Isles and on to continental Europe. The landscape was a guide in other ways as well. Did geography not affect human activities even now, in the twentieth century? How much more important it must have been in prehistory. The course of rivers and seaways, the disposition of peaks and marshy troughs, the location of natural springs, the type and relative fertility of soil, the rocky and the softer places, the plains where a human animal is vulnerable to attack and the escarpments where he has an advantage; all these things were likely to affect the distribution of prehistoric settlement and trackways. Old roads would surely tend to follow ridgeways, for example, such as those watersheds that meet – as Hippisley Cox's *Green Roads of England* points out – at the sacred site of Avebury. Roman roads, by contrast, displayed less sensitivity to contours and waterways, driving uncannily straight lines across the terrain, wilfully indifferent – on the whole – to geology, marshland, small streams and existing routes and settlements, their courses diverted only for the most insurmountable of obstacles. Roman roads were deliberately made, not formed through use. They were too much of a recent imposition to be of much interest to Peake and Cox; but they, too, left behind distinct imprints and disturbances in the landscape ready to be identified and deciphered.

Crawford and Peake thought prehistory should be approached not through texts (as many archaeologists preferred) nor through fetishized 'finds' (like those collected and admired by antiquarians), but through the spatial logic of *geography*. It made sense to think about the distribution of particular kinds of objects or sites over geographical space, rather than looking at them in isolation. The antiquarian John Abercromby had done something like this in 1904 when he plotted the distribution of prehistoric beakers; Crawford and Peake saw the potential for comparing such so-called 'distribution maps' against a map of geological and physical features. In 1911 Crawford tested the method by mapping the incidence of flat bronze axes and beakers across the British Isles, and found a geographical pattern behind their apparently random distribution. He presented a paper on the subject to the Oxford University Anthropological Society, and published it in *The Geographical Journal*. This was a way of spatializing prehistory, restoring geographical connections and the materiality of the landscape to a subject that was too often reduced to disjointed objects or texts; and it formed the basis of an approach to the subject that would come into its own in the years between the wars.

Crawford wrote up his work on the distribution of axes on a walking tour of Ireland, and later attributed its success to 'fresh air and exercise and the absence of books'. Right from the start of his career he preferred outdoor work. The distinction he gained in his Geography diploma in 1910 was due to a thesis based on intense fieldwork, which paid the kind of attention to landscape propounded by Peake. Sheet 283 of the 1-inch Ordnance Survey Map of England covered an area of just over 200 square miles of the district around Andover, including parts of Hampshire, Wiltshire and Berkshire. Crawford's thesis was a systematic study of the region mapped by this sheet; its geological structure, drainage system and vegetation; the distribution of its population, its communication network, and its industries in the distant past and in the present. In the autumn of 1909 he set out on foot from home, right at the top edge of Sheet 283 and headed south for Andover, walking west from there to Salisbury, beyond the western limit of the map, and to Blandford; back to Salisbury and on to West Dean along the Ridgeway, and through Stockbridge to the railway station at Sutton Scotney, and back to East Woodhay. For about three weeks Crawford traipsed around the countryside, across fields, down gravel pits, through scrubland, up hills and along old trackways and new roads, canals and railway lines. He noted place names that might encode forgotten pasts, and in pubs he probed locals for memories of old habits, beliefs and rites. Just west of where the Great Western Railway from Southampton to Newbury bisected the Roman Road from

Salisbury to Silchester, he found a forty-foot-wide raised causeway in a wood. In upland areas he looked for surface indicators of prehistoric settlements: ridges marking outlines of camps or ancient fields, the silted-up furrows of disused and forgotten trackways. If earthworks were covered by old thorns or turf of 'virgin closeness' they had to have been there for a long time. If the outlines of old fields bore no relationship to parish boundaries or existing arable and woodland you could be sure they were ancient. The 'gnarled thorns' and oaks on Litchfield Down he interpreted as virgin country, survivals from an ancient vegetative order, 'like old houses in the heart of a busy town'. His eyes were peeled for flints, and he found quite a few. In the exposed plateau gravel on the dip slopes at Sydmonton and Walbury, in gravel pits, and in drift deposits on the tops of hills he gathered stones which seemed to have been crudely worked, surely the earliest of tools, whose geological location suggested inhabitation of the region a million or so years earlier, if they were what they seemed to be. He filled his bag with this evidence, these stones, known as eoliths; sent them home by rail when they got too heavy. When he got home, weighed down with still more eoliths, he plotted the course of rivers, railway lines, and the incidence of long and round barrows inside the confines of Sheet 283. He measured the lengths of streams, the area, in square miles, of woodlands and copses. With the help of old documents, including Saxon charters published in the nineteenth century, he marked in the outlines of Anglo-Saxon boundaries, the extent of medieval forests, listed old names for new places. Crawford's study of Sheet 283 was a portrait, a survey and a history of a particular delimited region; an attempt to squeeze as much information out of a map and the area it represented as was possible. It was, he said much later, his first systematic piece of fieldwork, and it taught him 'how to look at a piece of country and to read from it, as from a faint and blurred palimpsest, the record of its prehistory'.

Oxford's Geography professor, A. J. Herbertson, was a keen promoter of this kind of regional work, looking closely at the distinctive configuration of geology, climate and vegetation of particular areas of the world. And he was so pleased with Crawford that he offered him the newly created job of Junior Demonstrator at the Geography School. After a few idyllic weeks in August, excavating on the Wiltshire Downs near Oxenwood with the Peakes, Crawford returned to Oxford. His first task was to move the Geography School from the Old Ashmolean building on Broad Street (now the Museum of the History of Science) across the road to Acland House, the former home of Henry Acland, Victorian physician and friend of Ruskin. The building was panelled with dark wood, much of it carved and inscribed; the panels in the roof of Crawford's new office were decorated with Pre-Raphaelite paintings. The row of houses of which it was part was pulled down in the 1930s to make way for the New Bodleian Library, with its vast basements, built to store the quantities of books that were accumulating at the old site. To excavate these basements, mechanical diggers removed great quantities of gravel laid down by the Thames in Palaeolithic times at the corner of Parks Road and Broad Street. The archaeologists that followed the diggers found fragments of medieval pots, seventeenth-century drinking glasses, the finial of a bird's feeding trough, fossilized sea urchins and three mammoth's teeth.

Crawford knew nothing of these fossils and finials under his feet as he settled in to his new quarters and began his new job. He spent most of his time teaching small groups of students; and he was also involved with the summer schools which attracted hundreds of schoolteachers to Oxford every year. The training of geography teachers might sound dull, but in the early years of the twentieth century it was theorized and practised in an astonishingly visionary way. As a new subject, geography had to be established in schools if it was to take root in universities, and a great deal of effort was put into defining the subject and how,

exactly, it should be taught. The emphasis in these early years was on the education of *vision* in the broadest and most radical way; geography was meant to train you to see. To think geographically was to visualize. The first Reader of Geography in Oxford, Halford Mackinder, called in the pages of *The Geographical Teacher* 'for the cultivation in geography and history of that visualizing power which in rudiment is natural to the child and the savage, but which tends to wither rather than to expand in the presence of the printed page and of the ribbons of landscape seen through the windows of a railway carriage'. Like certain strands of artistic modernism (with which it was more or less contemporary), geography sought to restore the innocent eye, distorted and dulled by the habits of modern life; and it was keen to develop pedagogical tricks of the most practical kind to effect this purity of vision in students.

No one took this further than the sociologist, city planner and sometime geographer Patrick Geddes, whose 'Outlook Tower' in Edinburgh made architectural space into a pedagogical tool.

Geddes's tower, at the top of the Royal Mile, was quite literally about outlook and insight. Its form and content embodied a philosophy of knowledge and how it is to be acquired; and its avowed function was 'to produce trained seers'. The Outlook Tower was a geography lesson in architectural form. Visitors were guided straight up to the top of the tower to a terrace, from which there were panoramic views of the city; on a clear day you could see as far as the snow-tipped hills of the Highlands. Afterwards, visitors were led to a camera obscura; Geddes thought that viewing the same scenery in this miniaturized way would recover the appreciation of beauty that had been dulled by modern life and routine education (it was also said to prepare the visitor for viewing the works of the Impressionists, Whistler and the 'Glasgow School' of painters in the art galleries of Edinburgh). The guide (often Geddes himself, or one of his assistants) would then take the visitor into a darkened room, furnished with just one chair. This cell was a place of 'insight'; it rested the eye and encouraged contemplation. Out on the panoramic terrace again, the visitor would find their observational capacity revivified and extended (with the help of the guide). They would observe the weather, the geology of the Castle rock, the trees, plants and flowers, the 'romantic beauty of the old town'. They would see that every thing exists in relations of time and space; and they would perceive connections and realities beyond appearances. A river would no longer be just a line of water in a scene. It would now be understood like Marlow's Thames in 'Heart of Darkness', as 'a geological consequence', the creator and refresher of towns, the obstacle of armies, the facilitator of industries, the conduit of goods from and to the ends of the earth. Visitors to the Tower would look out from the terrace with the eyes – in turn – of a poet, a historian, a painter, a geologist, a social reformer; and they would realize the unity of all of the arts and sciences, and the centrality of vision to them all. They would now *know* the city they were looking at, and its surroundings. The idea was that they would also *love* it, and thereby become not only better seers, but also better citizens.

As the visitor descended from the top of the Outlook Tower having looked both within and without themselves, they were guided from the top storey, representing 'Edinburgh', down through 'Scotland', 'Europe', 'The Empire', and finally 'The World', each occupying its own floor. The idea of this journey through ever-expanding conceptions of space was to give the visitor a visceral sense of their place in the world; and each floor was full of ingenious devices to bring this about. An episcope forced the visitor to 'visualise the world as if it were suddenly to become transparent beneath one's feet'; there was a 'hollow globe', a 'cosmosphere' and other 'appliances'. Elongated red spots on the wall indicated the direction of major world cities, and the size they would appear, if it were possible to see them. The idea was to 'see' the invisible; those parts of the world 'hidden by the curvature of the earth and sea'. Like the poet Matthew Arnold, Geddes wanted his visitor-citizens to 'see life steadily and see it whole' quite literally; but this was not an end in itself. Having grasped one's place in the world, there was an imperative to act; and as the visitor descended from the top floor of the tower various exhibits and tricks made the connection between sight and action, theory and practice. Allegorical stained-glass windows depicted Geddes's theories of the unity of the arts and the sciences, and the uses to which knowledge ought to be put; a bust of Pandora indicated the source of knowledge in curiosity, and the importance of applied knowledge for the future happiness of mankind, despite its risks; and at one point – lest the visitor be lulled into abstract reverie – the guide would open a door in the east wall of the tower, revealing to visitors, framed like a photograph, a view of Edinburgh's High Street, from the Castle to Holyrood Palace via 'churches, law courts, and slums', presenting 'a concrete summary of the Social fabric of which we form a part'; a social theatre in which we ought as good citizens to *act*.

Geddes was as obsessed as Peake by the question of social evolution, and the relation between human beings and their environment. Unlike Peake, however, Geddes did not want to rewind the historical clock; his goal was to bring about a better society through education, town planning and a number of other initiatives under the banner of 'Civics'. For Geddes what potentially lay at the end of the rainbow of human history was *Eutopia*, the good place, which unlike Thomas More's Utopia is not nowhere but here, this place, improved and perfected according to its particular character, history and needs. Eutopia was the next stage in the world's evolution, if we played our cards right, the 'neotechnic' phase to succeed the 'palaeotechnic' *Kakotopia*, or bad place, in which we are still stuck; and the Outlook Tower would quite literally be the nucleus of a future Eutopian University.

These ideas were part of the atmosphere of Oxford's Geography School under A. J. Herbertson, when Crawford was there. Herbertson had met Geddes when a student in Edinburgh, and became one of his 'disciples'. Later he worked as Geddes's assistant in Dundee and helped fit out the Outlook Tower; in the late 1890s he gave lectures as part of the summer schools Geddes organized in Edinburgh. When Herbertson took up his post at Oxford he re-created Geddes's summer schools, and invited his mentor to teach at them. Herbertson introduced Geddes to Crawford, and they had long talks together, for as Crawford later recalled, he was potential 'cannon fodder' for Geddes's war with society. Crawford remembered Geddes as a 'prophet with a mission', and he positively 'revelled in his talk'. Like Crawford, Geddes had been brought up in a religious hothouse (Scottish Presbyterian in his case) and he had replaced his faith with a distinctly visionary science. Geddes's vision, as embodied by the Outlook Tower, was the exhilarating dream of the panopticon, of seeing the world and its contents in their entirety; as if the all-seeing eye of God had been arrogated to the citizen of the world, the geographer, the social reformer, the planner of cities. The Outlook Tower aspired to overcome the obstacles of mortal vision: distance, the curvature of the earth, bricks and mortar; and it suggested that iniquity could be first perceived, and then rooted out by the actions of the enlightened. Crawford was later rather embarrassed about his youthful enthusiasms, and critical of the shortcomings of his early mentors. But the strains of geographical thinking that came from Geddes, and – in a slightly different direction – from Peake, practical, observational, epic in scope of time and space, and future-orientated, yoking the local to the global, set Crawford's path.

Crawford stayed on for a year as Junior Demonstrator at the Geography School. Herbertson could see that his assistant had other aspirations, and found him a post – unpaid – as archaeologist accompanying an expedition to Easter Island led by a Mr and Mrs Scoresby Routledge, who wanted to investigate the giant statues there. It was a precondition that Crawford took a diploma in Anthropology at Oxford, which he did, under R. R. Marett and J. L. Myres. He never got to Easter Island. After a number of delays and false starts, the *Mana*, a schooner built in Whitstable for the purpose, set sail in the spring of 1913. Crawford loved being at sea; he wrote to his aunts with descriptions of turtles floating on the ocean surface, whales and porpoises playing around the ship. The weather could be rough, supplies were inadequate, and he could not abide Mr and particularly Mrs Routledge, but he remembered night shifts where the indigo sea was lit 'by starlike diatoms falling out downwards, and by brilliant phosphorescence in our wake and sides'. On one such night shift, however, he felt so insulted by Mr Routledge that he decided to abandon the expedition before it got to its destination. At St Vincent, off the Atlantic coast of Africa, he left the *Mana*, wired Peake to underwrite his passage home, and returned to Liverpool on a cargo boat.

Back home Crawford considered his future. Paid posts for

archaeologists were practically non-existent in 1913; he was already 27, and the money he received from his father's estate had just about run out. Archaeology was, however, well funded in one distant quarter. Henry Wellcome had made his fortune with the pharmaceutical company Burroughs, Wellcome & Co., famous for its mass-marketed 'tabloid' pills, and for equipping expeditions into the dark regions of the world. Wellcome was also a philanthropist and collector with dreams of making important archaeological discoveries. At Abu Geili and Jebel Moya, Neolithic sites in the Sudan, he attempted to link philanthropy with archaeology by establishing camps where thousands of local men were employed to shift, excavate and sift through vast quantities of rocks and earth looking for settlement debris, which were then carefully sorted and documented. This kept the natives busy (it was also meant to keep them solvent, healthy and sober), and it kept warm Wellcome's archaeological ambitions. He hoped he might find in the sand of the Sudan 'an answer to the eternal enigma of man's beginning', and his excavations left no stone unturned, no soil sample unsifted. In 1913 Wellcome placed an advert in *The Times* for an archaeologist to assist the thousands in their work. Crawford got the job, but before he went to the Sudan, Wellcome arranged for him to spend a month in Egypt learning the principles of systematic excavation with the American archaeologist George Reisner. In January 1914 Crawford was put in charge of work at Abu Geili, a site on the Blue Nile which had never been excavated. The site turned out to be a settlement dating from the Meroitic era (c.300 BC–c.AD 400). Excavations also turned up a cemetery of the much later Fung period, with black-burnished bowls in each grave. But Crawford's record-keeping was made more difficult by the fact that not only did work have to be found for large numbers of men, Wellcome also insisted that nothing should be thrown away. At Jebel Moya, Crawford told his aunts, the very earth was made of thousands of stone hammers; no wonder, then, that at the end of the excavating season in 1914, Wellcome sent back to London a vast quantity of packing cases, sacks and baskets, full of fragments of artefacts.

Crawford returned to England in June 1914. Wellcome wanted him to take a holiday, and then start work in London on the excavated material sent over from the Sudan, returning to Africa for the next season. In fact he didn't return to the Sudan for thirty years. War broke out as he was excavating a long barrow on Wexcombe Down with his American friend Earnest Hooton (another regular at the Peakes'). Under an intransigent mass of chalk they had found some human bones, which seemed to have been broken when still fresh; a nearby round barrow yielded a cinerary urn and part of an Iron Age brooch. Hooton returned to America upon the declaration of war, taking the urn with him for the Peabody Museum at Harvard, while Crawford remained to wind up the excavations. He was surprised when Mrs Peake suggested he should enlist. He had long since discounted patriotic jingoism along with the exhortations of religion, and imagined his friends, as civilized people, would think the same. They did not; and such was the nature of their influence that when Harold Peake advised Crawford to 'get going early, before the rush', he did so. In September he enlisted with the London Scottish Regiment, citing his ancestry in Fife and Aberdeen; and soon he was on his way to France to reinforce the 1st Battalion, the first territorial unit to see action against the German army. Meanwhile the Peakes remained in Boxford, reading Jung and drawing up plans for a new world order.

# CHAPTER 2

At particular times of the day when the sun is low, the contours of trenches and craters from the Western Front can still be seen pockmarking the fields of Flanders and Picardy. Seen from the air, in certain seasons ghostly lines of the old front line wind across the landscape. When the fields of Thiepval are under plough in the winter, the trench lines of the Leipzig Redoubt show up pale against the dark soil where, just ninety or so summers ago, German soldiers dug tunnels and communication channels in the chalky ground. Trench warfare transformed this landscape into a mud which sucked up corpses, releasing long-buried seeds into surreal outcrops of flowers, burying dead men's bones, weapons, military buttons and mess tins for future archaeologists, farmers and souvenir hunters to find. Every year, they say, plough-ing brings forth an 'iron harvest' of rusted military hardware. Buried shells and grenades have a habit of working their way to the surface; as the earth repeatedly freezes and thaws over decades, any solid objects buried in it move upwards. Stone Age axes regularly appear here, too, for the same reason. Much like the Thames valley, with which it shares certain geological and archaeological characteristics, the whole area around the Somme valley was the site of prehistoric and Roman settlement. It was here in the 1830s that the Abbeville customs officer Boucher de

Perthes found flint hand-axes lodged in the bones of prehistoric beasts, sensationally suggesting the existence of an antediluvian man unaccounted for by the Bible. Here, too, in ancient times fields were ploughed along the sides of inclines; it was the gap between these that created the 'sunken roads' used in the Great War to hide the movement of troops and supplies. The terraces of ancient fields had soft interiors, useful for dugouts in this most atavistic of conflicts.

An excavation of the front line at Serre in 2003 uncovered the remains of a German soldier with a Bronze Age flint scraper in his breadbag. Men living below the surface of the earth must have become intimate with it to the point of madness, like the lance corporal in Crawford's regiment who, under fire and three feet underground, spent his time carefully and methodically packing earth into a spent cartridge case. In many places along the front, mud filled the entire visual field, forming a horizon beyond which no familiar sight by which a man could orientate himself was visible. A sharpened flint sticking out of the side of a trench may have been a reassuring sight to an amateur archaeologist serving his country; a human point of reference, an identifiable historical compass, an object comforting to the hand, more familiar perhaps than the unreal present. More often, after all, unspeakable and barely identifiable things would emerge from the mud: body parts of fallen soldiers 'known only to God' as the phrase went; men whose nameless remains had now become part of the archaeological record.

After a lot of marching around London with his regiment in their hodden grey kilts and spats, Crawford was keen, he said, to see some action; and he did not have long to wait. From the railhead town of Hazebrouck in northern France, Crawford's platoon was sent on a gruelling march to Béthune through the night of 19 December. While they didn't know it, they were to relieve the British line before La Bassée, which was being held largely by the

Indian corps. Crawford was billeted behind the front line at
Givenchy. The call came in the night for the London Scottish to go
to the firing line to relieve the Coldstream Guards. Crawford's time
in the trenches started as farce. As it began to get light he made out
some shadowy figures on the skyline, and began to fire his rifle
at them, until his sergeant passed an order down the line for him
to stop, as he was shooting at his own side. Crawford remained
convinced he was right, but reluctantly stopped firing. 'It was
several years,' he wrote later, 'before I had another opportunity.'

For the next month or so Crawford was in and out of the front
line. While it was not nearly so protracted or as bloody as the
major battles later on in the war, the defence of Givenchy suffered
from the same punishing conditions experienced in other operations of the war's first winter. It was cold, but not so cold that
snow and ice did not melt. Repeated freezing and thawing
resulted in an ankle-deep accumulation of water and mud in the
trenches. Spats and shoes were abandoned in favour of boots, but
that didn't stop trench foot. It was very muddy, and the trenches –
still quite new – required continual attention to keep them in
shape. As problematic as the Flanders mud was the uneven level
of experience of the troops, as Crawford's shooting gaffe suggests.
New recruits were trained in 'elementary squad drill and deploy-
ment' (all that marching around London) but not in musketry –
apparently there was no suitable practice range. As the regiment's
historian remarked after the event, with characteristic under-
statement, there were 'not a few casualties'. Altogether the battle
of Givenchy claimed the lives of 6000 men, counting both sides.
There was none of the famous Christmas Day fraternization
between the two sides along this section of the front. That happened further up the line; Crawford only heard about it later.
Around Christmas he got news that his aunt Do had died. On
Boxing Day he put on a brave face for his aunt Gertrude: 'I am
enjoying it all thoroughly,' he wrote, 'it is a wonderful experience.
No one can pass through it and be the same afterwards.'

Early in February Crawford was invalided home with flu and malaria (picked up in the Sudan). At a hospital in Birmingham he had his frostbitten feet rubbed with oil. When he was fit again he applied for a commission, and began to train as a cadet in Harrogate. He had an interview for the Royal Flying Corps at the War Office but was turned down as he was too heavy and had no experience of horsemanship (apparently regarded as a decent qualification in these early days of military aviation). He didn't want to return to the trenches, but a letter to the War Office applying for work in the army's map department went unanswered. He tried pulling some family strings (his grandmother's niece was married to Sir John French's Chief of Staff), and this time was more successful: he was offered a post as Maps officer in the nascent Third Army. Training for the job was a leisured affair at the War Office, followed by leave, which Crawford spent sculling on the Thames at low tide looking for stone and bronze implements that might have been washed up on the riverbanks. Early in July he was sent out to Beauval, near Doullens, where he reported to Major Winterbotham, who was in charge of the Third Army Topographical Section.

The Third Army was sent out in the summer of 1915 to take over the French section of the Western Front around the river Somme, a year before the famous battle that claimed so many British lives. Its Topographical Section was responsible for producing and distributing accurate maps of the area, containing up-to-date information about enemy lines and earthworks, the location of battery positions and other targets. Maps were, of course, a crucial instrument of war; and they became more and more important as this particular war progressed. The maps that the first British Expeditionary Force went out with in 1914 turned out to be distinctly inadequate to the task. They were on too small a scale; they were inconsistent; and they were seriously out of date. As trench warfare set in, victory depended more and more upon accurate mapping of the precise position of the enemy and its developing defences. The Third Army Topographical Section was small at first, with only three officers (Winterbotham, Crawford, and F. J. Salmon, who was in charge of trigonometry), but both it and its range of activities grew rapidly, and it soon became a Field Survey Company and later a Battalion. Its first task was to produce an accurate 1:10,000 map of the area, which it based on local cadastral maps and plane table survey. Aerial photography – a new technology – was used to locate the trenches and earthworks of the enemy, as well as its battery positions, observation posts, barbed wire, trench mortar and machine-gun emplacements. These were then plotted on the map, often using a camera lucida.

The map-making work was so intensive that three draughtsmen were sent home with impaired eyesight. The first edition of the new map was finished by December 1915. It overlaid grey topographical features (quarries, rivers, ditches, railways, forests) with the targets of war, printed in red, the lines of trenches cutting up the terrain like pinking shears, a landscape riven with scarlet sutures. These maps are exemplars of Alan Sillitoe's conviction that 'the soldiers of the British Army invariably fought and often died on the best possible maps'. They are the kinds of thing that map collectors swoon over, and that Great War enthusiasts take with them to the battlefields of the Somme to orientate themselves amid the beet fields, replanted forests and suburban sprawl. In 1916, of course, they were the tools of action. The degree of their accuracy and detail was potentially the difference between victory and defeat, life and death even, for the troops that used them.

Trench warfare was about invisibility; if you were visible you became a target. Each side dug in, each hid from the other's sight – and each side rendered itself blind in the process. It was difficult enough to know what one's own side was doing further up the line, let alone what the enemy was up to. As a result both sides developed techniques and technologies of vision, prosthetics of sight that would enable them to locate the invisible enemy across no-man's-land and, having found it, blast it out of existence. Maps were effectively just such a prosthetic device. The Tommies and their officers might have been in the dark; but their maps – built up from laborious observations from balloon, aeroplane or observation post – could see. That, at least, was the idea; pasted onto so-called 'artillery boards', maps told gunners the direction in which they should fire to hit unseen targets. Most survey and observation work was done to guide the artillery to the distant and invisible enemy. Under Winterbotham the Field Survey Unit used ever-more sophisticated techniques of locating enemy positions, observing and calculating intervals of the noise and gun-flashes of hostile batteries to determine their precise whereabouts. Gunners and HQ alike were frequently sceptical of these kinds of intelligence innovation. Apparently the gunners of the Royal Marine Artillery called Winterbotham 'The Astrologer', no doubt with heavy irony, when he assured them that he could get their howitzers to hit a distant and unseen target. But it gradually became apparent that there was (in Paul Virilio's phrase) a 'logistics of military perception' developing in this war, and that images were themselves becoming a kind of artillery. Sight became foresight, as Virilio points out; and foresight was at least half the battle.

Crawford's main job in the Topographical Section was the distribution of maps, and the supervision of a small printing press. Contributing to the war's artillery of images himself, his duties also included taking panorama photographs of the front line,

covering its length from the Somme up to the north end of the Vimy Ridge. Crawford took great pride in these photographs, describing them on occasion as 'quite artistic'; but they had the most utilitarian of functions, being used, alongside maps, in the planning of attacks. To take the photographs he positioned himself at observation posts, high up in chimneys or half-ruined church towers, or sometimes on the front line itself. He made himself vulnerable to the extent to which he was visible to the enemy, and so he often used a little periscope – a gift from Henry Wellcome – to see above the parapet. The camera he used revolved on a tripod to survey a scene, and he had to change its plate between exposures. Like his periscope, Crawford's camera was an extension of bodily vision, a revolving eye on a stick; and when it was hit by a sniper at Fricourt, he photographed its damaged bodywork, displaying it proudly in his autobiography many years later, almost as if it were a surrogate of himself.

Like the unknown German soldier dug up in 2003, Crawford collected prehistoric fragments as he travelled along the front line taking his panoramas. According to Winterbotham he 'displayed such an enthusiasm for unhealthy places that one wondered, until one came across a large bag full of flint implements which he used to find in the Somme trenches in the course of his duties'. A Mousterian flint sticking out from the side of a trench at Thiepval and a 'nice Merovingian brooch' from Bray ended up in the Museum at Newbury. But a fragment of shell sent home, perhaps accidentally, to Harold Peake turned out to be nothing more exciting than part of a modern mother-of-pearl button, made in France. Writing to Crawford in January 1916 in this most surreal of wartime correspondences, Peake told him that he had submitted it to 'two experts, Messrs Jackson and Elliott, Drapers of Newbury' who thought that the species of shell was probably *Lenis pictoris* or *Avodonela amatoria* (though these names were almost illegible), but that 'the cut edge' was 'quite modern'.

Meanwhile, history powered on. The activities of Third Army Maps at this time were part of the preparations for what was then being called 'The Big Push', the bloody advance in the summer of 1916 known subsequently as the Battle of the Somme. Having prepared the maps for it, in March Winterbotham's Field Survey Unit moved with the rest of the Third Army north to St Pol near Arras, where Crawford continued with his panorama work. Just before the British offensive began, Crawford's photographic skills were called upon for propaganda purposes, some of his pictures appearing in the British press. He photographed the howitzer guns getting ready at Humbercamp, for example, and was instructed to photograph the beginning of the British attack on 28 June. He waited at the top of a high chimney at Acheux, from which there was an excellent view of the scene on which history was due to unfold, but nothing happened. The attack had been postponed. Two days later he was sent to Beaumont Hamel; this time a mine was to be exploded under the Germans at Hawthorn Ridge first thing in the morning of 1 July as a sign for the troops to 'go over', with – as it turned out – appalling consequences. Crawford hung around in

the trenches long enough to take an unremarkable photograph of the distant blast, and then beat a hasty retreat during the fateful silence that followed, accidentally leaving behind Wellcome's periscope.

Crawford was not directly involved in the compiling of maps, but he watched everything that went on with the trained eyes of a geographer; and he was particularly interested in the batches of aerial photographs that were delivered to the map office at regular intervals by the Royal Flying Corps from behind enemy lines. Aeroplanes were still a recent invention in 1914, and the photographs they brought back from the field must have constituted a kind of visual shock, showing the landscape in a way often imagined but never before seen with anything like such clarity. This was how the earth and its contents might appear to a disembodied, astral eye. The most familiar of things seen from a human perspective – trees, fields, church towers, towns; the receding orders of earth and sky, foreground, middle ground and misty distance – were all made unfamiliar from the air, all turned inside out. Trenches appeared as crenellated lines running across the plain; when the sun was low, shell craters showed up in constellations of dimples and pockmarks like acne on a face. The aerial view flattened out the landscape, pictured it like a map, and with such resolution, such detail! In the right hands, aerial photographs could be read like maps; but unlike maps they were records as well as diagrams, containing photographic information that was sometimes unexpected, and always up to date. An officer in the front line might not be able to see much beyond his sandbagged parapet, or have knowledge of the state of the trenches further up the line. An aerial photograph could show just how far away the enemy was, how complex its earthworks were, and what effect any recent shelling might have had on both sides. It brought visual news from beyond the frontier of natural sight.

What evolved on the front line – as a matter of urgency – was the work of specialist interpretation of photographic information. The novelist and science fiction writer H. G. Wells visited Third

Army Maps as part of his tour of the Western Front in 1916. It was Crawford who showed him around. Wells could see how remarkable aerial interpretation was, in a report of Crawford's tour:

> An air photograph to an inexperienced eye is not a very illuminating thing; one makes out roads, blurs of wood, and rather vague buildings. But the examiner has an eye that has been in training; he is a picked man . . . Here, he will point out, is a little difference between the German trench beyond the wood since yesterday. For a number of reasons he thinks that will be a new machine gun emplacement; here at the corner of the farm wall they have been making another. This battery here – isn't it plain? Well, it's a dummy. The grass in front of it hasn't scorched, and there's been no serious wear on the road here for a week. Presently the Germans will send one or two waggons up and down that road and instruct them to make figures of eight to imitate scorching on the grass in front of the gun. We know all about that. The real wear on the road, compare this and this and this, ends here at this spot. It turns off into the wood. There's a sort of track in the trees. Now look where the trees are just a little displaced! (This lens is rather better for that.) *That's* one gun. You see? Here, I will show you another . . .

War precipitates and develops new technologies, new skills. As Wells wrote in his autobiography, Crawford would later apply this kind of skill honed in war, the trained interpretation of visual evidence, to the peacetime work of archaeology.

Aerial photography made the terrain legible, to those with eyes to see. It wasn't just the identification of enemy positions, manifested to the eye through graphic, coded signs. Aerial photographs also revealed networks, distances and connections that existed but which couldn't be seen by earthbound mortals. As such they lent their viewers a thoroughly modern but somewhat inhuman sense of visual mastery of space, something modernist artists like Malevich and Marinetti found very exciting. Crawford was excited, too. Not long after arriving at Third Army Maps, he wrote enthusiastically to his aunts about the aerial images of German trench lines he'd seen. He was astonished to see how plainly the trench lines showed up, he said, being dug in chalk. 'One could hardly believe the trenches were full of men,' he added, 'they looked so peaceful and lifeless.' As W. H. Auden later remarked, it was precisely this sort of effect of the aerial view – its tendency to desensitize human values, reducing history to nature – that enabled the aviator to drop his bombs.

It was aeroplanes – along with the tank – that rescued the First World War from stalemate, adding a vertical dimension to the field of battle. As a tool of observation and reconnaissance, aviation revolutionized the field, even if commanders were slow to realize its full potential. Military intelligence, after all, had always looked to the highest vantage point. Before aeroplanes there were information-relaying balloons anchored on the battlefield (these were still being used in 1914–18); before balloons there had been watchtowers. The principle is primitive enough: it was the same impulse, at root, that propelled early man to a high point in the landscape from which to survey the territory, looking out for enemy tribes, or searching for better pasture. Military intelligence is always looking for the point from which the whole picture is visible, while camouflaging itself. It has a horror of perspective; it wants nothing to hide from its sights. Its history is the search for an Archimedean point which has been pushed ever further into space, residing now in the remote-sensing capabilities of spy satellites; in 1914–18 the closest approximation to that point was an airborne camera just beneath the clouds.

In a war bound as this one was to the physical terrain, geography and archaeological fieldwork weren't bad training for intelligence work. Fieldwork sharpened the eye in a way that could prove very useful in wartime. For all his dedication to peace, the visual pedagogy of Geddes's Outlook Tower was arguably an apt preparation for a branch of military activity in which vision and topographical survey played such an important part. Thanks to his geographical training, Crawford had a strong sense of the importance of a good visual sweep, seeking out the highest and best observation posts for his panoramas. In fact he soon wanted to go higher. In the autumn of 1916 he went up in a plane 3,000 feet over the Somme front as the battle raged below. 'It was a wonderful sight,' he told his aunt, 'especially flying over the battle area. The whole country there is brown, there is a great brown belt all along the front, about a mile wide, where the ground has been turned up by countless shells.' The experience of flight was so thrilling that in January 1917 he applied to join the RFC as an observer. 'I am very excited about it,' he wrote to his aunt. After a course in aerial gunnery at Hythe he was posted to 23rd Squadron, stationed at first near Beauval, and then at Baisieux. His first stint as an observer did not last long. On his maiden observation flight Crawford's FE2b plane was attacked by Fokkers and had to make an emergency landing after gliding northwards to the right side of the front line, guided by the dark outline of Adinfer Wood. Crawford and his pilot were safe, but Crawford's right foot was 'a gory mess'. An enemy bullet had cut across his instep, breaking the bone of every toe except one. For the rest of his life the right sole of his shoes wore out most quickly in the middle where there remained a bony lump in his foot.

Crawford's foot injury put him out of action for the best part of six months. In May 1917, after passing through a series of hospitals in France and England, he was sent to convalesce at the RFC Auxiliary Hospital at Heligan House in Cornwall, before the legendary gardens there were lost. Here he had a lot of time on his hands, and he started to write a book. The book, as he explained it to his aunt Edith, was ambitious enough. 'It deals with the classification of knowledge,' he wrote, 'and the place of archaeology in that classification – then its aims and methods.' It was conceived by Crawford as a summary of conversations held with Harold Peake about the evolution of civilization understood from a geographical viewpoint. It aimed to consider how this viewpoint might shed new light on historical and archaeological problems, and then it would get round to 'more practical things like town-planning and garden cities'. He'd been thinking about all these things ever since his first meetings with Peake, and his enforced leisure at Heligan gave him an opportunity to write them up. But it was H. G. Wells who was seemingly the immediate catalyst and ongoing inspiration for his book.

Fandom came naturally to Crawford as a young man. He was particularly susceptible to social prophets, especially those who – like him – had rejected a religious upbringing in favour of Science. And so it is not surprising that he had long been a fan of H. G. Wells, whose utopian fiction and other writings were propelled by an understanding of evolutionary science promoted with the passion and the rhetoric of an evangelist. Science, in Wells's work, would quite literally save the world. Following apocalypse and mass destruction, only a higher intelligence – in the form of extraterrestrials or scientists – could redeem the planet. Wells had a big following among the middle-class young in the closing years of the nineteenth century and the early years of the twentieth, and it's not hard to see why. In an age when, as George Orwell wrote, 'science was faintly disreputable and religious belief obligatory', Wells's vision was exhilarating:

It was a wonderful experience for a boy to discover H. G. Wells. There you were, in a world of pedants, clergymen and golfers, with your future employers exhorting you to 'get on or get out', your parents systematically warping your sexual life, and your dull-witted schoolmasters sniggering over their

Latin tags; and here was this wonderful man who could tell you about the inhabitants of the planets and the bottom of the sea, and who knew that the future was not going to be what respectable people imagined.

Crawford was just such a boy; Wells's influence was, he said later, 'profound and lasting'. He wrote his first fan letter to the great author from the airless confines of Keble College in 1908, thanking him 'for the encouragement your books are to the lonely wayfarer who feels that he is not, as he feels in Oxford, the only one who does not bow the knee to Baal; and hopes some day to do some service to the only living cause'. Eight years later Crawford got to meet his idol. When Wells toured the Western Front in the autumn of 1916, Crawford showed him around the map section at Arras, explained aerial reconnaissance to him and gave him some panoramas. The following May, after Crawford had been invalided home with his wounded foot, he spent a weekend at Wells's home at Dunmow in Essex; and it was soon after this that he began work on his book.

Wells was by this point becoming very vocal in the British press on the subject of the war and the future; and Harold Peake was keen to get an audience with him too. During the war Peake and his associates had been giving the future a lot of thought. Under the banner of 'regionalism' (inspired by Herbertson and Geddes) they held a series of conferences to discuss the division of England into provinces after the war, each province corresponding to 'regions' determined by vegetation, geology, industry, historical settlement and so on. Existing villages were to be regenerated, and new ones designed from scratch. Peake drew up blueprints for the 'ideal township' of the future, geometric designs for future utopian living. The idea was to stem the flow of metropolitanism, and the rural decay which inevitably followed, by resuscitating regional consciousness. These were the ideas Peake wanted to discuss with Wells, together with his hopes for a post-war world capital at Constantinople. Constantinople was the ideal place, thought Peake, situated between two continents, 'a bridge, as it were, between the Old World and the New', near to the major sites of ancient history. It's clear that Peake saw himself in this picture, as curator of a new world museum, ushering in the spoils of empires, so that they might illustrate five or six millennia of world history under his eye. This would be a global version of his unique displays at the Newbury Museum, in which each century of 5,000 years of history was given the same amount of space, tracing the evolution of life forms up to modern man, represented by a mirror in which the museum visitor saw themselves reflected. Peake had kept Crawford informed of his thoughts and schemes throughout the time he was at the front, and he urged him to press his case with Wells when he got to spend his weekend with him in Essex.

The future Wells was beginning to envisage, by contrast, was one in which the various nations would be replaced by a single Federal World State. The nationalist rivalries that had caused the First World War were superfluous in a world increasingly united by science and technology, according to Wells; they were the hangovers of an evolutionary tribal stage that had already been superseded. An increasingly globalized world required a World Government, and an end to such superstitious nonsense as flag-waving and leader cults, especially since these things had led to the insanity of the current war. Fresh from the front, in his 1917 book *War and the Future* Wells expressed his vision with the fervour and language of a preacher:

> I think that mankind is still as it were collectively dreaming and hardly more awakened to reality than a very young child. It has these dreams that we express by the flags of nationalities and by strange loyalties and by irrational creeds and ceremonies, and its dreams at times become such nightmares as this war. But the time draws near when mankind will

awake and the dreams will fade away, and then there will be
no nationality in all the world but humanity, and no king, no
emperor, nor leader but the one God of mankind. This is my
faith. I am as certain as I was in 1900 that men would
presently fly.

Perhaps Wells was trying to convince himself that the future
was brighter than the war's carnage portended. His 1916 novel
*Mr Britling Sees It Through* has the Wells-like Mr Britling struggling to make sense of the death of his son in the trenches by
attempting to write an essay 'of preposterous ambitions' entitled
'The Better Government of the World'; but he is haunted by
visions, doubts and grief, and ends up just doodling. Yet in his
non-fiction writings Wells was clear enough. The war, for him,
was both a crisis point in the history of the world, and also an
opportunity for change; it was a chance for the human race to
decide what sort of future it would have.

As he sat on committees for the proposed post-war League of
Nations, Wells realized that it was going to be impossible for a
new world order to be conceived, and nationalism to cease,
unless history started to be thought about in a different way.
National histories would have to stop being taught in schools and
universities, since they perpetuated nationalist sentiment, and
gave a skewed picture of the whole. They should be replaced by
a new 'Universal History'. This would not be just a collection of
histories of, say, modern America, medieval France, the British
Empire, and so on, but a synthetic History of the World, from its
beginnings to the present day. Such a history would need to be
written; and so, astonishingly, he did. Wells's 1920 *Outline of
History: Being a Plain History of Life and Mankind* was followed in
1922 by *A Short History of the World*. This was world history written at a moment of crisis, in which the standard historical
determinants – monarchy, nationhood, individual religions,
empire-building – were subsumed into a much bigger picture, as

if world history were being viewed at a great distance from which such things appeared as little more than flickers in the night. As a contemporary journalist remarked, Wells's history showed the stages of civilization move past 'like shadowy films of a world-cinematograph'. The idea was to rewrite history from a different perspective in order to throw the present and future into clear relief. This was history as prophecy, or at least a history from which the future was to be extrapolated; and it was to be a great evolutionary tale of science triumphing over religion, irrationality and superstition in all human life, leading to the better government of the future. *The Outline of History* traced the evolution of the social units into which human beings have combined, from the family tribes of the Neolithic Age through to nation states and their tragic culmination in the Great War, to be replaced by – what? The final chapter considered 'The Possible Unification of the World into One Community of Knowledge and Will'.

Wells's history books turned out to be a huge and apparently unexpected publishing success, which their author put down to an immense yet untapped public thirst for world history in a digestible form. Amongst writers and intellectuals some – notably Hilaire Belloc – were appalled, but others were pretty impressed. George Bernard Shaw recommended *Outline* to Trotsky as a thoroughly new kind of politically sound history; but Trotsky was not convinced. He described Wells's book as the product of an uninformed and unrigorous so-called historian 'roaming far and wide over the history of a few millennia with the carefree air of a man taking his Sunday stroll'. Crawford, however, saw an affinity between Wells's conception of history and his own. History – as he told him – was Crawford's gospel as it was becoming Wells's; and he, too, took the big scope, putting nations and empires into perspective. At Oxford, Herbertson had preached an approach to geography that sought to replace nations and empires with natural regions. Crawford was thrilled to hear that Wells took seriously the influence of geology and geography on the history of civilization; and that he, too, sensed that discoveries in the realms of archaeology and palaeontology were rewriting that history. What's more, Crawford was in line with Wells politically. He agreed that Universal History was 'the necessary educational fore-runner of a world-federation', as he told Wells in a letter in 1919, and he effusively justified to the great writer his devotion to archaeology, an apparently

> 'useless' branch of knowledge by the thought that it will provide new material for the education of future generations – material that, if it is used at all, *must* help to weaken the consciousness of nationality and strengthen that of universal brotherhood. It has done that for me at any rate.

Wells's historical vision, like his science fiction, championed the scientist and scholar, among whose ranks Crawford placed himself. After his experiences at Marlborough, at Keble and at the front line of war, he was delighted to think that religion, superstitions and jingoism were to be swept away by the great and unstoppable tides of history, making way for a brave new world of scientific reason; and he was keen to play his part.

The book that Crawford started to write at Heligan after his weekend with Wells was eventually published in 1921 as *Man and His Past*. The book bears the imprint of both Peake and Wells, calling for the study of Universal History to be taken up in schools, and for a World Museum to be established. Overall, Crawford's book is a kind of manifesto and justification of a particular approach to history. This is a history mistrustful, like Peake, of written sources; a history outside language, outside texts. History is not so much that which is written in books, but something which awaits discovery in the world itself; and it does not mind how long it waits. And if individual discoveries (a small stretch of Roman road, a medieval parish map, a bronze sword dredged from the Thames) might seem mundane or insignificant, what they contributed to – the vast plan of Universal History – could hardly be more important. The work of the archaeologist or historian was to piece together clues to this plan, a profoundly satisfying task Crawford compared to the work of a craftsman putting together a building whose blueprint he can't see the whole of. It is as if history were a jigsaw puzzle, which must be put together without the assistance of the picture on the lid. It is a painstaking and often dull business, but the rewards are immense. For the picture that is so slowly formed is a visionary one that encompasses all of the past, present and future, too. The archaeologist's work may seem tedious, wrote Crawford in the closing passage of his book, but 'he travels through time upon the magic carpet of imagination'; and the view is marvellous.

The idea of history as a massive jigsaw puzzle could hardly sound more misguided to modern archaeologists and historians. Few believe in the big picture any more, let alone in our ability to piece it together. The most we can do is try to make sense of fragmentary evidence, never forgetting that the story we tell about it is always contingent, is always going to be affected by our particular standpoint, is only one of many possible stories. History as it is currently taught in schools and universities insists that historical knowledge is constructed in discourse, not 'found' in the world; and that we can never really know the truth about the past. In their more extreme formulations, postmodern thinkers see historians as little more than glorified storytellers, who are foolish to think that they can ever know or tell it 'how it really was'. Historians nowadays realize they are 'forever chasing shadows', according to Simon Schama, 'painfully aware of their inability ever to reconstruct a dead world in its completeness however thorough or revealing their documentation. We are doomed to be forever hailing someone who has just gone around the corner and out of earshot.'

Crawford, like Wells, indulged in none of the epistemological doubts described by Schama. The past may have been elusive but it was certainly not unknowable. History was effectively a *science* for these men, and it surely followed certain laws, most notably the laws of evolution, which applied to the world of culture as well as nature. Wells's *Outline of History* began its story with the disposition of the planets, going through the origins of life on earth before the beginnings of man, as if these were all guided by the same laws, susceptible to the same scientific approach. 'The rocks bubbled and the sea smoked,' wrote E. M. Forster in a review of Wells's book, 'presently there was an inter-tidal scum: it was life.' Nations, empires and entire civilizations were represented – in Wells's own words – as 'things which have appeared and disappeared almost incidentally in the course of a longer biological adventure' of which they were just a tiny part.

Crawford's *Man and His Past* also perceived all knowledge as one, and he, too, saw human history as a small part of a much greater sweep. He imagined a great Museum with one immense Time axis along which could be arranged everything from the formation of the solar system through the Jurassic period, early Man, ancient civilizations and on to the present day (and beyond). What the scientific approach of both writers implied was that if our picture of the past was hazy in places it was just because we did not yet know enough about it. Nor was this ever likely to be final. More information could always, in theory at least, be found; new archaeological discoveries might elucidate hitherto obscure corners of the past. New technologies, too, might be developed through which those dark corners might be illuminated: illegible scripts might yet be read, lost conversations might one day be heard. If the past was 'out of earshot', as it were, we must invent a telecom system so that we can listen in! History would reveal itself to the diligent historian possessed of the right tools as surely (if slowly) as the physical world revealed itself to the diligent scientist, equipped with microscope or telescope. No historical incident was necessarily altogether lost to us. There were no lost races, no lost scrolls, lost libraries, lost languages or lost cities; they and everything else were just waiting to be found, waiting to be intercepted by tools which had not yet been invented.

The past itself is, of course, littered with those who dreamed that this might be possible. None more, perhaps, than Jerome Harrison, a Victorian photographer so in love with his medium, and so confident of its prospects, that he could see no reason why, if a camera, pointing towards the earth, could be propelled into space faster than the speed of light, it would not be possible to create a photographic record of the whole of history. If it were pointing to the right place at the right moment in its journey spacewards, the camera could take a photograph of Mary Queen of Scots, so we could see how beautiful she really was; it could document Julius Caesar's landing on the shores of Britain, and so show exactly where this historic event took place. Harrison imagined that it might be possible for the camera even to record stages in human evolution that were still, in the 1880s, being argued over. If there really had been a 'missing link' between the 'fruit-eating ape-like creature' that lived in the primordial trees, and the 'reasoning omnivore' that was the true ancestor of mankind, then a photograph of such a beast would settle the debate. The photographic survey imagined by Harrison – a sort of space-age version of the project he was at the time carrying out in Warwickshire – would be a record against which there could be no appeal, no argument. It would keep the babbling historians quiet. And it would prove right the antiquarian Sir Thomas Browne, when he wrote in 1658 that 'what song the Syrens sang, or what name Achilles assumed when he hid himself among women, although puzzling questions, are not beyond *all* conjecture'. The Syrens, after all, were the bird-women of ancient myth who sang of all that had ever happened, all that is, and all that shall be; the very archetype of the sublime idea that there might be no limits to knowledge of the world.

For Crawford and Wells historical knowledge may have been a challenge, but it was not an abstraction. It was a real and solid thing, and not a chimera that looked different depending on which way you looked at it. They did not worry that their particular historical and geographical co-ordinates, or their class and gender credentials (as – in their case – white Western middle-class males writing in the early twentieth century) might unduly affect their view, any more than it would have done had they been physicists or astronomers. In fact the whole idea of a Universal History implied the existence of a universal observer, like one of those extraterrestrials with 'intellects vast and cool and unsympathetic' in Wells's *The War of the Worlds*, that scrutinize the affairs of men from afar. What was aimed for, in fact, was an approach to history that was the equivalent of the aerial view or the panorama, the view from a great height or an immense distance which would deliver the broadest sweep. This was an Archimedean viewpoint from which the underlying patterns of historical processes would become plain, just as the terrain was made visible in an aerial photograph of a battlefield. The course of world history may be no clearer to its human participants than the battlefield was to those men crouching in the trenches of the Somme valley. Seen from a great distance, though, the bigger picture emerges.

This picture comes at a cost, however. Universal History, like the aerial view, claims a privileged viewpoint. From its cool distance it perceives broad historical processes, just as the aerial view detects spatial configurations imperceptible from the ground. But the surveying eye in both cases has its blind spots. Crawford, flying over the battlefields of the Somme, was unable to see the soldiers in their trenches. And in a similar way, Universal History mapped out a chronology in which human experience counted for less than impersonal forces, as if gauging the rapid currents of a river were of more importance than describing the fate of those who were drowning in it.

Oswald Spengler's epic *The Decline of the West*, like Wells's and Crawford's books, came out in the wake of the First World War;

it, too, saw patterns appearing out of the historical panorama. Spengler's prognosis for a world in which civilizations follow cycles of growth and inevitable decline may have been rather more pessimistic than Wells's, but the assumed observational position is the same. It is the position, so to speak, of the aerial observer, intoxicated by his sense of mastery of space and time. No wonder, then, that the final passage in *Man and His Past* likens the historian to 'the traveller who has reached at evening the summit of a lofty pass', who 'scans with eager eyes the new landscape opening out before him'. It's hard to imagine a historian or an archaeologist describing their work in such grandiose terms nowadays; they know that the most magnificent of views can turn out to be mirages.

The seeds of *Man and His Past* were planted at Heligan in the spring of 1917; but by the autumn Crawford's foot had healed, and he was ready to return to the front. In September he joined the RFC No. 48 Squadron as an observer. The planes flown by this squadron were the new Bristol fighters, in which observer and pilot sat back to back, both of them armed. Crawford's main job was to escort the naval squadron as it carried out bombing missions. He went out on reconnaissance missions, too, taking photographs, and recording the locations of enemy positions. He turned out to be uncommonly good at this kind of work, recording so many more details than the other observers that the Wing Commander suspected him of faking them. Crawford put his success down to a novel method he had devised, in which he recorded his observations directly onto a hand-drawn map, rather than using map references. He also made full use of his geographical and archaeological knowledge, using the straightness of Roman roads at times, for example, to help orientate himself.

Every day in the autumn and winter of 1917 he went up, recording some of his impressions of flight in a diary. Looking down, the cloud layer 'looked like a vast snowfield, and the shadow of our machine was visible upon it, surrounded by a small circle of rainbow

light'. Flying at 20,000 feet or so with no enclosed cockpit may have
been spectacular but it was also chilly, and Crawford made himself
a face mask from a black cat-skin after his nose got frostbitten. The
icy temperature could be hazardous. Crawford's mounted Lewis gun
often used to freeze up; and on one occasion this happened when his
plane was under attack. It landed with a dead engine, covered with
ice; but Crawford and his pilot were unhurt.

Once again, Crawford – who was by now Squadron Intelligence
Officer – had had a lucky escape; others in his squadron were less
fortunate. It was, after all, dangerous work. In these early days of
aerial reconnaissance, observers were at the mercy of darkness, fog
or cloud. They were obvious targets for anti-aircraft guns and fighter
planes. As a result, observers had a short life expectancy; and were
therefore only allowed to do it for six months of continuous service.
Even with this safeguard, there were many casualties. Some were
recorded in Crawford's diary without much apparent emotion, but
when one observer named Hardie and his pilot, Maclaren, were
killed, it had an impact which made its way onto the page. Crawford
glimpsed Maclaren's burned body through the door of the mortuary,
alongside 'several forms wrapped up in blankets and sewn tight'.
'I . . . felt very much upset for some time afterwards,' he wrote. 'The
image has photographed itself on my mind.' Hardie and Maclaren
had been flying beneath the clouds, where they were particularly
vulnerable to attack from above. After seeing their bodies in the
mortuary Crawford was more nervous when flying under clouds:
'I sit the whole time with my eyes on the clouds behind and above
and my finger on the trigger.'

As he got towards the end of his six months, Crawford was
entrusted with a reconnaissance mission that involved going
deep behind the enemy lines, to collect intelligence on preparations for a major German offensive. This was obviously a perilous
operation. The plan was to fly above the clouds, calculating the
direction and distance to get to the destination, coming down at
that precise spot to carry out the reconnaissance under the

clouds. Crawford and his pilot would head for Le Cateau, where they would descend, then along the valley of the river Oise to Hirson, and back home, guided by maps. They waited for the right day; and on a day in February when the cloud cover seemed adequate, they set off. After flying in what they had calculated was the right direction, for what they believed to be the right duration, they came down at a dramatic tilt through the clouds. Their calculations were wrong, however, for which Crawford later blamed his pilot, who had not taken into account the plane's retardation of speed in ascent; they were not where they should have been. Emerging from the clouds they saw a German soldier hanging out his washing. They had no idea where they were; and they began to be shot at. They landed and set fire to their aeroplane, with no one in sight. Escape was not possible; and before long they had both been taken prisoner.

Ten days later, and weak from lack of food, Crawford was taken to a camp on an island at Landshut in Bavaria where he was to receive various regulation inoculations. Within a week or so he began to feel slightly stronger, and started to think about how he might escape. He hatched a plan; and on 6 March he attempted to carry it out; the escape attempt, including a map, is described in his autobiography. Disguising himself as best he could by turning his army tunic inside out, he hid himself in a ditch until nightfall, having put a dummy in his bed. During an especially noisy evening sing-song by his fellow prisoners (who were in on it), he got across the yard and squeezed through the barbed wire that surrounded the camp. His plan was to swim across the river Isar to the mainland, but the current was too strong; he was carried downstream, and ended up back on the same shore. He set off again by foot; when challenged by a sentry he pretended to be a drunk German soldier, but he was soon found out. He was taken to the civil prison at Landshut, where he was put in a cell. He stayed there for a week. He tried, he said, to start work on his book again; but he was too hungry to think.

Not long after returning to the camp from prison, Crawford was sent to the POW camp at Holzminden, near Hanover. It was at Holzminden that the biggest mass escape of the war took place; when Crawford arrived there, the secret tunnel was still being dug. As a recent arrival, Crawford wasn't allowed to join in; but he helped out as a 'soil consultant' to the tunnellers and, after the big escape in July when 70 or so captured officers tried to get away, he smuggled food and news to those who had been caught and were returned to the camp. Crawford was in fact planning his own escape. In a smuggled-out letter he asked Harold Peake to send him maps and a compass; he also arranged with Peake a secret code. It's certainly possible to imagine that Peake's letters to Crawford while he was at Holzminden were encrypted; that his musings on the course of the ancient Amber Route that ran near the camp, for example, was really a set of instructions on possible escape routes. Archaeology – as Agatha Christie knew – makes an excellent decoy. But it is just as likely that the letters really were what they purported to be: discussions of regionalism, village reconstruction and prehistory, with suggestions for further investigations. For despite the fact that Holzminden was described in the British press as the 'worst camp in Germany', its inmates 'at all times' the 'victims of brutal treatment', Crawford found it not only companionable, but also remarkably conducive for studying. It was certainly preferable, he thought, to Marlborough. 'Imprisonment is not at all a bad thing,' he wrote to his aunts. It at least 'gives one [the] chance of quiet reading'. And read he did, with most of his books sent to him care of Peake, who arranged for them to be posted direct from their publishers, as was the rule. He read books on psychology and 'semi-philosophy', anthropology, archaeology and town planning; he read Samuel Butler, Jung and more H. G. Wells. He wrote down extracts in a notebook, 'fine, confused stuff', as he later called it; and he discussed his reading with a major who was teaching him German. And in the light of this reading, and these discussions, he started to think about his book again.

Crawford remained at Holzminden until the end of the war in November, a total of seven months. He returned home to his aunts, who had by now moved to Donnington, near Newbury. He was thirty-two; he had no job (Wellcome's work in the Sudan had been indefinitely postponed), but he had his war gratuity and some back-payments. Alongside finishing off *Man and His Past* he spent the next year or so doing fieldwork, first in Wiltshire and then in Wales, under the auspices of the Cambrian Archaeological Association. He camped out alone in a sheepfold in the hills above the Merionethshire coast, where there were chambered cairns, stone circles and a hill fort. When members of the Cambrian Archaeological Association – 'a motley crew of amateurs', according to Crawford – visited his excavations on their annual outing, they found him eccentric in dress and diet. The geologist William Boyd Dawkins explained to the group that he had surely been traumatized by the war. Crawford later laughed off the incident as an example of a bourgeois distaste for working attire. But it's possible that the war had indeed taken its toll. Images like that of the burned bodies in the mortuary, and untold others, had imprinted themselves onto his mind as irrevocably as onto a photographic plate. Fresh air was the best tonic; and, unlike the visiting amateurs, it passed no judgement. After packing up camp in October 1919 he walked home to Newbury, a journey which took several days over the Welsh hills and across western England, following the Roman road from Gloucester to Boxford.

Throughout this time, Crawford had made full use of the fact that the Ordnance Survey had decided to issue 6-inch maps free of charge 'to certain qualified persons' in exchange for archaeological information inserted on them, to add to and correct what was already there. Just as in his wartime observation work, Crawford located and marked many new sites on these maps. He also pointed out a large number of 'archaeological errors and deficiencies' on them. So regular a visitor to the Ordnance Survey offices did he become, and so many corrections did he make, that apparently Sir Charles Close, the Director General, 'thought that he might do worse' than offer him a permanent post. After more excavations in the summer of 1920 in Hampshire (where he was again accused of wearing 'funny clothes'), and then on the Isle of Wight (assisted by an ex-serviceman badly injured in the war), he went to Southampton to start work as the Ordnance Survey's first Archaeology Officer. He moved into a house named Hope Villa in Nursling, a village outside the city. He kept both the post and the house for the rest of his working life.

# CHAPTER 3

Nothing that has happened or existed has left no trace, no material consequence. We may not have the tools or the skills to find these consequences, or the wit to know them when we see them; we are always mistaking signs for things, stories for objects, processes for their products. The labyrinthine ways in which things and people are connected are largely obscured by the veils of time and space, even if there are moments when, like the author G. K. Chesterton, we perceive with a flash of recognition that the things we encounter in life are the fragments of something else which would be immensely exciting were it not too vast and too well hidden to be seen. The day-to-day sights, sounds and events of ordinary existence, thought Chesterton, are really the mixed-up tag ends of an infinity of tales which are never likely to be told. A stranger sitting opposite us on a train; what are the events that propel him onwards? A piece of chalk in our hand; who can tell the provenance of the millions of skeletons of sea creatures that once crept across prehistoric seabeds, compacted, now, into a mark on a blackboard?

What, after all, are objects and appearances but stories in disguise? Is not the most mundane of things crystallized history? A broken mother-of-pearl button found in a muddy trench was once sewn on to a garment, was, before that, manufactured, from what was once – according to the Newbury Drapers – the shell of *Lenis pictoris* or *Avodonela amatoria*, once stuck to a nameless coastal rock. A bend in a road may owe its existence to a fallen tree – long since gone – that caused ancient wayfarers to divert their path around it, on an old way that was later made permanent in tarmac. Only occasionally is one of the infinite number of undocumented historic events or mute tales pulled out of the obscurity that would otherwise be its fate; in a forensic investigation, for example, when the pollen grains on the sole of a dead man's shoe tell the story of a journey from an olive grove to the boot of a car. Such investigations, whether forensic or archaeological, serve the needs of the present, in this case the nailing of a murderer; they leave untouched the millions of untold stories with which they are not concerned, all of the infinite strands of historical cause and effect whose frayed and matted ends comprise, precisely, the world of appearances.

Historical causes continue to produce their effects regardless of whether or not we recognize them as such, like the cherry trees that grow still on the ground where a family once threw their pips after a meal, or the deformed insects whose minute symmetry has been derailed by the emissions of a nuclear power station. Neither does anything quite disappear. Matter, like radioactivity or love, transmutes or is dispersed but can't become nothing; and it continues to produce effects in the world, whether or not those effects are ever discerned. The inventor Charles Babbage was so convinced of this that he deemed the very air to be full of the pulsations of atoms, permanently set in motion by everything that has ever been said, just as the earth and the ocean are the eternal witnesses to every event, geological, meteorological and historical. The air keeps a record; it is the 'never-failing historian' of all that has ever been uttered. It may have been this idea that sent Babbage's friend Charles Dickens off on his reading tours around Britain and America, in search of sonic immortality, his voice vibrating in the ether for ever. The eternal aerial pulses, as Babbage remarked, may be unheard by the acutest ear, unperceived by human senses; but their existence is demonstrated by reason.

What kind of being, with what kind of tools, might ever be able to tune in to this 'vast library' of the air, land or sea, and be able to pronounce, with absolute certainty, that they could identify the songs the Syrens sang? If it is not us humans it is because we are ourselves part of the library; we, too, are crystallized, pulsing history.

The Southampton offices of the Ordnance Survey on London Road were rather emptier in the early 1920s than they had been before 1914; staff numbers were down by more than half. Having swung into full military mode for the duration of the war, producing a constant flow of maps, artillery boards, and trained surveyors between Southampton and France, the county revisions that were the Survey's normal peacetime activity had fallen behind. Post-war cuts in personnel meant that there were far fewer staff to get the backlog of work done. It was in this environment of low morale and staff cuts that Crawford took up his newly created position; no wonder it caused resentment. Antiquities had been included on Ordnance Survey maps since the beginning, but there had never before been a dedicated Archaeology Officer overseeing them. As a civilian – despite his war service – Crawford was in a minority in this organization; and archaeological work continued to be seen as unimportant by many of the Royal Engineers who were Crawford's new colleagues.

The Ordnance Survey owed its existence, in the eighteenth century, to the need to know in geographic intimacy those dark parts of the British Isles – especially the so-called Celtic fringe – where rebels might hide and collect, and the borders where the King's realm might be vulnerable. With its theodolites, plane-tables and compasses it calculated contours, plotted the course of rivers, calibrated distances, tracked roads; it drew up and printed maps, and punctuated them with standardized place names. Right into the twentieth century, when Crawford joined it, the Ordnance Survey trained soldiers how to survey theatres of war or enemy terrain. Its peacetime work of domestic survey was seen as excellent preparation for the war that was its main reason to exist. Despite the civil status it now had, a large proportion of its staff were military personnel, and it was as rigidly hierarchical as any military organization; a chain of command ran from the Director General through the colonel who was Executive Officer down through all the ranks, various, of officers, NCOs and men. Maps were produced in series of scales; quarter-inch, half-inch, 1-inch, 6-inch, 25-inch; and in ranks of editions: the 6-inch town plan, the 1-inch 'Contoured Road Map' that classified 11 types of road, the hachured 1-inch 'Tourist Map', the quarter-inch *Atlas of England and Wales*. Counties underwent revision in rotation: Essex, Northumberland, Gloucestershire, Oxfordshire, Buckinghamshire, Derbyshire, Durham, Herefordshire; the shires of England taking precedence in the post-war backlog over the sparser regions of Scotland, Wales and Ireland.

The Ordnance Survey was the latest in a line of Establishment bodies – Marlborough, Oxford, the army – in which Crawford took up somewhat uneasy residence. When he arrived he was provided with the barest of rooms to work from (one table, no chair), and no official assistance (he got an assistant in 1938). His position within this hidebound organization was unprecedented, anomalous and insecure. At least once his job threatened to be cut to part-time; his salary in any case was low. Yet he could see the advantages of symbiosis with such a powerful, if intransigent, host. There were very few paid jobs in archaeology available in 1920; and in many ways, for all its difficulties, it was an ideal position for him. Working within the Ordnance Survey offered him the perfect opportunity to put British prehistoric archaeology quite literally on the map.

The appointed task of the Archaeology Officer was to correct
and update the archaeological information of each county as it
was revised. The antiquities marked on OS maps were patchy.
Some counties had been very thoroughly done thanks to the
labours of particular individuals. Wiltshire, for example, had
been well covered by William Colt Hoare in the early nineteenth
century. But other counties needed a lot of work. Some sites had
not been marked on the map; others had been wrongly positioned, or falsely identified. Too often, untrustworthy sources had
been accepted without question. In some cases, sites identified
in books had been inserted on the map without their position
and identity being checked on the ground, or their names – often
inventions – given a second thought. At worst there were sites
that were named with wild inaccuracy as 'Druids' Altars' and
the like. Crawford found plenty of work to do. Mindful of his
vulnerable and unprecedented position, perhaps, he made it
his business to broadcast the need for a centralized authority –
himself – who would weed out the errors, fill in the gaps, and
rationalize the entire operation.

It seems to have been expected that Crawford would follow
protocol and rely on a mixture of printed sources and local
informants, without ever leaving his office much. The Director
General was 'rather taken aback', Crawford wrote later, when he
asked him for permission to do fieldwork. But there were so
many blank spaces on the map, so many dubious attributions,
names perpetuated by the Chinese whispers of generations, lent
authority by the permanence of printed text. The map had to
be returned to the terrain it was supposed to represent, paper
and print checked, wherever possible, against earth and stone.
Gloucestershire was being revised when Crawford started his
job, and in the autumn and winter of 1920 he claimed to have
personally inspected two hundred and eight ancient sites in and
around the Cotswolds, many of them unmarked. Eighty-one
new barrows were added to the map. Encouraged by this early

success, and having established a precedent for it, Crawford made fieldwork an essential part of his job, even though his long absences from the office were often frowned upon. As each county's turn came up he went out, in all weathers, to Wiltshire, Hertfordshire, Northumberland, Buckinghamshire, Cumberland, Warwickshire, Bedfordshire, Northamptonshire, Somerset, Yorkshire, Lancashire, Leicestershire, Sussex and Dorset; he visited Roman sites in Scotland, and prehistoric sites in the Scilly Isles, plotted long barrows and megaliths against geological and vegetative features; he compared symbols with monuments, maps with views, and views with old records found in county archives; he pencilled in his corrections and additions, filed his report at the end of each year.

His preferred mode of transport was the bicycle, with which, when adapted for his use, he claimed he could survive for a month or more at a time. Two lamp brackets fixed to the handlebars enabled him to carry up to five bags at once. A curved hook stopped the bags from knocking against his knees as he cycled. He strapped a raincoat onto the back carrier, and wrapped the all-important 6-inch maps around the crossbar. His trousers were tucked in, and the outfit on occasion was completed by furry mittens and a pilot's helmet, both from his war service. Decked out in a similar fashion, he said, he once cycled the seventy-two miles from Stonehaven, south of Aberdeen, to Blairgowrie, in a day. Substitute a Bristol fighter for the bicycle, and it was not so different an activity from Crawford's wartime observation work; and certainly – in his eyes at least – no less urgent.

He got help, of course; from regional antiquarian societies, and from a network of so-called 'honorary correspondents' who knew their corner of the country, and who supplied information in exchange for maps. Crawford called them his 'ferrets'. Some of his prize ferrets were barely out of short trousers, and were inspired by Crawford's example to become archaeologists themselves.

Other correspondents were retired surgeons, ex-colonels, land-owners and country curates, drawn from those ranks of the middle and upper classes that had long maintained antiquarian interests, and who took upon themselves the responsibility of recording antiquities in the shires. This they continued to do – but now when their identifications were questionable, the new Archaeology Officer made it his business to double-check their work in the field – 'a very necessary but very thankless task', as Crawford reported to the Royal Geographical Society in 1922.

It was as an attempt to reduce the need for such thankless double-checking that Crawford drew up some field archaeology 'Notes for Beginners', which were first issued by the Ordnance Survey in 1921, and reprinted many times throughout the following decades. Like the bird-spotter's field guide, instructing the amateur ornithologist how to tell the difference between, say, a marsh and a reed warbler, Crawford's 'Notes' issued guidelines on how to know an antiquity when you see one, and how not to

mistake for it a logan stone, rabbit warren or chalk pit. A low round swelling might indicate a round barrow, a common type of prehistoric burial site, easily recognized on open and unploughed land like the Wiltshire Downs. If, however, there is a shallow pit of the same sort of size nearby, the swelling is more likely to be earth dug out to make a pond, since run dry. Tumuli, like certain birds, occur in groups, and so if one is found, then others should be looked out for nearby. Instructions were given on how to identify the most easily overlooked types of site, those most camouflaged from view. The elusive remains of the Bronze Age burial mound known as a disc barrow manifests itself to the eye as a ring of lighter coloured soil in chalky land where the soil is ploughed; in late spring where there is grass it appears as a circle that is greener than its surroundings. Long barrows were likely to be more conspicuous: readers of Crawford's 'Notes' were advised to look out for mounds of around one hundred feet long, slightly broader and higher at one end. Long barrows take different forms in different geological zones; in Wiltshire, where there is little stone, they were made of earth; there the field-worker was told to look out for broad ditches running parallel to an earthy mound. In rocky country long barrows were made of large stones as well as earth. Cornish 'dolmens' and Welsh 'cromlechs', Crawford told his readers, are the exposed burial chambers or portals of such barrows, all that remain of much larger structures. Since the portals were almost always to be found at the eastern end of the barrows, fieldworkers were advised to look carefully to the west of them for traces of the original mound. Crawford's 'Notes for Beginners' were a kind of natural-ists' guide to prehistory.

The field archaeology promoted by Crawford's 'Notes for Beginners' was an activity as much as a body of knowledge. In principle, it was most democratic – as long as you followed the rules, of course, and didn't go imagining that dolmens were altars built by Druids or ancient Egyptians. It encouraged participation, with no special equipment required; and it implied that discoveries by informed non-experts might well be possible. It had as much in common with rambling, birdwatching, scouting and landscape appreciation – pursuits with which it could easily be combined – as it did with scholarship. And so it found favour in a nation that was notoriously both suspicious of abstraction or bookishness and convinced of the wholesomeness of outdoor activities of all kinds. 'Field archaeology,' wrote Crawford later, reflecting on its development in this country, 'is an essentially English form of sport.'

Field archaeologists look at the landscape differently; they have to both see – really see – and *see through* superficial appearances. They try to perceive the outlines of ancient fields beneath modern ones, the old roads that might, or might not, coincide with roads that are still being used; they keep their eyes peeled for evidence of old boundaries or ditches, the slight contours of burial mounds, the buried foundations of Roman villas, or the ground-down ramparts of hill forts. 'The surface of England,' wrote Crawford, 'is a palimpsest, a document that has been written on and erased over and over again; and it is the business of the field archaeologist to decipher it.' Field archaeologists traipse, sniff and track; they learn to see beyond the lines of tarmac, pavement, hedge and fence through which the landscape is framed to the eye; they get away from the road. They focus their gaze upon what, in the 1920s and 30s, was invariably called 'the face of the land', looking out for scars, symptoms, visual disturbances. Faint wrinkles or pimples might only appear when, as the fieldworker moves across the landscape, they rise up on the horizon, or when the sun is low in a cloudless sky, and they are thrown into relief as shadows on the land. The task is to deduce causes from effects, origins from appearances. A pattern under the turf of a sheep run of closely set hummocks and banks emerging at dusk may be the remains of an ancient settlement, the slight protuberances of half-buried foundations. If the earth of rabbit scrapes here is black, or if potsherds turn up in molehills, it is likely to be an ancient site. But if there are stinging nettles growing on the site, and if the hummocks respect existing field boundaries, the soil has probably been recently disturbed, and it may be a quarry of a more recent date. Field archaeologists know that vegetation grows differently on soil that has been disturbed, even if that disturbance happened centuries ago. They know that crops grow more luxuriantly over silted-up ditches, and more stunted where there are buried remains. The site of a Roman villa might go unnoticed until a field of wheat grows and ripens, to reveal most strangely the outlines of buried masonry, only to disappear again at harvest. Slight contours or indentations on the land marking out the site of a lost settlement might be invisible to the eye until a low sun throws them into sharp but momentary relief. These are the sorts of thing the field archaeologist looks out for, like the shadows cast by oats growing on uneven ground, photographed by Crawford on an unusually clear summer evening in Northumberland.

The archaeologist's 'field sense' involves all of the senses, sharpened like the hunter's. His eye is trained, and like Sherlock Holmes he is alert to things that are invisible to others. He may spot, for example, a belt of gritty soil in a ploughed field, and it may be all that is left of this portion of a Roman road that is visible as a raised causeway in the neighbouring meadow. He may know, too, the best season in which to detect different kinds of site in different types of landscape. Fieldwork is impossible in parts of Wales after May, wrote Crawford, since bracken hides the surface of the ground. A dry afternoon in March is the best time anywhere, since vegetation is low, and 'every fold in the ground is plainly visible' in the low sunlight. January in Scotland might be cold but, wrote Crawford, 'the low, yellow sunlight in midwinter is ample compensation for the slight discomforts endured, and ideal for photography'.

And how beautiful they are, the photographs Crawford took

in the field. How well he knew the way in which the low Scottish
sunlight could illuminate a scene, how the light shone differently
in a denuded Fife wood on a February afternoon to a leafy
Southampton suburb on a July morning, how shadows are the
result of a unique meeting of time and place, and how they had
history in them. Clarity of information was their purpose, not
beauty. Yet Crawford's photographs make it seem as though he
had a particular knack of finding the remains of the past, however inauspicious their guise; as if he knew that it was *here*, where
there is now a line of trees, that there was once an earthwork, and
that it would be at just this moment as the sun's rays pierce the
canopy of leaves that the telltale ledge would be illuminated. His
photographic eye seems oracular, seeing things that are hidden
to ordinary sight, reminding us of Walter Benjamin's remark that
photographers are all the descendants of 'augurers and harus-
pices', those who read omens and portents in the stars, in the
flights of birds and the entrails of animals, uncovering guilt – and
foreseeing the future. So sure does his eye seem of locating the
traces of the past that it seems as though if only we were per-
ceptive enough we too could see the layers of the palimpsest, the
marks of the ancient builders, the labourers, and the passers-by,
every fold and scratch in the ground all coming out in shadows
and shining sunlight.

The eye of the field archaeologist is evident in Crawford's photographs. And he was, by all accounts, astonishingly observant.
The artist John Piper and his wife once shared a car with him, and
were amazed by how much he saw in the landscape that passed
by their windows. He saw things where others saw nothing.
But it was not just a question of *seeing*, the action of the trained
eye in the landscape. The observation of the field archaeologist
involved tactility as much as vision, feeling the land as well
as just looking at it, like the time that Crawford took soundings
with a walking stick along the bottom of a ditch on the Silchester–
Speen road in Berkshire, looking for the rounded hump of a Roman

causeway. What is sought is a visceral knowledge of the land that is as intimate as the farmer's knowledge of his fields. Crawford knew that field archaeologists had to acquire and develop the sort of knowledge possessed as a matter of course by countrymen, and he often consulted local people about the land they lived on. A woman who lived in a cottage in Avebury on the old road – long since disappeared – to East Kennet told him that the plants in her garden grew differently in the place where the road was said to have been. What was important to field archaeologists was to really *know* different kinds of landscape – chalk downs, fenland marshes or gravel flats; how they behaved in different circumstances, how fast and in what manner old monuments might degrade in them. They sought to know how, for example, tracks in chalky country might sink over time; how, after rain, silted-up ditches hold moisture for longer than the surrounding earth; or how ploughing on an incline – as was the case in the Somme valley – creates visible banks known as 'lynchets'.

Is it any wonder that so many medical doctors have pursued archaeology? Substitute the landscape for the human body, and an archaeologist's 'field-sense' was precisely like the 'physician's acumen', according to Cecil Curwen, one of Crawford's 'ferrets', and a doctor himself. One of the earliest tracts on field archaeo-logy, the seventeenth-century *Hydriotaphia* or *Urne-Buriall*, was penned by a physician, Sir Thomas Browne. And the very term 'field archaeology' was coined by Dr J. P. Williams-Freeman, one of Crawford's early mentors, in the title of his 1915 book *An Introduction to Field Archaeology as Illustrated by Hampshire*. It was while doing his rounds as a country doctor on the edge of Salisbury Plain that Williams-Freeman began to observe the way in which crops grew differently over silted-up ditches, and how the outlines of ancient fields were visible within the boundaries of newer ones. On the surface of the land, as on the human body, superficial symptoms betray underlying causes. Prehistoric, Roman or medieval sites 'present', like medical symptoms; the site of an ancient burial 'presents' as a dark ring in dry grass or, under other circumstances, as a chalky ring in ploughed earth. The field archaeologist, like the medical doctor, needs to know what questions to ask about such symptoms, what combinations they appear in, what form they take under different conditions, or in different areas, what further tests might be carried out before delving deeper. The diagnosis takes place without surgi-cal intervention, although there might be tools that can be used to get a better idea of the nature of the underlying cause, like the percussive use of an iron pick on the ground to hear whether it hides an underground ditch or pit, a technique known as 'bosing', developed by General Pitt-Rivers and his helpers in the nine-teenth century. Excavation is archaeology's surgery, the search for proof; field archaeology is non-invasive, the identification, in the first instance, of symptoms – and the divination, through the senses, of the presence of historical remains.

Unlike his famous contemporary Mortimer Wheeler, Crawford
was not really an archaeologist who did a great deal of digging
himself. 'His prime interest,' recalled Glyn Daniel, 'was the face
of the countryside in its archaeological aspects.' It was not just
where ancient sites and monuments were to be found that interested him; it was how they related to each other, what constellations
they formed, and how the siting of those constellations related
to topography – geology, vegetation, trade routes, sources of water.
Working at the Ordnance Survey was, in this sense, ideal; for he
was at the very source of the most up-to-date cartographic expertise. Crawford could build up a database of sites and plot them
on the maps that it was his employer's business to produce. Not
long after he began work at the OS, on his own initiative
Crawford revivified a plan to produce so-called 'Period Maps'.
He drew up a model for a map of Roman Britain, plotting all
the known routes of Roman roads and the settlements they
connected against a background of physical features, and submitted it for approval. The Director General was not pleased,
apparently, to discover that the new Archaeology Officer had
used office hours to pursue what was an unsanctioned project.
The map, though, went ahead; it was published in 1924. The
*Daily Mail* described it as 'one of the most wonderful maps ever
produced', suggesting – rather surreally – that it would open up
'a new era in motor touring'. It sold out so quickly that the
Director General was forced to concede. This sort of success
was, in fact, just what the Ordnance Survey needed. After the
First World War the Survey was under considerable pressure
to broaden the market for its maps. The artist Ellis Martin had
been brought in to design map covers, part of the popularization
drive of the 1920s; he designed the cover of Crawford's Map of
Roman Britain, which was quickly reprinted, and a second edition produced in 1928.

More 'Period Maps' followed in the 1930s, including England
in the Seventeenth Century, the Celtic Earthworks of Salisbury

Plain, Neolithic Wessex, and Britain in the Dark Ages, which mapped the settlements, burial sites, tracks and trade routes of the British Isles after the Romans left, plotting them – where possible – against physical topography and the surface vegetation that was thought to exist at the time. Crawford considered these maps to be the chief accomplishment of the Archaeology Office during his time there. It was not just that they sold well, although this was important to Crawford as part of his own popularization drive. It was also that they were, for him, works of art, and the very embodiment of the sort of non-textual history that he had long believed in.

He was not the only one. The 1920s and 30s saw a great flowering of British field archaeology, with Crawford and his maps a central part of it. Young archaeologists like Stuart Piggott, Charles Phillips, Grahame Clark and Christopher Hawkes (to all of whom Crawford was 'Ogs', or sometimes 'Uncle Ogs'), as well as others like Cyril Fox, E. Cecil Curwen and Williams-Freeman, were actively and systematically investigating the British landscape in the spirit of a whole lineage of antiquarians stretching back to the sixteenth century – Leland, Stukeley, Colt Hoare, Pitt-Rivers – but with better tools at their disposal, especially aerial photography. Like Crawford and Peake, they were interested in landscapes of settlement, not just in isolated remains or finds. Cyril Fox, for example, plotted the hill forts, dykes and ancient tracks of Cambridgeshire against a reconstruction of the county's vegetation and coastline in prehistoric times, when Ely was still an island, and Cambridge not far from the coast. His work on ancient landscapes was published as a series of maps in his strangely titled book of 1932, *The Personality of Britain*. Others – including Crawford – were obsessed by prehistoric agriculture, and the patterns of ancient field systems, many of them still visible on the plains of Wessex and elsewhere; many more turned out to be visible from the air.

Crawford made his office at the Ordnance Survey the epicentre of this sort of work, the first port of call for workers in the field. He built up a collection of photographs of cadastral maps, old maps of country estates which – like the maps drawn in the eighteenth century by Stukeley or Colt Hoare – often included invaluable archaeological information, which had since been lost or built over. After coming to an arrangement with the Air Ministry that any RAF air photograph showing archaeological information would be transferred to the OS Archaeology Office, he created a centralized archive of aerial archaeology of the entire British Isles, accessible by archaeologists and members of the public. He encouraged young archaeologists to use these resources, and to add to them. And in 1927 he began his own journal, *Antiquity*, as a publication in which new work, and new findings, both on the ground and from the air, could be published.

Crawford conceived of his work, and the work of a select group of his fellow archaeologists (described by him as a 'heroic band'), as a new wave in archaeology. The 'heroic band' filled the pages of *Antiquity* in its early years, and included Piggott, Clark, Hawkes, Fox, Gordon Childe, Mortimer Wheeler and T. D. Kendrick. These names would one day become the archaeological establishment. But in the 1920s they were the rebels, the 'young turks' who would rather be out in the field than in the comfortable reading room of the Society of Antiquaries. Crawford was amongst them. Archaeology, he felt, had for too long been in the hands of gentlemen amateurs and genteel county societies, who followed their own whims and interests; it had for too long been a regional, amateur concern. And it was far too important to be left entirely to them, with their predilection for brass rubbings and genealogies. It required a scientific outlook, a clear mind, and a willingness to get your boots dirty; it also required a knowledge of certain basic and established facts. Training was required. Effectively Crawford and his 'heroic band' represented the professionalization of a field that had hitherto been the province of just about anyone with the leisure and the inclination to pursue it. As the historian Adam Stout has shown, these archaeologists sought to establish *authority* in a hitherto largely unregulated field. And they pretty much succeeded. Theirs was a kind of archaeological modernism, that left its mark on just about every major ancient site in Britain.

As for Crawford, his work at the Ordnance Survey – the 'Notes for Beginners', the Period Maps, his Occasional Papers, and his county-by-county collecting of archaeological data – was just such an exercise in the establishment of authority. He identified the different types of sites, and standardized the way in which they were represented on maps. His office decided the proper names for different sites, and printed them – with unassailable authority – on the 6-inch maps. Crawford was very anxious to establish the authority of the Archaeology Office – that, in a sense, was the purpose of his 'Notes for Beginners' and his other publications and broadcasts, warning of the dangers of false identifications and wild ideas. The amateurs and the county societies had their role, but after Crawford came to office, it was radically redefined. They could (and should) collect information – as long as they knew what they were looking for – but they were warned against interpreting it. That was the job for a trained archaeologist. It was no longer acceptable, thought Crawford, for just anyone to have a go at prehistory.

If Crawford was defensive, it was because his own position was insecure. There were hardly any paid positions for archaeologists before the Second World War; most archaeologists did it for nothing. The subject had not yet been established in universities, and its public role was not yet a given. Crawford's post at the Ordnance Survey was new, and it was by no means guaranteed. For the first few years of his job Crawford was paid at a daily rate of twelve shillings, since the Treasury did not think it necessary to sanction a proper wage; indeed, they suggested in 1922 that the work ought to be done on a part-time basis. To be

fair, the Ordnance Survey (after an intervention from the
President of the Society of Antiquaries) fought Crawford's corner
at this point. 'The archaeological information on Ordnance
Survey maps is quite an important feature, in a country like ours,'
wrote the Director General, 'and it ought to be dealt with by an
expert instead of being left more or less to amateur effort as it
has been in the past.' The Treasury agreed to fund the post for
three years. In 1926 – by which time Crawford was forty – the
Ordnance Survey sought to make his post permanent. The
Treasury agreed; but the correspondence between the Lords of
the Treasury and the Ministry of Agriculture and Fisheries, writing on behalf of the Ordnance Survey, shows a distinct reluctance
at every stage to value in principle the work of the Archaeological
Officer, and bring his pay up to date throughout his time there.
The ministry and the Ordnance Survey argued repeatedly that
Crawford's work brought credit to the organization, and money,
too, thanks to the 'Period Maps' which sold in their thousands.
Crawford's work was framed as an essential part of the Survey's
modernizing process, and its public profile. Yet the Treasury
certainly needed convincing. Even when it was agreed to grant
Crawford an assistant in 1938, the Treasury had to be persuaded
that a decent wage would need to be advertised in order to attract
a properly qualified person.

In the meantime, the volume of Crawford's work at the OS was
increasing enormously, largely thanks to his own industry and
initiative. The build-up of the archive of aerial photographs collected from the RAF, the production of 'Period Maps', the listing
of megalithic monuments, the rounds of fieldwork for county
revisions, communication with honorary correspondents; all of
these kept him very busy. The volume of letters received by the
Archaeology Office from members of the public increased enormously, too. Correspondents from the fastnesses of the British
Isles wrote with questions about their localities, suggestions for
identification, requests for information, or for work experience.

Crawford tried to answer them all, although – as the poet Geoffrey Grigson found out when he approached him – he did not have much patience for whimsy or wild ideas. He was clearly not easy to work with. His successor, Charles Phillips, wrote later that Crawford was likeable but exasperating, and that the Archaeology Office was much more peaceful when he was out of it. At the Ordnance Survey his irritability seems to have derived, in part, from a conflict between his archaeological ambitions – which became more urgent as urban development threatened to destroy ancient landscapes – and the institutional intransigence he encountered. This conflict reached its peak in 1940 when bombs fell on Southampton, and the Ordnance Survey – having made no preparations for such an event, according to Crawford, despite his warnings – lost much of its irreplaceable accumulation of papers, printing plates, photographic negatives, and archives, including Crawford's own library.

For all his complaints, though – and there were many, from the illiteracy of its typists to the bureaucracy of the Stationery Office – there were advantages to being part of the State machinery of the OS; and Crawford knew it. He had been keen from the start to democratize archaeology as an activity, and to make available its findings to the broadest public. He wanted to promote an understanding of archaeology against a geographical template, to put archaeology firmly on the map, and to get the map into as many hands as possible. The OS was a place from which he could carry out these ambitions, with its cartographic expertise, its privileged access to the RAF, and – from the 1920s – its marketing drive. It was a good place for one of Geddes's students to set up shop, its maps, like the Outlook Tower, promoting a certain sort of informed citizenship. His was, in fact, in a position of considerable power. His separateness from the various archaeological societies and the handful of universities in which Archaeology was taught suited him. As Mortimer Wheeler wrote after Crawford's death, he had an 'inability to work in harness'.

If he received little official encouragement for those projects which would become his legacy – aerial archaeology, the 'Period Maps' – the fact that the administration took relatively little interest in his work ensured an environment in which he could largely do his own thing.

It was aerial archaeology that – with Crawford's encouragement – really kick-started British field archaeology in the 1920s and publicized its findings. Seen from the air, this old country certainly showed its age. Old pathways, ploughed-over burial mounds, and the craquelure of ancient field systems might not be visible from the ground, but in an aerial photograph they could be seen with extraordinary precision. Seen from the air it was easier, too, to distinguish old networks from subsequent developments. The ridged outlines, or 'ribs' of older cultivation systems, in Crawford's words, showed up through the network of modern field boundaries 'like the bony skeleton of an old horse'. The palimpsest of the British landscape could be photographed like an ancient text, especially in the deforested regions of southern and central England. The gravel flats of the Thames valley, the marshy fenlands of East Anglia, or the chalky Southern downs all gave good results. And how spectacular and strange it looked, this old country that we thought we knew so well; how astonishing it was to see through this most modern of lenses these ghosts of history. It was quite literally a kind of revelation. As the historian G. M. Trevelyan told Crawford in 1929, 'I think the discovery of these old Celtic fields, from under the palimpsest of later agricultural systems, is the most romantic thing that has come to stir our historical imaginations since the first Cretan finds.'

Before the invention of flight, archaeologists and antiquarians had certainly imagined the benefits of an aerial view; and one or two experimented with balloons and kites. Crawford's experience of flying in the First World War reinforced his conviction that

aerial photographs might be of quite some interest to archaeologists. But it wasn't until 1922, when Dr Williams-Freeman
showed him some RAF photographs of Hampshire, that he realized just how interesting they could be. Pictures of Windmill Hill,
near Crawley, taken at 10,000 feet revealed an entire system of
ancient field boundaries, or lynchets, which was insensible to
the earthbound observer. This was just the kind of thing that
Crawford had dreamed of. So clearly marked on the photographic plate was this pattern that he could make a map out of
it, in exactly the same way as enemy trenches had been mapped
during the war. This was a map which – as he announced to the
Royal Geographical Society in March 1923 – was nothing less
than an accurate plan of the 'fields of a group of communities
which ceased to exist about 1,500 years ago'. It was like having
access, for the first time, to a lost world. The invention of aerial
photography, Crawford announced, would be to archaeology
what the invention of the telescope was to astronomy. It was the
instrument archaeology had been waiting for.

The lynchets had turned up as if by accident on the RAF
pictures of Hampshire, which was why Air Commodore Clark-
Hall had shown them to Williams-Freeman. How many more
faint constellations of ancient settlements might turn up almost
casually on the practice aerial photographs of the RAF, how
many burial mounds, field boundaries, enclosures, fortifications,
lost villages? Crawford lost no time in finding out. There was
an army school at the Old Sarum airfield on Salisbury Plain, where
pilots were trained in the arts of aerial reconnaissance and artillery
spotting that had been developed in the war. Looking over their
practice negatives, Crawford found something remarkable on
some shots taken over the fields near Stonehenge. Nobody in
1923 knew for sure the course of the Eastern branch of the
Stonehenge Avenue; nobody had known for hundreds of years.
What Crawford thought he saw on these negatives were the faint
lines of the bank and ditch of the Avenue leading away from the

famous stone circle towards the river Avon. The corn grew differently over this bank and ditch in the dry summer of 1921
when the photos were taken, and while the difference was so
slight that it could not be seen from the ground, it was clear
enough from the air. Back on the ground, Crawford and the
archaeologist A. D. Passmore used the aerial photographs as a
guide to where they might look for the remains of the Avenue. 'It
was like steering a ship by means of sounding,' wrote Crawford,
for there was no sign on the ground of where the Avenue might
be. Trenches were excavated in three places, revealing the chalk
ditches filled with soil they hoped to find, along with a whole
load of flint scrapers pocketed by Passmore for his collection,
later left to the Ashmolean Museum. Out in the stubbly fields in
the autumn of 1923 other archaeologists who came to have a
look were 'quite satisfied' that the course of the Avenue had been
proved. The advantage of aerial photography, as Crawford
announced, was not just visual revelation, thrilling though that
was. It was also that it provided a key to excavation; X marks the
spot where to start digging.

It was not accidental that one of aerial archaeology's first vic-
tories should have been connected with Stonehenge. At the
aerodrome at Old Sarum, Crawford was looking for something
dramatic, something, surely, that would capture the public imagination and publicize the new technique; and anything connected
with Britain's most celebrated prehistoric monument – already in
the news in the early 1920s as it was being excavated by Colonel
William Hawley – was bound to do that. The whole story of the
discovery of the course of the Avenue as it unfolded was written
up in the *Observer* and in the *Illustrated London News*, where
it was accompanied by these most remarkable photographs.
Aviation was still new, aerial photography even newer; both had
a glamour which now infected the image of domestic archaeology, hitherto the province, in the public imagination at least, of
the grave-fossicking antiquary. Air travel had a futuristic quality

to it, still. The fusion of flight with Stonehenge was heady and headline-grabbing; especially when it promised to reveal something completely new about the old stones. Aerial archaeology came not just as a tool to the working archaeology, but as a boost to its public image. And Crawford's name – itself given weight by his association with the Ordnance Survey – was firmly associated with the new technique.

It was as a result of reading about the aerial discoveries in the *Observer* in 1923 that Alexander Keiller, heir to the family marmalade fortune, wrote to Crawford. Keiller was a trained pilot with antiquarian interests who had worked in intelligence during the war, and he proposed to finance an aerial survey. Crawford and Keiller hired a plane, installed a captured German camera in the observer's cockpit, and set up their headquarters at Andover. In the spring and summer of 1924, accompanied by a pilot, Captain Gaskell, they flew over Berkshire, Dorset, Hampshire, Somerset and Wiltshire, looking out for visible remains. They mounted the photographs resulting from these sorties on cardboard, and walked over the ground each covered, looking out for evidence at ground level, drawing up a schematic map for each one. The photographs and the plans were compiled and published, with commentary, as *Wessex from the Air* in 1928, a strange and beautiful tome. It turned out to be too wet for crop sites to appear, but Crawford and Keiller learned how to catch the banks and ditches of hill forts or ancient fields either early in the morning, or just before dusk, hours of the day they called 'lynchet time'. 'On a June morning before breakfast the greater part of Salisbury Plain is seen to be covered with the banks of abandoned Celtic fields,' wrote Crawford, in his introduction to *Wessex from the Air*, 'but afterwards they "fade into the light of common day".'

The quotation is from Wordsworth's 'Intimations of Immortality'; it is one of the moments in which Crawford's Romantic sensibility surfaces in what is otherwise the spare prose of a diehard empiricist. Such moments appear throughout Crawford's writings and in the visual logic of his photographs. They formed a link between professional archaeologist and non-specialist reader, something he was keen to maintain; but they also betray a poetic imagination which was sometimes at odds with, and sometimes in marvellous tune with, his professional activities. (Scratch the rationalist, and a romantic appears; this was the man, after all, who as a teenage boy was bullied for believing in ghosts, which – as he told his aunt – he believed were 'all over the place, only not visible . . .') He saw the astonishing beauty of aerial archaeology no less than those artists in the 1930s – John Piper, Paul Nash – who were so fascinated by it; but he had little time for visual art himself. Aerial archaeology – unlike art – had a purpose from which its beauty was inextricable. And perhaps it was precisely because he saw the perfect beauty of aerial photography – its exquisite fitness to the purpose of archaeological revelation, a 'vision splendid' – that he picked it up in 1922 and ran.

The basic premise of aerial archaeology is the fact that when earth has been disturbed, when a post hole or ditch has been dug, or a bank built up, that ground is never quite the same again. This is true whether the disturbance happened recently, or thousands of years ago; the die is cast. That particular bit of earth has been differentiated from the surrounding earth, although we might not be able to see it. Under certain conditions the difference becomes visible to an aerial observer. So at certain times of day, when the sun is low in the sky, the outlines of ancient fields become visible over Salisbury Plain, as shadows throw their ridges and dimples into sharp relief; these are known as 'shadow sites'. So-called 'soil sites' appear when the disturbed earth retains more moisture – or less – than the surrounding earth, and so appears darker or more pale. 'Crop sites' appear when surface vegetation registers the difference in the underlying earth. The roots of plants will not be able to penetrate the earth so deeply where there are subterranean remains, for example, and as a result the plants will grow stunted. In times of drought these stunted plants will dry out more quickly than the others, and will appear pale to an aerial observer. Likewise, plants that grow over silted-up ditches will grow more luxuriantly, and will be the last to wither in a drought, retaining their colour when the others have become pale. Surface vegetation can act like the dust of the detective, or photographic developing fluid, but only under certain circumstances that are not always easy to predict. Barley is a more sensitive 'developer', for example, than oats, wheat or grass, but only in certain soils. Dry spells can bring about remarkably sharp crop sites, like the outline of the medieval tithe barn, complete with buttresses, that appeared in the grass at Dorchester in June of 1938. But sites like this one are only spectacular if there is an observer to see them. The aerial archaeologist has to be in the right place at the right time; he is a geomancer in collusion with the sun, the weather and the crops in the fields.

It was Crawford who categorized sites according to how they reveal themselves to an airborne camera – as shadow site, soil site, crop site – or, more rarely, through the patterns of melting snow. Crawford explained and showcased the discoveries of aerial archaeology in two buff-coloured OS pamphlets in 1924 and 1929, by which time his name was firmly identified with the new technique. He did not take many aerial photographs himself; flying in these days was largely confined to the military forces. But he encouraged the RAF to look out for sites on practice flights, and he tirelessly publicized the new technique and its findings, not least in *Antiquity*.

One of the most exciting things about aerial photography was that it showed mysterious features that had not been seen before and that could not be identified, like the large rectangular enclosures that showed up in the Thames valley, at Dorchester, Benson and Sutton Courtenay. Another new type of site revealed by aerial archaeology was represented by Woodhenge, found by Squadron Leader Insall, a pilot stationed at Netheravon on Salisbury Plain.

Flying near Amesbury in the winter of 1925 he spotted a circle with a curious series of concentric white dots within it on a ploughed field. Returning late the following June the field was full of wheat, and now both the circle and dots appeared dark. The site was later excavated, and the dots Insall saw turned out to be pits that had once contained wooden posts, in a structure thought to be like nearby Stonehenge, but constructed from wood rather than stone. Prehistoric timber circles like Woodhenge are a type of monument that owe their discovery to aerial archaeology, since their scant traces are rarely visible from the ground. It was discoveries like Insall's that caused Crawford to encourage any 'young archaeologist who wants to make discoveries' to 'join a flying-club and learn to fly. Not until then,' he said, 'will the harvest be reaped ... England is still, for the archaeological aviator, an almost unexplored country.'

Someone who heeded the call to explore this unknown country was Major George Allen, after picking up a copy of one of

Crawford's Ordnance Survey pamphlets in a Southampton hotel. Allen was the wealthy managing director of Messrs John Allen and Sons, his family's engineering firm in Cowley near Oxford. He had his own plane, based in a private airstrip at Clifton Hampden; and he was willing and able to respond quickly as sites were identified, or when the circumstances were propitious for discovery. In consultation with Crawford and other archaeologists he went on photographic expeditions all over the Thames valley in the 1930s. Time and money were little object, and so he could return again and again to the same site under different circumstances. In July 1932, for example, he photographed the big circles – due to the silted-up ditches of a prehistoric henge monument – that had appeared in the arable fields at Dorchester between the Abingdon and Oxford roads; and he returned again and again between April and August of the following year as the circles slowly emerged but only in certain fields; and again in the summer of 1938 when, since the entire site was planted with cereal crops, the whole monument was visible from above. (There is nothing there now; the site was turned into a gravel pit and flooded.) Allen's circumstances meant that he could fly off at a moment's notice. 'There is a plum waiting to be picked,' Crawford told Allen in a letter of April 1933, 'and that is Castor, near Peterborough.' Allen sped off, although, as he told Crawford a couple of weeks later, 'I doubt if the plum was quite ready.' Later that dry summer he had more luck. 'I have been overwhelmed with air work,' he told Passmore in a letter. 'The whole of the Thames valley and its tributaries have come out in a violent rash, circles and marks everywhere.' A single photograph of Stanton Harcourt showed twenty-six new circles. Crawford was delighted by Allen's results, like the lovely photograph he took in 1936 of Headington, near Oxford, where medieval strip lynchets line up like waves on a petrified sea, about to break over an orderly line of villas and their gardens. As he told the Prehistoric Society in 1938, 'When I see his handwriting on a large packet amongst my morning letters, I know that there will be no work done until the contents have been examined and the new discoveries duly gloated over.'

The photographs that Major Allen took in the decade before his sudden death, in a motoring accident, in 1940, were taken with a large camera that he designed and built himself. This camera, now in the Ashmolean Museum, was made out of aluminium; it was fitted with a large handle on each side, and took one plate at a time – the plate had to be replaced after each exposure. Allen flew his plane single-handed, Ordnance Survey map across his knees. Flying hands off ('there is no risk,' he wrote, 'in letting go the controls'), he would lean out to take each photograph. This resulted in an oblique image, rather than the vertical shots – much better for mapping purposes – that were taken for *Wessex from the Air*. Allen's technique was novel; but the results were stunningly beautiful. There is a photograph of fields near Royston, taken in the winter, just after rain. Two

lines divide the image horizontally; one is the railway line from
Royston to Baldock, and a train is just passing, a plume of white
smoke drifting behind it. Parallel to the railway line is a modern
road, a solitary car making its way along it. It is a scene of
modernity and movement; but other landscape features, invisible to the driver of the car or passengers in the train, can clearly
be seen. Iron Age ditches, silted up over the centuries, bisect
both the road and the railway; they have absorbed the rainfall
and so appear as dark stained lines across the ploughed fields.
And just below the road, and running alongside it, are the ruts
of the old Icknield Way. What is astonishing to the point of
uncanniness is the way in which these ancient features, invisible from the ground, secretly share the landscape with the
living, as they go about their business. The appearance, in a
photograph, of these traces of the past is like the casual way in
which ghosts appear alongside the living as they pose in their
drawing rooms in Victorian spirit photography. Perhaps this was
why, in the early days of the new technique, Crawford was at
pains to tell the audiences he lectured on the subject that there
was nothing magical about it, and no photographic tricks
involved. The camera simply recorded what the aerial
observer saw.

When Major Allen returned after a month to the same fields,
the marks of the ditches were gone; more rain had fallen and the
dampness of the field had been levelled out. Similarly elusive
was the double enclosure known as 'Caesar's Camp' on
Greenfield Common in Middlesex. Stukeley knew of this site in
the eighteenth century – he recorded it, and gave it its misleading name – but by the twentieth century its precise location
was unknown. Flying back from Scotland in June 1930,
Crawford spotted the site – he recognized it from Stukeley's
drawing – in a field outside Staines. He had no camera with him,
however, and the moment was lost. Not until the spring of 1933
did Major Allen manage to photograph it, a faint figure in a

ploughed field. The back gardens of a strip of new suburban villas abut the fields in which this strange figure persists, after so many centuries; but the occupants of those houses presumably do not know that they are living in such proximity to a site that was there long before they were. They cannot see what the

STAINES.I. 15. 4. 33.

aerial viewer can see. It is a disjuncture of perspective that has revealed the ghost. And yet here it is, this ghost; and the uncanny thing is surely that this 'lost' relic has been there all along, unperceived.

All his life Crawford was fond of cats. And his analogy for the disjuncture of perspective of the aerial view was that it was like the difference between a cat's view of a patterned carpet, and a man's view of the same carpet. The man, standing over it, can see quite clearly the pattern on the carpet. The cat, however, has only a blurred awareness of the pattern, being so close to it. So pleased was he with this analogy that Crawford took photographs of a patterned carpet, as seen by a cat, and the same carpet as seen by a man, and published them in his contribution to a scientific volume on aerial archaeology. The photographs demonstrated how shapes that are only partially sensible from the ground become clearer from the air. This cat-on-the-carpet analogy reinforces a sense felt in front of the photographs of Royston and Staines that aerial archaeology defamiliarizes the landscape we know, making the familiar scene of roads, fields and suburban life strange indeed. It implies that we earthbound humans are like the cat on the carpet, with only a partial perception of the earth we tread upon, and live in. It takes another kind of eye, another viewpoint to reveal to us the truth about the world. And does this not have a theological resonance? Does it not remind us, once again, that there may be a vantage point – God's, surely, and the great eye in the sky – from which things are perfectly clear? If anything, Crawford would have claimed a military rather than a theological precedent, the lessons of the battlefield in the First World War when it became clear that only from above was the mazy network of trenches visible and intelligible. It's the same logic as that which underpinned the dream of Universal History. The participants in history may not have a clear view of the vast processes of which they are just a tiny part. Yet seen, as it were, from a great distance, the pattern of those processes comes into focus.

One of the most remarkable things about aerial archaeology is that very few human processes will completely remove a site from view for ever. It might be decades – centuries even – before the right combination of crop growth, rain, sun and aerial observer results in a site manifesting itself and being photographed. But unless deep excavations or quarrying are carried out, removing all traces of the site, the possibility remains that one day, under new conditions, it will reveal itself. As the President of the Society of Antiquaries told his listeners in 1925, aerial photography had 'emphasized one thing, not quite

appreciated hitherto, namely, how sensitive the soil is, how slowly nature heals the wounds made by man'. Even if it is built over, a site can potentially persist, unless deep excavation has removed it when the foundations were dug. For all that it depends on chance, human ingenuity and the practical restraints of finance, technology and skill, there is a sense in which aerial

archaeology suggests that we just have to wait for the right combination of circumstances for the revelation of even the most
elusive traces of the past. Certainly more recent technologies of
remote sensing have captured images of sites which are not only
invisible from the ground but are also invisible to the ordinary
aerial observer. But a sense of this possibility was there from the
start, at least in Crawford's less guarded writings on the subject.
Describing two aerial photographs taken over Woodbury in 1929
showing an Iron Age crop site, Crawford described them as 'her-
alds of innumerable queer resurrections. They assure us that no
site, however flattened out, is really lost to knowledge.' Aerial
archaeology was the perfect visualization of a faith that the past
is never quite lost to us, for all that our desires to find it may be
thwarted. It implies that history – like the secrets of astronomy
and molecular biology – will surely reveal itself, given the right
tools, the right technological aids, the right viewpoint. Nobody,
surely, hoped for this more than O. G. S. Crawford. And perhaps
this is why, in his 1933 book *The Shape of Things to Come* (a
vision of a future World State ruled over by Air-men), H. G. Wells
had a survey aeroplane named Crawford locate the ancient wreck
of the mythical glider of Icarus under the sea in the year 2104.
What was lost shall be found; even if it takes hundreds or thousands of years.

# CHAPTER 4

The dimension of time was to Crawford just as real as the dimension of space; the only difference, as he was fond of pointing out, was that you could not go to the past for a holiday. Historians and prehistorians were therefore at something of a disadvantage compared to geographers or geologists, who just had to sally forth into the world in order to survey it. The business of mapping the world's coastlines, contours and geological strata was, he wrote, nearly complete; and this was thanks to the fact that we are able to travel in space. Mapping the time dimension was taking rather longer; for, as Crawford wrote, 'We cannot travel in Time. We cannot live in ancient Greece or in Ur. It is impossible to compile a chart or chronological table of the past as complete and accurate in its own way as was our world-map. The most we can do is to laboriously piece together such fragments as survive, in written records or in the rubbish-heap of buried cities.' But a complete and accurate chart – a historical map, in fact – was certainly the goal, extraordinary though that might sound to modern archaeologists and historians. And the 1920s were, in Crawford's view, an exciting time. So many fragments of the past had been discovered, that at last something like an accurate picture of history was beginning to emerge. It was to present this emerging picture to the public that in 1927 Crawford started his own journal.

*Antiquity* was a quarterly with a printer but no publisher, enabling Crawford to speak in an unusually direct way to his readers. It contained no adverts, depending on subscription fees to survive; and, rare for what was essentially a scientific journal, it was affiliated to no subsidizing scholarly society or institution. A loan from Alexander Keiller helped to start it up; but thereafter it had to make its way in the market – a fact of which Crawford was quite proud. *Antiquity* had no shortage of subscribers in its first decade. There was an audience for archaeology in the 1920s and 30s, as Crawford had discovered through the success of the Period Maps. Archaeology was in the news, especially the more glamorous finds like the discovery of the tomb of Tutankhamun, Leonard Woolley's excavations at Ur in Mesopotamia, or the Minoan civilization uncovered by Arthur Evans in Crete. But the popular newspapers could not, according to Crawford, be trusted to represent archaeological work accurately. Too often the press fed a public thirst for drama at the cost of accuracy. Less spectacular but more significant advances – new theoretical ideas, or apparently minor discoveries that nevertheless shed light on human development – were rarely reported on at all. The public's appetite had been whetted – but who would put it straight on hoaxes, who would point out the significance of archaeological discoveries large and small, directing attention away from the glittering prizes of grave-robbers towards the bigger picture of world history of which these were just a tiny part? Most existing archaeological journals were too specialist, and were not aimed at the general reader. This was where *Antiquity* positioned itself, somewhere between the learned societies and the popular press.

The discoveries of archaeology were, to Crawford, so very important in their implications that they ought to be part of every thinking person's knowledge. The missionary purpose of *Antiquity* was to spread the news from the field into the broader culture. To win readers Crawford knew his new journal had to look good on the shelf. And so its materials and typography were very carefully chosen. *Antiquity* was printed by the Quaker printer John Bellows of Gloucester on thick, high-quality paper, using the sort of well-spaced Bembo-ish typography associated with literary journals. It had its own distinctive logo, a woodcut silhouette of Stonehenge, designed by Ellis Martin, Crawford's colleague at the Ordnance Survey, and the man responsible for the cover design of many of their most popular maps in the 1920s and 30s. Crawford had learned the importance of an immediately recognizable brand from the entrepreneurial Henry Wellcome. And perhaps most strikingly of all, compared to other periodicals, *Antiquity* was stuffed with marvellous, high-quality photographic illustrations: stark images of landscapes studded with burial mounds, disinterred idols, shadows scudding over ancient fields. After war broke out in 1939, paper shortages meant that the text became more cramped, the photographs allowed less room; and *Antiquity* – like its editor – never quite recovered its visionary confidence. But for the decade or so after its inception, which was also the decade in which Crawford's vision of history was at its most strident, *Antiquity* was as visually stimulating as any artistic journal.

Crawford's first editorial read like the manifesto of an avant-garde. It staked out its territory in the most grandiose of terms: 'Our field is the earth,' he wrote, 'our range in time a million years or so, our subject the human race.' The time was surely ripe for survey. 'Never before has so much been known about the past; never has the desire of knowledge been greater.' The scope of *Antiquity* was vast; its approach scientific and modern. 'We employ methods of research undreamt of before; we call in the aviator, the photographer, the chemist, the astronomer, the botanist, to assist us.' It was only a few years, after all, since aerial photography had first shown its potential for archaeological research. *Antiquity* would report on aerial discoveries as they happened, and would keep readers informed about other applications of science and technology to archaeological problems.

Disciplinary boundaries meant nothing. There should be no real division between archaeology and science, just as there was none between history and prehistory. All knowledge was one; and any tool capable of producing historical knowledge – like the aeroplane – could be called upon to produce it.

There should be no division, either, between the study of supposedly 'advanced' civilizations – including Western civilization – and supposedly 'primitive' peoples. When Crawford did his anthropology diploma in Oxford, he absorbed a Victorian perspective of cultural evolution that organized all of the cultures of the world along a great evolutionary ladder. His tutor, Marett, insisted that there should not be 'one kind of history for savages, and another kind for ourselves, but the same kind of history, with the same evolutionary principle running through it, for all men, civilized and savage, present and past'. What this meant was that so-called 'primitive' peoples were seen as the living embodiment of the prehistoric tribes who once roamed Europe, for they were at a similar stage of evolutionary development. And so anthropology and archaeology were one. Studying the savage was studying ourselves, as Marett put it, as we were thousands of years ago. It was effectively a way around time travel; you might not be able to visit prehistoric Europe, but you could study the tribesmen of the Sudan. In anthropological circles this idea – so crudely put – may have already been looking rather quaint by the 1920s. But it remained one of the guiding principles of *Antiquity*, adding considerable colour to its pages. Crawford's first editorial set the tone: 'We shall not confine ourselves too rigidly within the conventional limits of archaeology. The past often lives on in the present. We cannot see the men who built and defended the hilltop settlements of Wessex; but we can learn much from living people who inhabit similar sites to-day in Algeria.'

For a periodical whose field was the earth, however, *Antiquity* in its first decade had a decidedly British accent. Most of the early issues had a disproportionate number of articles – about half – on

British sites, landscapes and cultures. The national bias was due, in part, to the nature of Crawford's position. It was clearly the cause of some friction at the Ordnance Survey that in addition to his roaming absences, the Archaeology Officer had begun his own publishing venture. But Crawford effectively turned his day job into the ideal base from which to edit an archaeological journal. In practical terms the fieldwork he undertook as part of county revisions could double up as material for articles, notes and news. He often reported on finds he made during his official work in the pages of his journal. What's more he ensured that after the dramatic findings at Stonehenge he was inevitably the first to know of any aerial discoveries by arranging for the RAF to send him any practice shots that included archaeological information. Exploiting the Ordnance Survey's status, in 1930 he visited every RAF station in the country equipped for photography, and drew up for each one a list of sites within a 25-mile radius that were to be where possible the subjects for practice work. If anything interesting turned up in these practice photographs, *Antiquity* was the perfect way of making it public. But it was not just aerial findings that Crawford managed to oversee. His job kept him in touch with archaeologists all over the country, from whom he could solicit reports and articles; and his position at the centre of a network of government officials, local correspondents and antiquarians ensured that he usually knew what was going on in the field.

And quite a lot *was* going on. *Antiquity*'s early years coincided with (and contributed to) a great flourishing of British archaeology; and it was designed by its founder as the platform for the new generation of workers in the field, the 'heroic band'. In 1928 the excavation season included Woodhenge (newly discovered from the air) by Captain and Mrs Maud Cunnington; the Iron Age village of Chysauster in Cornwall by T. D. Kendrick; the Belas Knap Long Barrow near Winchcombe by HM Office of Works; and the sites of four Romano-British towns: Colchester,

Caerleon, Richborough and Alchester. Throughout the 1930s
there were major excavations of British sites: Mortimer Wheeler's
work at Maiden Castle in Dorset, and at Verulamium; Alexander
Keiller and Stuart Piggott's excavations at Avebury and their
reconstruction of the avenue of stones that led there; Gordon

Childe's uncovering of the Neolithic village of Skara Brae in the
Orkney Islands; the excavation of Woodbury near Salisbury led
by Gerhard Bersu; and then, just as war was about to break out,
the discovery of the Saxon ship-burial at Sutton Hoo in Suffolk.
All of these were written up in *Antiquity*, usually by the protag-
onists themselves; in the case of Sutton Hoo an entire issue was
dedicated to it. There were reports, too, on fieldwork in progress
from all corners of the nation: from Cyril Fox in Cambridgeshire,
from Cecil Curwen in Sussex and in the Hebrides, and from
Crawford himself in Oxfordshire, the Scottish borders and wherever else he happened to be on official, or unofficial business.

   *Antiquity's* British bias was popular with its readers, if the letters to its editor are anything to go by. Some of this may have
been due to the fact that many subscribers were landowners with

local antiquarian interests, chaps like Colonel Sir Courtney Vyvyan, who had been second in command alongside Baden-Powell at the Siege of Mafeking, and who in 1927 ordered the re-erection of the so-called 'Dry Tree Menhir' on his land at Helston in Cornwall. This was exactly the sort that served as honorary correspondent for the Ordnance Survey. But *Antiquity* had a more democratic appeal than this; it had to if it was to survive, and carry out its editor's mission. Like the field archaeology 'Notes for Beginners' Crawford wrote up, the tone and content of *Antiquity* gave the impression that just about anyone in any part of the country could go out and find barrows or Roman roads; you just had to go about with your eyes open. It gave the impression that fragments of the ancient past were quite accessible to those with eyes to see; and that there were mysteries waiting to be investigated in every town and village. Crawford effectively tapped into a market for Old England, a market that was fed – if not created – by the growth in car ownership between the wars. Motor transport put the old country within reach; Albion was no longer just something you might read about, or imagine – it was a place you could visit.

*Antiquity* was begun in the same year as H. V. Morton's phenomenally successful book, *In Search of England*, was first published. Morton's book described how the author set off from London one morning in his Bullnose Morris to find England, the 'real' England that you had to leave the big cities to find, a sort of 'Deep England' equivalent to the idea of '*la France profonde*'. Morton more or less invented the powerful idea that a car could take you to an older and more authentic country. *In Search of England* was the progenitor of an entire genre nicely described by the geographer David Matless as 'motoring pastoral'. Shell, seeing the potential, started to advertise its petrol as offering exclusive access to a mysterious and ancient land. Artistic lithographs depicting idyllic and deserted historic sites like Stonehenge and the Long Man of Wilmington invited motorists to 'See Britain

First with Shell'. And there was a whole explosion of books with titles like *The Undiscovered Weald* or *Unknown Cornwall*, which promised to open up to their readers places that were off the standard tourist track, sights and sites that you could imagine yourself to be the very first to find.

All of this was small beer when compared to the Britain revealed by *Antiquity*. Truly strange images and objects filled its pages: a chariot wheel, found in the riverbank at Ryton; remains of a bear and an Arctic fox discovered in caves near Inchnadamph in Sutherland; modern troglodyes in West Kilbride. There seemed to be no end of such things; *Antiquity* implied that just about the whole of Britain was littered with them. Photographs of unimpressive-looking mounds and lumps, the sort of thing one might not notice as one went past in a car or a train, turn out to be burial mounds, still for all we know containing crouching skeletons or buried treasure. You just needed to know where to look.

And often *Antiquity* told you: readers were informed where they might be able to see crop marks or ridge-and-furrow field patterns from the window of a car, and which train lines gave good views of chalk hill figures like the Cerne Abbas giant. Even the most suburban of places had its curious and ancient relics, like 'Caesar's Camp' in Staines, visible only from the air. The country *Antiquity* showed its readers was one far stranger, far less well known than anything described in the topographical literature of armchair tourism. This was the real 'unknown' country, appealing to the surrealist as much as the motorist or rambler.

Reading *Antiquity* in the late 1920s or 30s you might believe that people in some parts of the British Isles were still living under conditions that had barely progressed, evolutionarily speaking, from the Dark Ages. An article on 'Prehistoric Agriculture in Britain' in 1927 was illustrated by a photograph of a Skye crofter using the caschrom, as if to illustrate the author's contention that the traction plough had not yet superseded the older implement in the remoter islands of Scotland. Another article entitled 'The Hebrides: A Cultural Backwater' described how the region had only emerged from the Iron Age at the end of the nineteenth century. Flour had been ground on querns on Lewis until fairly recently, readers were told, and primitive facsimiles of Royal Doulton china were hand-moulded out of clay until the arrival of Woolworth's in Stornoway. Photographs of shielings and black houses – some of them still inhabited in 1938 – accompanied the article. Perhaps then you *could* go to the past for a holiday after all. But city-dwellers didn't have to go as far as the outer reaches of Scotland to come across remnants of a superseded way of life. 'Possibly the most primitive dance in Europe' was reported still to be taking place in the Midlands in 1933. And one issue of *Antiquity* had a note on 'Primitive Huts near London' which described how conical huts in Epping Forest ('within twelve miles of Charing Cross') had been used by charcoal burners until 1910.

Modern life had not, then, completely blanketed out the old ways, the old roads or the old dwellings; they were still there, if you knew where to look. We might even be living in them, or alongside their remains, without realizing it, like the inhabitants of the villas in Major Allen's aerial photograph of Staines. In fact we could hardly avoid the remains of the past. For as *Antiquity* demonstrated, some thirty years before W. G. Hoskins's book (and TV series) *The Making of the English Landscape*, just about the whole of the British Isles was *made*, the product of human ingenuity and labour as much as of nature. Field systems were the product of enclosure, town layouts were often medieval in pattern, and new roads might follow the course of much older ones. *Antiquity* showed how even those towns that seemed the most suburban, the least 'historic' – like Staines or Croydon – were embedded in much older networks of roads and settlements, occupied the same ground, used – often – the same transport routes.

Many in the 1920s and 30s feared that urbanization, road-building and unchecked development were gradually but effectively wiping out an ever-diminishing 'old country'. The Campaign for the Preservation of Rural England (CPRE) had been founded in 1926 to counter the effects of development on the countryside, and its voice was a powerful one among the middle classes from which *Antiquity* drew its readership. In a sense Crawford's journal partly reassured its readers that the lineaments of the old country were still there, for all that they were increasingly hemmed in or built over by roads, railway lines and urban sprawl. But *Antiquity* also shared its readers' anxiety about changes to the 'face of the land'. Crawford's particular concern was that ancient landscapes with their irreplaceable field patterns or other traces of prehistoric life might be developed or built over, making his work and that of other field archaeologists more difficult. The Office of Works had the power to take specific ancient monuments into its guardianship. But until the Ancient Monuments Act of 1931 this power did not extend to areas of land, no matter how valuable a historical record that land was of agricultural, industrial or religious practices. Crawford was conscious of the threat to entire ancient landscapes as well as individual monuments, and he urged a programme of preservation. The need, he told his readers in 1929, was really urgent,

> for with the approaching electrification of Southern England, the coniferous activities of the Woods and Forests Department and of private planters, the demands of the Services for land for aerodromes and manoeuvres, the spread of bungaloid eruptions, and the threat of arterial roads and ribbon-development – with all these terrors imminent, it is unlikely that any open country or downland will be left in Southern England in a hundred years' time.

It was not enough, Crawford insisted, to preserve a monument or part of a site leaving its broader landscape context to go to the dogs. 'Who cares for Oldbury and St George's Hill now that they are infested with villas?' he asked his readers. Too often efforts were misdirected; unimportant or unthreatened sites were excavated when, elsewhere, whole landscapes were being destroyed. It was a question of mismanagement of resources, and an unfortunate provincialism which divided up archaeological work by county. An enlightened policy, Crawford told his readers, would buy up large portions of still unspoilt areas like Dorset and Dartmoor before the price of land rose still further. This was what Alexander Keiller had done in 1923 when he bought Windmill Hill near Avebury, as a 'patriotic act' to prevent the possibility – mooted in the early 1920s – of a wireless station, or worse, being built there. But then the British authorities were far from enlightened. When it came to what would later be called heritage management, wrote Crawford grimly, 'Our loyalties hark back not even to the Heptarchy but to a yet earlier prehistoric period of the tribal organization.'

Crawford mobilized the preservationist sympathies of his readers when it came to saving the landscape immediately around
Stonehenge. In 1927 this bit of land was described by the CPRE
as a 'mess': right up near the stones there was a gaudy café of the
sort routinely derided by preservationists, and nearby a decom-
missioned aerodrome was being used as a pig farm. The whole
area was earmarked for development, which, it was feared, would
spoil for ever the stones' 'loneliness' against the skies. The
government claimed its hands were tied. A public appeal was
organized in the name of the National Trust to buy up the land
and save it from the indignity of a row of 'Druids' Bungalows'.
Crawford publicized the appeal and urged his readers to respond,
which they did: the appeal was successful, and the land was
bought for the nation.

Crawford successfully utilized his readers' patriotism when –
as with the campaign to save the Stonehenge landscape – it suited
his purposes. He knew that articles on the more iconic monuments of the British landscape – the White Horse of Uffington,
Avebury, Cerne Abbas and Stonehenge – would be popular with
his readers. And of course British field archaeology was effectively
his day job. But Crawford really wanted *Antiquity* to have a truly
international outlook. Nationalism was, after all, a primitive
tribal sentiment. If he invoked it in his readers it was with what
he considered to be a higher purpose in mind.

Crawford travelled abroad whenever he could, both on official
OS business and when on leave; and his autobiography is full of
accounts of foreign travels. In 1928, for example, he visited the
Middle East on an OS-sanctioned trip to recover and preserve
aerial photographs taken there during the war. Many trips to
Europe in the 1930s came out of the initiative – raised by
Crawford himself in 1928 – to create a Map of the Roman Empire
as an international enterprise. The ever-pragmatic Crawford
hoped to exploit the nationalism of fascist Italy by suggesting that
the first sheet be Rome itself. Mussolini – whom Crawford met

in November 1932 – was predictably quite keen (Crawford later humorously suggested to a friend that it was he who had given the Italian dictator the 'big idea' of starting up the Roman Empire again). But only a few sheets, none of them Italian, were completed by the time war broke out. War prevented the map's completion. But before that happened, Crawford attended meetings in connection with the project in Florence, in Frankfurt-on-Main and Berlin, in Budapest, Vienna and Basle, along the way visiting Pompeii, Herculaneum and Ostia. All of this was part of Crawford's official work. He also took holidays in Algeria, Malta, Corsica, Tunisia, Germany, Austria and Romania, among many other places, including Cyprus, where he bought a house in 1936. In his autobiography he is rather defensive about the number of holidays he had, but almost everywhere he went, whether on official business or vacation, he visited archaeological sites or undertook some fieldwork of his own, taking photographs of ancient monuments, like megaliths in Schleswig; inscriptions, like those in Pompeii; or 'survivals' of outdated agricultural practices, like the primitive plough he saw still being used in Sadowitz in Bulgaria in 1937. Some of these finds ended up in *Antiquity*; so, too, did articles he solicited from archaeologists, anthropologists and others whom he made it his business to meet when he was away from home. Crawford was very keen for *Antiquity* to be a world journal.

Thus it was that alongside pieces on British subjects *Antiquity* carried articles on the pit-dwellings of Hungarian gypsies, underground villages in Southern Tunisia, and the way in which the Konyak Nagas of Assam dispose of their dead; there were reports on excavations from around the world, and comparisons between the formation of ancient tracks in Wessex, Malta and the Sudan; images of the furrows of prehistoric fields in Denmark, Siamese earthworks, Iraqi scarecrows and 'Donegal Survivals'; and considerations of more general topics such as 'the Role of Birds in Early Navigation', the significance of ship graffiti, and the origins

of bronze and wheat. Crawford certainly had a talent for striking juxtapositions. In its prime *Antiquity* was full of poetic resonances and visual correspondences, like the juxtaposition for no obvious reason of a modern Tunisian brush and a Norman stone arch, their formal resemblance surely not a coincidence. At times Crawford's journal looked as if it could have been a sourcebook for a native Surrealism. It certainly appealed to artists like Paul Nash and John Piper. 'Each number was an excitement concentrated in an article,' remembered the poet Geoffrey Grigson in 1978, 'it might be on the Uffington White Horse, or the travels of the Celtic Saints, or fortified churches in Transylvania, or megaliths in Assam, or the origins of cultivated plants, or waterclocks, or Cornish fish-cellars, or the Cerne Giant, the flasher of Dorset, or querns, or roses in antiquity.' Crawford in Grigson's

eyes was a sort of poet himself; 'archaeology's Eliot', he called him.
And even though Grigson sensed that there was a thread connect-
ing all of these fragments – just as there was in T. S. Eliot's poetry –
it was the marvellous oddities of *Antiquity*, and their surreal
juxtapositions, that thrilled him.

But *Antiquity* was supposed to be far more than a miscellany.
The whole point of starting a new journal was that all of these
fragments added up to something. When people in the past had
tried to see patterns in history they had failed, according to
Crawford, because there simply was not enough historical information available. Now, however, there had been so many new
discoveries that the pattern of history was becoming clear. Many
of these discoveries were fascinating in themselves. But one
shouldn't become distracted by details, however seductive they
might be. 'To see the sweep of history rather than its details,' he
told his readers, 'you must stand back and view it from a height
of detachment.' It was the aerial view again, the cat and the
carpet. You had to take the distanced view. And then, like someone getting up from a prone position on a carpet and looking down
at it, the pattern would become clear. It was as if, for Crawford, all
of the accumulating facts of history, all of the unearthed coins,
the Iron Age pots, roots of words, Roman ruins, the querns and
the earthen circles and the scythes and the myths and the har-
vesting devices of the world were at last beginning to fall into a
pattern which – like those 'Magic Eye' illusions popular in the
1990s – came into focus if you squinted, if you pulled back to the
right viewing distance. And the figure that emerged was so very
important that it deserved to be brought to the attention not just
of professional archaeologists but of every thinking person, for
it concerned everybody. 'What is to be the end of it all?' asked
Crawford towards the end of his first editorial. 'What new idea
is to emerge from all this vast accumulation of facts and give
them coherence? Has it already emerged? We shall return to this,
the most important subject of all.' The big idea; the figure in the

carpet; the most important subject of all. What would emerge out of all these facts, Crawford half-believed, half-hoped, was nothing less than the identification of the path along which the human race was treading, from its murky beginnings towards its future. It was an answer to the questions *Where Have We Come From?* and *Where Are We Going?* – questions that only the bold or the cranky dare to answer.

Baldly put, history's pattern – in Crawford's eyes – was one of evolutionary progress, in which science would triumph over all kinds of superstition and folly (including nationalisms). In an ambitious article entitled 'Historical Cycles' published in *Antiquity* in 1931, he elaborated further, with a nod to Flinders Petrie, Spengler and others. The history of civilization, he wrote, can be regarded as the recapitulation of the process of evolution. The different stages of civilization, in other words, correspond to different stages of the evolution of life. The argument went something like this. Since the earliest times human beings have organized themselves into ever-larger and ever-more complex groups, from the family to the tribe, the tribe to the village, village to town, town to city, city to nation, nation to empire, federation and league (such as the League of Nations). A 'solitary tool-using hunter' for thousands of years, the discovery of agriculture and the domestication of animals meant that *Homo sapiens* came to settle in small communities which later became villages, towns and eventually cities, these cities combining to form nations and so on. The process, argued Crawford, is directly analogous to that of evolution, where cells have arranged themselves into ever-more complex organisms, from the most primitive of unicellular life forms to multicellular organisms. As these organisms evolve the cells that comprise them become increasingly specialized as they are organized into groups, and elaborate systems such as the circulation of blood or the glandular system evolve to service them. So it is, wrote Crawford, with human society when it has advanced to city life, where different individuals and groups take on different professions or trades, and systems of transport and communication networks evolve to service them.

It is not surprising, thought Crawford, that human society should obey the same laws of development of all living things; it is exactly what you would expect. The process is spasmodic rather than continuous or uniform, just as it is in the natural world. Some communities have recapitulated more of the process of evolution than others, which are still closer – by analogy – to the unicellular stage. 'Palaeolithic hunters are now extinct,' wrote Crawford confidently, 'but Neolithic collectors survive in the Australian aborigines and elsewhere; just as primitive forms of life abound in every pond.' But even those communities (like Great Britain) which have become imperialist nations have probably only advanced to the equivalent of the stage of vertebrate or mammalian life. Movement towards the next stage would come when – as would surely happen – a single world state comes into existence, and the whole human race is 'organized as a single social organism'. Didn't the units of life – the cell, the organism, the community, the nation – always inevitably band together into ever larger and more complex units? Was it not in the very *nature* of life that it should progress towards ever-larger, ever-more co-operative systems? There would doubtless be casualties, as there were in the natural world, evolutionary dead ends. It was not guaranteed that modern European states would not be left behind if they weren't careful, as the Australian aborigines had been. It was quite conceivable that the 'torch may be picked up later on by some now obscure racial group on the confines of western civilisation'. Being left behind would effectively mean extinction, according to Crawford: human societies and entire races that could not be assimilated by the world state would eventually die out. If this was true then it had tremendous implications for everybody. Evolution held the key to the future development of the planet, and it was imperative that the findings of its scholars were conveyed to the citizens of the world so that they would know the truth, and be prepared. Evolution, the master plot of world history, was the very oracle of the new World State; in this sense *Antiquity* was seen by its founder as a sort of newspaper, its reports on the past really tidings concerning the future.

Scientific research was already truly international by its very nature, according to Crawford. As such it was both the herald of the future World State and the foundation upon which it would be built. Science was going to be the new culture, replacing the limp-wristed and moribund 'Culture' of the 'literary gents' as Crawford called them. While the literati were fiddling about with their experimental poetry and prose, archaeologists had discovered the origins of civilization, the roots of urban life and of writing; they had outlined the rise and fall of entire empires, the birth and disappearance of world religions. 'It is not literary people so called but those who are advancing the bounds of knowledge who are the creative artists of today,' wrote Crawford in an *Antiquity* editorial. Scientists (including archaeologists) were the true avant-garde; *Antiquity* was an avant-garde journal that would see all of the artistic ones turn to dust. Whether they knew it or not, scientists were workers in the 'universal Intelligence Department, for the use of future Directors of Operations'. It was unfortunate, wrote Crawford, that at the moment scientific discoveries were being put to sectarian ends, including warfare, and nationalist competition. Nation states and their interests created obstructions to the free development of scientific research; nationalism had warped the spirit of scientific enquiry. Unfortunately the political and economic organization of mankind was dragging behind advances in science and technology, but was still determining their development. But government would inevitably catch up with technology. Civilizations, like organisms, flourish and die; and out of the ruins of the present order a new phase would surely begin – and it would be the phase equivalent, on the evolutionary scale, to the dawn of humanity itself. Science would secure a new world civilization drawn up on the most rational of lines. This for Crawford was the logic, the great cosmic fractal of life, the Good News promised by history. It had to be true. It would surely come to pass.

Although he claimed some originality for it, Crawford's vision of world history riffed on fairly standard nineteenth-century ideas of cultural evolutionism, filtered through H. G. Wells, whose 1905 book *A Modern Utopia* described a World State run on rational lines and overseen by a caste of scientist-rulers known as the Samurai. In private Crawford was struggling to accommodate Marxist ideas within his overall theory. Whether he was up to the job is another matter, as he himself wondered. It seems that he could conceive of the existence of a pattern in history more easily than he could back it up with the writings and findings – fully absorbed and acknowledged – of philosophers, economists or natural scientists. He mentioned Spengler in his 1931 article, for example, but he had never read his work, as he confessed to a friend. It is probably fair to say he was no great intellectual (one archaeologist recently described him rather damningly as 'a practical man with academic interests') but he had always had a taste for big ideas. He enjoyed seeing how far he could take the evolutionary analogy; and he couldn't help himself from speculating on a Wellsian inter-planetary future in the next turn of the evolutionary helix. 'What is to be the next integration,' he asks, 'in which the world-state will be the single unit?' Where else but in one's own magazine could one air such theories, ask such questions – where else could one invent, in effect, one's own wheel and see how far it could go?

Still, after 1931 Crawford never again spelt out the nature of his vision of the path of world history in *Antiquity* in quite such depth. Pontificating about the state of the world and its future may have been endemic in the 1930s but taking a stance one way

or the other – and occasional references to socialism in his writing showed which way Crawford was tending – was bound to
alienate at least part of the readership on which *Antiquity*
depended to survive. Crawford tended to confine his stronger
views to the odd editorial remark or review to minimize the
damage. Perhaps he also realized that his passion was not always
matched by his erudition; and that he was better advised to leave
public theorizing about the nature of history to his friends R. G.
Collingwood or Gordon Childe. Childe, in particular, had a gift
for synthesis, and Crawford knew it; he later wrote that he was
'more influenced by his writings than by those of any other
person', an influence that was political as well as archaeological.
But if little was said directly about the future of the world in the
pages of *Antiquity*, Crawford's vision and enthusiasm continued
to structure its contents and fuel its production. The global
future, free from superstition, religion and nationalism, was what
made sense of all of *Antiquity*'s apparently disparate fragments; it
was effectively the vanishing point around which they fell into
perspective.

What was irritating was that not everybody saw it that way. It
was not just the Little Englanders, who complained when
*Antiquity* stopped including so many articles on British topics, the
ruralists who like H. J. Massingham believed that the country's
future lay in its pre-industrial past, or the artists like John Piper,
who snipped out articles and images that interested him and
stuck them into scrapbooks. There were others, those who
squinted at the miscellany of *Antiquity* and saw not Evolution but
proof of other sorts of patterns: the occult trigonometry of the
Pyramids, the migrations of the lost tribes of Israel, the whereabouts of lost continents, the coming-to-pass of the Book of
Revelation, the identification of Britain as the true Holy Land,
secret genealogies of the Royal Family. Weren't archaeologists
always finding new things that upset accepted outlines of history
and geography? Were there not any number of unsuspected sites

and artefacts coming to light as new tools were invented to uncover them? And could some of them not be the very proof of the most unlikely hypotheses? The lost villages and 'queer resurrections' of aerial archaeology, for example, might suggest hidden knowledge, proof of an arcane geography indicating the presence of anyone from ancient Phoenicians to extraterrestrials. Out in the West Country, for example, Katherine Maltwood was convinced that she had found in aerial photographs around Glastonbury a vast zodiac, its outlines inscribed in field boundaries, hedges and other landscape features. Air photographs, she wrote in her 1935 *Guide to Glastonbury*, showed the 'ancient landmarks of a forgotten civilization, and thus amplified what the Ordnance Survey Maps had for long delineated, unknowingly'. Crawford filed all such things under 'Crankeries'; and urged his crankier correspondents not to bother to go on writing to him.

This included those who continued to believe in the existence of 'ley lines', the idea promoted by Alfred Watkins in the 1920s that ancient monuments across the British Isles were joined up by remarkably straight lines that had been mapped out by prehistoric surveyors. Watkins, who was a flour manufacturer and inventor of photographic equipment, had this revelation while inspecting an Ordnance Survey map. He suggested that Stone Age surveyors had plotted straight lines across the landscape using various sighting devices, marking out these lines with natural features and piles of stones as waymarkers. They were used, thought Watkins, for a multitude of purposes, for trade, for orientation, for finding flint sources. In the ensuing centuries, temples and burial places were established at the markpoints along the leys. By the time the Romans came, the ley system was no longer in use, but the Romans built some of their roads along the old lines; and later still, churches were built where older temples had been. That was how it was that the sites linked up by leys dated from different periods. And memories of the archaic system lingered on, in place names, and in folklore. Watkins published a number of books on the subject – *Early British Trackways* (1922), *The Old Straight Track* (1925), *The Ley Hunter's Manual* (1927) and *Archaic Tracks around Cambridge* (1932) – and soon ley hunting had become a pastime for Watkins's devotees. Enthusiasts signed up for the 'Old Straight Track Club' and spent their weekends squinting at horizons and drawing up alignments, an activity that had ironically been made possible by the increased availability of cheap Ordnance Survey maps. Crawford was scathing, despite Watkins's attempts to establish a dialogue. Until the end of his life he continued to receive letters on the subject. Did ley lines exist? As Archaeology Officer of the Ordnance Survey and editor of *Antiquity* Crawford was deemed well placed to know for sure, but he swatted off his many correspondents on this topic. 'The Editor acknowledges with thanks the receipt of your letter on the 9th and assures you that there is no significance in the facts stated. It would be possible to align factory-chimneys or haystacks; probably someone has already done so.' People *would* persist in seeing patterns where there were none.

Crawford could not bear the fact that perfectly well-educated people were so susceptible to fancy, so easily distracted, so stubborn in their adherence to views and beliefs that had no grounding in hard science. But if he attracted their attention – and he certainly did – he had himself partly to blame. What could he expect when he adopted such an oracular tone in his editorials (a voice given extra credibility by his position as a government employee), especially with all this talk of patterns coming into view? The sort of outdoors fieldwork he encouraged his readers to go out and try for themselves, measuring, looking, walking and plotting, with scant regard for book-learning, was very much the method of Watkins and his followers, even if their conclusions were somewhat different. What's more, he may have disdained the cranks, but in an attempt to get a bigger audience and more subscribers he deliberately chose topics that would get their attention. 'Leonard Woolley has found The Flood', he announced provocatively to his readers in 1929. Indeed *Antiquity* made a speciality of examining the archaeological evidence for legendary or mythical events, or lands such as Lyonesse, the land of Arthurian legend that was supposed to have existed between Cornwall and the Isles of Scilly. Articles on these sorts of subject were usually meant to debunk the myths heralded by their beguiling titles – 'The Work of Giants', 'Noah's Flood' or 'The Lion and the Unicorn' – but readers of *Antiquity* might not, of course, read on that far. In fact the success of *Antiquity* – in terms of garnering a non-specialist audience – was surely largely due to its skilful blending of the mythical and the scientific, the way in which it delivered its most astonishing announcements through the deadpan language of science and the apparent objectivity of photography, seemingly proving that the marvellous does indeed exist. *The wooden seat is for the soul to sit upon*, ran the caption to a photograph of the burial place of a Konyak chief's skull published in *Antiquity* in 1929. Could readers be blamed for failing to take the appropriate distance from such an image?

Crawford, though, kept his focus on the big picture. 'What new idea is to emerge from all this vast accumulation of facts and give them coherence? Has it already emerged?' Perhaps it had; everything pointed to Russia, where the organization of society had finally caught up with the possibilities of science, and where the future had already begun.

# CHAPTER 5

Going to Russia from the West in the 1920s and 30s was not like going to any other country. For those who saw the Soviet experiment as the forerunner of a worldwide socialist revolution, going to Russia was a journey not only across space but also across time. It was a journey to the future. You could read about it in books like Sidney and Beatrice Webb's 1935 *Soviet Communism: A New Civilisation?*, which when republished in 1937 was so sure of itself that it dropped the question mark in the title; but it was best to go and see this brave new world for yourself. The capitalist media could be so misleading, with its tales of forced collectivization, state-sanctioned theft and deliberately induced famine. You couldn't believe what you read in the papers. Far better to see for yourself, to tour Soviet prison cells and see the bowls of fruit on the tables, to visit the much-maligned collective farms and see the day-care provisions for infants, the communal dining rooms and medical facilities, to witness the enthusiasm of voluntary workers putting in the hours on their days off, building roads, railways and tramways for the greater good of state socialism. Here was proof that human beings *could* create a better society than the one that seemed to be cast in stone in Britain: a grimly class-ridden, ossified society, one's passage through it determined by accidents of birth, wealth or sex; the whole at the cruel mercy of the vicissitudes of the market. Human beings could organize themselves differently; paradise need not forever be postponed, but could be brought down to earth, as it had been in Russia. Russia, in the words of *Are You Going To Russia?*, a 1934 guidebook published in London, was 'the greatest travel adventure accessible to the average person to-day'. It had to be seen to be believed.

The new world had its offices and outlets in Britain, places where you could go to peruse guidebooks and phrasebooks, copies of *Russia Today* (the English-language magazine for the Friends of the Soviet Union), workers' literature, and the works of Marx, Engels and Lenin. These outlets had their own geography: in London there was the Library and Workers' School at Marx House on Clerkenwell Green (where you could take a course, attend a lecture, buy Russian handicrafts, borrow books or order them wholesale from the Workers' Bookshop); a string of other radical booksellers; and in the recently completed Bush House in Aldwych (the home, after 1940, of the BBC World Service), right in the centre of the modern metropolis, was the Modern Russian Bookshop (*Kniga*), next door to the offices of Intourist, the Russian travel agency. It was through Intourist that you bought your ticket. Many went in the summer months by boat, which sailed from London to Leningrad twice a week.

The boats were moored near London Bridge, their red flags flying at the mast; islands of Soviet communism within sight of the palace of Westminster. Six boats were built in the shipyards of Leningrad to ply the London–Leningrad line: the *Cooperatsia*, the *Smolny*, and the *Sibir*, the *Jan Rudzutak*, the *Felix Dzerzhinsky* and the *Alexei Rykov*. These cargo-passenger diesel ships brought hundreds of tons of butter and eggs to London in special refrigerator holds, and transported British tourists to Russia throughout the 1930s. They were staffed by Soviet crews, who greeted their foreign passengers as 'comrade'; inside, portraits of Lenin replaced those of the King, wall-newspapers were available for crew and passengers to read, and there was a dedicated 'Lenin room'. If there was first- and second-class accommodation for passengers, it was only as a concession to old-world prejudice. If the very best materials had been used to fit out the passengers' quarters it was with the commendable aim of demonstrating the capabilities of Russian workmanship. And if the names of the only two of these boats (the *Jan Rudzutak* and the *Alexei Rykov*) to be named after living Bolshevik heroes had to be changed after 1937 when their real-life counterparts were arrested on suspicion of conspiracy against Stalin and later executed – it could surely be done without anyone noticing.

In May 1932, having taken his entire annual leave from the Ordnance Survey in a single block, Crawford embarked for Leningrad on the *Smolny*, accompanied by a friend and fellow geographer, Neil Hunter. It was the summer in which, as the editor of the *New Statesman* remarked, 'the entire British Intelligentsia' seemed to have gone to Russia. Sidney and Beatrice Webb were also travelling on the *Smolny* on that day in May; Crawford watched George Bernard Shaw (who had made the trip the previous year) wave his friends off from the wharf. Also on board was John Shaftesley of the *Manchester Guardian*, who after the war would become the editor of the *Jewish Chronicle*. There is a photograph taken by Shaftesley of Crawford and Hunter on the landing raft as they arrived in Leningrad. Crawford is clothed quite differently to how he appears in other photographs. And it's hard not to think that he had dressed most deliberately for entry to a workers' state and a new world. Unlike Hunter, and most unconventionally for a civil servant, he is wearing a worker's flat cap. And is that a *zippered* jacket? Aldous Huxley's futuristic *Brave New World* of 1932 may have been full of zips, where their speed in getting clothes on or off made them the very symbol of enlightened and uninhibited sexuality, of the sort that was rumoured to be rife in the Soviet Union. In England zips were so modern in 1932 as to be quite outlandish, unless confined to handbags, tobacco pouches or naval uniform, which is in fact

Hunter     Crawford

what Crawford appears to be wearing. He had always been in favour of the most practical clothing, including bits and pieces of army or navy gear if it suited his purpose, regardless of bourgeois protocol. And here he is, hands in his pockets, bag on his shoulder, feet apart, full frontal, ready for action in a new world of worker-scientists, rationality and zips. His enthusiasm is surely there in his very stance.

And he was most enthusiastic, although you would not know the extent of it from any published source. There is no explicit mention of it in *Antiquity*. In his autobiography, written twenty years later, his enthusiasm is reduced to a single regretful sentence. Describing his trip to Russia he notes that 'We saw much that was both new and old, and I was greatly impressed and for a time fooled by the imposing façade of the structure; that phase passed, I am thankful to say . . .' He goes on to describe his (pretty standard) tourist itinerary, which took in Moscow, Nizhni Novgorod (renamed Gorki in the year of Crawford's visit), Stalingrad, Rostov-on-Don, and on to Tiflis in Georgia where, when Hunter fell ill, Crawford travelled alone across the Caucasus to Armenia. Together they went on to Batum, on the Black Sea coast, and travelled by steamer on a round trip to Sukhum in Abkhasia. The account of this trip given by Crawford in his autobiography makes much of the privations, the discomforts and the mishaps he suffered while in the Soviet Union: the paranoid officials and inept bureaucrats, the trains that did not run on time, the theft of his wristwatch in Tiflis, the bugs in the hotel rooms. Reading Crawford's autobiography you might well not guess just how enchanted he was, in fact, by what he saw – or what he thought he saw – in Russia in the summer of 1932.

In 2001 the Sackler Library opened in Oxford. It was built to house the University's hitherto disparate collections of books on art, archaeology and Classics, and when these collections were catalogued and put online, an item entitled 'A Tour in Bolshevy' by O. G. S. Crawford appeared. It turned out to be the bound typescript of a book, which Crawford had written but which was never published, inscribed on the flyleaf to his friend, the classical scholar Stanley Casson in November 1934. 'A Tour in Bolshevy' is an account of Crawford's trip to Russia, described in the most glowing of terms. There are no complaints, here, about bed-bugs, late trains or petty theft. Here such things are brushed off as irrelevancies in the greater scheme of things, the sort of thing that only an ill-informed bourgeois tourist would dwell on. The people of the Soviet Union were, he wrote, far too busy to pander to the comforts of mere tourists. What was important was the way in which a completely new civilization was coming into existence through the will and the actions of the people. This new civi-lization was most evident in places like the new factory towns and State farms, places like Traktorstroy, where the tractor factory of Stalingrad had gone into production just two years earlier, in 1930. Crawford was very impressed by his tour of Traktorstroy, including its Dispensary (with its open-minded attitude to birth control and venereal disease), its Factory Crèche, its communal kitchen built in the Constructivist style, filled with cheerful and contented-looking worker-diners. 'There are no pale faces at Traktorstroy,' he noted, 'or indeed anywhere that we went in the Soviet Union.' Before leaving he took photographs of a family group to prove to disbelievers that communism had not done away with such things, and of a trainload of tractors off the production line, to prove that the workers of Stalingrad were indeed capable (as some in the West doubted) of producing them.

Wherever they went, Crawford and his companion peered at the masonry of new buildings, turned taps on and off to test the water flow, opened and closed doors to see how well they fitted, observed clothing, measured food queues, noted the price of cinema tickets, assessed food quality, listed the components of meals. Whenever possible they interviewed workers, asking

questions about their wages, rent and other monthly expenses, holiday provision, their degree of contentment with the new system, and so on. By the time they left Rostov for Georgia, Hunter had accumulated a sheaf of notes, and Crawford had taken nearly 200 photographs, which he developed in hotel rooms along the way, since it was not permitted to take undeveloped film out of the country. They carried on like this for the remaining three weeks of their tour, gathering material, priding themselves on their objectivity. It was this material, collected in the spirit of what Crawford called 'dispassionate scientific observation' (rare, he said, among his fellow tourists), that formed the basis of 'A Tour in Bolshevy'. This was the method of the archaeologist, the anthropologist and the social scientist. It was only appropriate, after all, to use such methods. This was a completely new sort of civilization; and one had to come to one's own conclusions, based on sound empirical evidence, about this great social experiment. 'The tourist can see much,' wrote Crawford, 'if he talks to everyone, keeps his eyes open and looks beneath the surface.'

It was particularly important, thought Crawford, to look beneath the surface of modern Russia. One had to see beyond the dirty and unkempt appearance of buildings and people. The poverty was only apparent; it was not – from a truly historicist viewpoint – real. In fact to judge by material evidence – the archaeologist's method – communist Russia was precisely a civilization which favoured essentials over appearance, wrote Crawford approvingly. That was why no effort was spent on beautifying shop fronts; it was the quality and usefulness of the goods rather than their presentation that mattered. The façades of historic buildings might be peeling but only the bourgeois tourist's sensibility would be affronted by this; there were far more important things to attend to than cornices and gilding. And if few Russians wore collars on their shirts it was not – as some foolish visitors might think – a sign of their degradation, but of their liberation from unnecessary adornment and expense.

The benefits of the system were clear enough, even to tourists. A civilization in which production was for use not profit meant that you could get decent tobacco (in the tourist shops, at any rate), not like in England where the tobacco leaves were mixed with chemicals; and there was enough room for one's legs in the theatre, since there was not the business-driven incentive to pack in as many punters as possible. In Russia, wrote Crawford, 'a chair is made to sit on, not to supply parasites with unearned increments'. Some things – especially technical matters – were clearly still not fully evolved. Russian plumbing, for example. It was important – in the spirit of dispassionate scientific observation – to be honest about these things. But it was equally important – in the historicist spirit of Marxism – to compare them not with Western standards but with those of Russia under the Tsars, equivalent in evolutionary terms to the Middle Ages. Seen in that perspective, Russia had made astonishing – not to say miraculous – progress.

In general it was fair, wrote Crawford, to judge the system by its *best* products, on the basis that in the future these would be standard. So it wasn't so much of a problem that Intourist guides showed their tour groups only the finest showpieces of Soviet communism in action. Crawford realized that not all Houses of Culture were like the one his tour group was taken to in Leningrad – a spectacular building designed for the purpose in the Constructivist style, complete with foreign workers' room, military room, crèche, anti-religious room, students' library and cinema theatre. Other Houses of Culture in other towns were housed in old buildings, and may well have been less impressive. For the time being the new order – like the hermit crab, making its home in the discarded shell of a dead crustacean – had to dwell in the ruins of the old culture that it had overthrown. But one day all Houses of Culture would be like the Leningrad one. A new civilization was being born out of the corpse of the old one. This was how it happened. You could see it in the streets, where new buildings and construction sites rose up beside the soon-to-be-demolished husks of pre-Revolutionary hovels. You could see it, most startlingly, as churches were demolished and

their bricks cleaned up and re-used as the building blocks of communal apartment blocks. Evolution was happening so fast you could document it photographically; the astonishing spectacle of a civilization coming into being before your very eyes. You could see the future, too, in the faces of young people, a sure sign of the direction in which history was heading. Watching children play at the Karl Marx school in Rostov, Crawford noted with envy their apparent 'absence of repression', their lack of any 'galling inhibitions of class or sex': boys and girls played together, 'members of a community of equals which is carrying out the greatest task that any community has ever attempted since human society began'. Crawford was in no doubt that what he saw in Russia would come to pass throughout the world. 'A system has been devised,' he wrote in the final paragraph of 'A Tour in Bolshevy',

> by which the real wishes of the majority, guided by their most advanced and intelligent members, can be carried into effect. It is called the Soviet system, and it already operates successfully amongst 230 million people in Russia and China. We shall not have to wait very long before it operates everywhere.

Crawford's visit coincided with a period of massive accelerated industrialization of the vast territories of the Soviet Union. Stalin's first Five-Year Plan was launched in 1928, its goal to turn Russia from an agrarian economy into an industrial one in record time. 'We are becoming a country of metal,' announced Stalin in 1929, 'an automobilized country, a tractorized country.' Factory towns, steel plants, dams and power stations were planned with the help of foreign advisers and built by brigades of so-called 'shock workers' who competed with each other for greatest speed and productivity. Ernst May, the architect of a number of Weimar housing settlements, was invited to plan Soviet cities including

the socialist city of Magnitogorsk, whose steel plant was based
on the factory at Gary, Indiana. The tractor factory toured by
Crawford in 1932 had been prefabricated in Detroit by the Albert
Kahn Company (which had built factories for Ford, General
Motors and Chrysler) and assembled in Stalingrad. Foreign help
was a necessary stage in Russia's transition to an economy that
could 'make the machines needed to make the machines'. And
once these factories were established, annual targets of productivity
were set for automobiles, tractors, ploughs and beet-diggers,
pig iron and steel. At the same time, a sustained campaign of collectivization and 'de-kulakization' of the countryside had begun
in 1929. Volunteer party activists went out in groups to confis-
cate the private property of the wealthier peasants (*kulaks*) and
move farmers and their livestock into collective farms or State
farms, equipped with modern machinery and communal facilities.
All existing food supplies and grain stores were to be pooled; food
production was to be mechanized and centrally controlled. The
new farms had their quotas to fulfil, too. Their productivity – like
that of the new factories – was trumpeted and urged on in wall-
newspapers, on posters and banners, and through agitprop street
sculptures and constructions.

If the goals and achievements of the Five-Year Plan were conveyed to the people through the iconography of vast public
sculptures, posters and theatrical performances, it was partly
because so many Russian citizens were barely literate. They were
still at the stage of a medieval peasantry that understood the
teachings of the church through wall paintings and devotional
icons; the Party adopted the same language. But this stage would
not last much longer, according to the many pronouncements on
the subject. The 'liquidation of illiteracy' was high on the agenda
of the Five-Year Plan, part of a drive to educate the Russian
people so that they might read the many books on technology,
workers' organization and communist philosophy that were
filling up the libraries at the factories, *kolkhozi* and Houses of

Culture. Collectivization and industrialization demanded a new generation of well-trained, literate workers that could keep accounts and read the newspapers as well as fix tractors and deliver the party line in the workplace. Literacy was one of the goals of a new public education system that was designed to create exactly this new type of worker, who understood their historic role, and why it obliged them to work hard – and why it obliged them to denounce those who did not. In a public garden in Sukhum, Crawford photographed an assemblage which encouraged the denouncing of all slackers and drunkards, opportunists, *kulaks*, hooligans and petty thieves, whose names were to be chalked onto a blackboard.

The Five-Year Plan aimed to construct not only factories but a new sort of society as well, composed of a new kind of person; and it left no aspect of life untouched in its ambition. In order to create this society, planning – on the basis of something defined as science – would filter through everything from the management of the economy, industry and agriculture to public health, education and childcare. It had long been in the interests of the Soviet Union to impress foreign visitors, especially any 'opinion-formers' like writers, journalists, scientists, trade unionists and educators. Certain 'techniques of hospitality' (to use Paul Hollander's term) were used to persuade and flatter these tourists, making them feel important while they were shown carefully filtered aspects of the Soviet project. When H. G. Wells visited Russia in 1920 he was taken to a very well-equipped school where every child assured him that their favourite writer was – H. G. Wells. Wells smelt a rat; but others were simply delighted by the way in which they were honoured in the Workers' State. George Bernard Shaw was greeted by a crowd of thousands and a brass band when he arrived in Moscow in 1931. The Webbs – whose early scepticism had been assuaged by a visit, to their London residence, from a very persuasive Soviet ambassador – also got special treatment. Crawford saw them 'whisked off at

once in a special conveyance' when the *Smolny* arrived in Leningrad. But less exalted tourists got special treatment, too. It does not seem to have struck Crawford as odd that two English-speaking Armenians turned up at the hotel where he and his guide were staying in Erivan, gave them 'a most hearty welcome', and escorted them to a restaurant, where they had an excellent meal in a separate room that was found for them by one of the men. But it certainly must have softened him up for their subsequent tour of the town in the company of the two comrades, who pointed out new building and tram works, told them about the major construction schemes in progress outside the town and, appealing to Crawford's professional interests, showed him the site where the archaeologist Ashkharbek Kalantar (who, within a decade, would perish in prison as an enemy of the nation) had not long before found some fragments of ancient pottery. Crawford was certainly impressed. 'The archaeologists I met at Erivan are to be envied,' Crawford told the readers of *Russia Today*.

Given the crudeness of some of these 'techniques of hospitality' it is hard to see how so many foreign tourists were won over. But if they were, it was largely because those tourists – including Crawford – had a powerful will-to-believe in the Soviet dream before they ever got there. Free market capitalism did not seem to be working, after all. Unemployment had rocketed after the Wall Street Crash in 1929. The Depression in the West made Russia look good; there was full employment, industry was powering ahead, public health and education were taken seriously. But more than this, Soviet sympathizers and fellow travellers like Crawford clung to a belief that human beings could perfect themselves and the way in which they organized things. They were, as David Caute says in his book *The Fellow-Travellers*, children of the Enlightenment, and they were seriously disillusioned by the fate of its ideals in Britain, Germany, France or the USA. Many had particular axes to grind: supporters of curriculum reform,

free love, Esperanto, veganism, birth control, and health through
dance all sought – and usually found – a receptive audience in
Russia, even if it was just among the kindred spirits they met in
their tour groups. Malcolm Muggeridge described how the boat
he took to Leningrad in 1932 echoed with the 'resonant, don-
nish-demagogic voices' of just such a party of intellectuals, whose

> tweedy suits and coloured ties were everywhere. They had
> the shambling gait, the roving eye, the air of being the elect
> or chosen ones, which I had come to associate with those
> who felt they knew the answers, and could steer us aright to
> peace, prosperity and the everlasting brotherhood of man.

When such groups arrived in the promised land, they were
already predisposed to find exactly what they had come looking
for, and they saw what they expected (or longed) to see: a society that was trying to pull itself up by the bootstraps, that was
taking control of itself, applying to society in all of its aspects the
lessons of science, rebuilding a broken world on the most
rational and enlightened of principles: from each according to
their ability, to each according to their need.

Such a vision – even if it was just a vision – was bound to exercise a powerful attraction for the many teachers, thinkers and
reformists who made their way to Russia in the late 1920s and
30s. Apart from anything else, this seemed to be a society (unlike
their own) that would take them and their work seriously, a civilization in which they would have an important role to play. The
Soviet Union believed in planning, on the basis of the best and
most progressive thinking on any given subject; and this
delighted the visiting experts – the social scientists, the town
planners, the doctors, the teachers, the architects – who felt
themselves to be marginalized and impotent at home in the West.
In Russia academics were directly involved, or so it seemed, in
public policy. Anthropologists, for example, advised on the

collectivization of particular ethnic groups; biologists advised on agricultural policy. New settlements like collective farms and factory towns were designed by engineers and architects, according to principles of utility, social space and public health. How much could Britain be improved, thought the visiting intellectuals to this planned paradise, if it would only do a bit of planning itself.

It may be that the spring of 1932 was the best time ever to get a good impression of the Soviet experiment. Things seemed to be going well for Stalin and his modernization drive; great advances in industry, education and public health had been made in an impressively short time. The cost of those advances was not yet apparent to foreign observers. 1932 was before the purges and the show trials; before the period that became known as the Terror, although terror had already begun behind the scenes. It was before Stalin's clampdown on artistic experimentation was fully realized, although it had certainly started. And it was before terrible famine, the direct result of the agricultural policies of the Five-Year Plan, swept across the Ukraine and other grain-growing regions, killing millions. To be sure, the seeds of that famine had already been sown, as peasants resisted forced collectivization and the official confiscation of grain supplies. Many Ukrainians were already hungry in the spring of 1932. But in the Soviet press, if it was mentioned at all, any food shortage in the Ukraine was blamed on *kulak* sabotage of the harvest, any starving peasant was said to be play-acting for anti-Soviet purposes. And for some time, it seems that it was quite easy for foreign sympathizers either to agree, or to turn a blind eye.

On their visit Crawford and Hunter were shown round one of the showpieces of Soviet collectivization, the vast State Farm of Zernograd (literally 'Wheatville') near Rostov. They faithfully jotted down all the reams of statistics they were given there, the 'sacred digits of socialism' (to use David Caute's phrase): population, crop yields, area of cultivation, output percentages taken by the State in each year, percentages kept. They were pleased to note that the output of the State Farms was 'increasing by leaps and bounds', that soil cultivation was overseen by an Institute of Agricultural Engineering, staffed by female scientists (*so* progressive). They saw that the workers seemed to be housed comfortably, and fed adequately. They didn't see the process through which workers were brought to this farm and others like it; or what happened to those peasants who did not make it that far, those arbitrarily defined as *kulaks*, who ended up as forced labour on schemes like Magnitogorsk, or who were deported to beyond the Arctic circle where they were left to perish. They didn't see raw hunger, the tangible results of a policy of the forced removal and redistribution of grain supplies that was still going on; presumably they believed Stalin when in 1930 he distanced himself from the most brutal implementation of Party principles in the countryside, and gave his suave assurance that it would stop.

Crawford did not see these things. He only looked beneath the surface when it suited his purpose. Yet he prided himself on seeing; he was trained to see. The Outlook Tower in Edinburgh was designed to remind the trainee visionary that entire social worlds hid behind closed doors. And whichever way you look at it, what he saw in Russia was what he wanted to see. Sight failed him, for he had *faith*; and the will-to-believe was blinding.

Among the papers connected with Crawford's trip there is evidence that for all his talk of the scientific objectivity of the eye-witness, he knew before he went to Russia what he would find. He wrote a draft of the first pages of 'A Tour in Bolshevy', for example, three months before he went there. He knew what he would find because Russia represented the beginnings of the World State that had been foretold, the promise of history. It was surely with the Soviet Union in mind that he wrote his article on 'Historical Cycles' in *Antiquity* early in 1931, with its premonition of a new world order. Political organization was lagging behind advances in science and technology in most of the world, but in

Russia it had caught up, and politics and economics were run on scientific principles. Religion, superstition, and even the idea of the nation had been liquidated in this fore-runner of the World State. This was evolution in our time; and if it was happening a bit faster than usual that just made it more exciting. 'Here in Russia', wrote Crawford in 'A Tour in Bolshevy', 'has occurred a change greater and far more abrupt, because consciously effected, than that which took place in prehistoric times when the agriculturist superseded the hunter and the collector.' Surely this was something to interest anthropologists and archaeologists everywhere, not to mention the ordinary citizen. Russia had effectively pole-vaulted history, going straight from feudalism to a planned socialist economy, without bothering with those stages of industrial capitalism through which the West had passed, and in which it was now mired. If it was possible to inspect prehistoric man in the deserts of Australia or Africa, it was now possible to study the man of the future – *Homo sovieticus* – in the cities and collective farms of the USSR.

Crawford in fact shared the conviction of the Bolsheviks that they were at the very vanguard of history. Lenin, like Crawford, believed that the course of world history was now knowable in its entirety. He, too, thought that history was coming into view like a vast landscape seen from a cockpit. Communism had been conceived in just such a way. Was not Marx's conception of class struggle based on an understanding of history in the broadest possible scope, from the slave relations of the ancient world to the feudalism of the Middle Ages through the bourgeois revolutions of the seventeenth and eighteenth centuries, through industrialization, and on to the inevitable triumph of the proletariat? Was the Russian Revolution not the fulfilment of a historical prophecy? For Marx, in one of his best-known dictums, communism was the answer to the riddle of history, and knew itself to be the answer. Not only was it the latest – and possibly the last – stage in the evolution of human society, it was the first to be conscious of itself *as* evolution. It was the first to seize control of history, as if history itself was just another science to be mastered and put to use. As indeed in the minds of the early Communist Fathers, it was.

It was surely the Soviet Union's faith in science, and its rejection of superstition, religion and tribalism that identified it as the harbinger of the World State in Crawford's eyes. Communist Russia believed so fervently in science that it preserved the body of its first leader so that he could be brought back to life when – as would surely happen – the technology was invented to do it. Everywhere in Stalin's Russia, science was forcibly supplanting religion. Just as Christian churches were once built on pagan sites in order to destroy but also tap their power, the superiority of 'scientific atheism' was theatrically promoted in precisely the places where Russians once worshipped. De-sanctified holy sites, expropriated by the State, were put into the charge of the League of the Militant Godless to teach the public the value of rational thought and the dangers of fetishism. St Isaac's Cathedral in Leningrad, which Crawford visited, had been turned into the State Anti-Religious Museum in 1931. Inside, a huge Foucault's pendulum showing the rotation of the earth around its axis took the place of a bronze dove, the symbolic representation of the Holy Spirit, which had once hung beneath the cathedral dome; the index of an irreducible law replacing the representation of a superstitious abstraction. Nearby was a painting entitled *Galileo Before the Roman Inquisition*, an icon of a martyr to science.

It's easy, in retrospect, to see how the Russians in fact made a fetish out of science and technology, how, as Nicholas Berdyaev remarked, they converted scientific positivism 'into a primitive metaphysic, . . . a special religion supplanting all previous religions'. One only has to see images of those rituals through which newborn babies were not christened, but 'Octobered' with names like Tractorina or Elektrozavodsk, or names inspired by revolutionary heroes, accompanied by the laying-on of the red flag. But the Soviet commitment to scientific research – Marxist science, of course – was real enough; and one of the most enviable things about it, from Crawford's point of view at least, was the way in which the research of Russian workers in the fields of the historical, material, and social sciences – no matter how abstract or esoteric those fields were considered in capitalist countries – engaged directly with contemporary social, political, industrial and agricultural life.

Something of the dynamism of Soviet science had been brought home to British scholars at the Second International Congress of the History of Science and Technology, held in London in the early summer of 1931. The Soviet delegation to the Congress stunned the audience with its fervour, exposing the bourgeois bias of science and its applications under capitalism, and revealing the radical nature of the Soviet worldview. The audience was apparently largely made up of historians of science and antiquarian gentlemen of leisure, with only modest claims for the importance of their subject – it mattered, but not *that* much. And here was Nikolai Vavilov, talking enthusiastically about his research into the origins of agriculture – a topic long dear to the antiquarian – not as a fascinating aspect of the history of civilization, best contemplated in an armchair, but as a way of engineering the future. The grains of wheat that could be found wrapped up with Egyptian mummies were not to be valued for their aura of antiquity, but for the potential information they stored, useful for plant-breeding programmes in the collectivized agriculture of the Soviet Union. This was Soviet scholarship in heroic, constructivist mode. In Leningrad, Vavilov and his co-workers were amassing the world's biggest seed bank, from samples gathered in every part of the globe. So committed were the staff of this seed bank, that they famously starved to death rather than feed on the grains they guarded through the Siege of Leningrad in the Second World War. By this time, though, Vavilov – unknown to him in the heady days of 1931 – had been sentenced to death by execution; he died in January 1943 of emaciation and dystrophic diarrhoea.

Crawford had a go himself at Soviet-style scholarship soon after the London Congress (which he didn't, in the end, attend), in a rather odd article called 'The Dialectical Process in the History of Science', published in the *Sociological Review* just before he went to Russia. In an ambitious argument he grappled with a dialectical reading of the invention of aerial archaeology, and considered the deleterious effects of capitalism on the advance of archaeological knowledge. It was, he wrote, the large-scale digging brought about by the Industrial Revolution and carried out by the working classes that had led to archaeological discoveries; but the bourgeois class that was also the product of industrialization had – in terms of archaeological knowledge – brought about only private collections and sterile typologies. How much more, muses Crawford, might have been discovered had Britain been a socialist country, its children taught – as they were in modern Russia – the history of tools, the principles of scientific method, and the outlines of human evolution. Science was simply not taken seriously enough in Britain, its research programmes and its findings too often affected or eclipsed by received wisdom, the vested interests of church or property-owners, or rank indifference.

The idea conveyed by the Soviet delegates to the Kensington Congress was that scientists in the Soviet Union were active *workers*, not passive scholars; an idea that exerted a powerful attraction to Crawford – hence, surely, the cap he wore on the landing raft at Leningrad. He liked the idea that persons like himself might have an active role to play in the construction of a new sort of society. He had always felt awkward about the fact that archaeology was regarded by most people as a sort of hobby. He was one of the first professionalized archaeologists, and like members of other new professions, was rather defensive about the fact that he was paid to do something which others would do for free. In Russia he would be somebody important – no more important, of course, than anyone else; but important nonetheless.

Among the minute hierarchical gradations of the British middle classes Crawford had never in fact been sure quite how important he was. He had always occupied a somewhat uncomfortable position within the institutions of the Establishment and, racked by contradictory impulses, had become a very British combination of a snob and a rebel. He was not the only one to find in Russia a liberation from a class system in which he was never quite sure of his place. It was plainly quite exhilarating to him to be relieved of anxieties over proper comportment, deferral and attire. He had always 'had a flair for wearing the wrong tie', quite a peril in the parlours and dining rooms of Britain. The relief was felt as soon as he stepped on board the *Smolny*, and felt himself to be – like the captain and all his crew – a worker among fellow workers. And it continued throughout his holiday, in which – as he noted later – he experienced a 'definite modification of my character (for the good)'. It was a relief not to have to bother with the perplexing and irrational extravagances of evening dress ('a subtle form of class propaganda'). It was a relief to be able to speak to working people without awkward condescension on one side and servility or embarrassment on the other. It was a relief not to have to contend with the obsequies of waiting staff, and to bypass all of the class tensions involved in transactions in shops and hotels. And it was a huge relief both social and financial not to have to tip every waiter, hotel lackey or station porter as one did in capitalist countries. One marvellous by-product of communism, he found, was that one could be sure – as one could not at home – that one was not being ripped off. In fact, as he reported to the Basingstoke Rotary Club in a lecture given on his return, everything was remarkably cheap in Russia; he came home with twelve pounds out of the twenty he took with him unspent. So excited was he by the favourable rate of exchange, and so convinced of the eventual fate of capitalist nations, that he – like Sidney and Beatrice Webb, apparently – bought bonds in Russian currency so that he would gain by the inevitable fall in the exchange rate of the pound against the rouble. The idea of making a profit out of the fall of capitalism appealed to him enormously. It was a sort of prospecting on evolution, in effect, in which cognoscenti like himself – and about time too – would get a head start.

The spectacle of communism in action seems to have brought out a certain sanctimoniousness in Crawford, as well as a native parsimony. His enthusiasm for the Soviet experiment had an undeniably evangelical flavour. Revolution could have an almost Biblical righteousness as the idle rich get their come-uppance and the meek inherit the earth. In Leningrad, for example, he was taken to a grand house that had formerly belonged to a prosperous bourgeois; it was now a 'Rest House' where workers could go for a holiday. Seeing these workers occupying the opulent rooms of this house made quite an impression on him. 'To me it was a most dramatic moment,' he wrote in 'A Tour in Bolshevy'. 'Here indeed was the Revolution in being. Here were the mighty put down and the humble and meek exalted . . . I had not expected to see so impressive an example of history in the making. It was as if one could have seen a Saxon family living in a Roman villa.' It was similarly gratifying to visit the lavish palace occupied by Catherine the Great at the place the Bolsheviks renamed 'Detskoe Selo'. Crawford and his tour group were taken round this relic of the former order, and made to gasp at the vulgarity and tastelessness of the palace interiors, the kitsch chapels, the room, later lost after Nazi looting, clad entirely with amber, another room covered entirely with mother-of-pearl. These rooms were kept as showpieces of the bad old days; but other parts of the palace complex at Detskoe Selo were used as rest houses for workers, and a sanatorium for children. Again, the contrast between the shell of the old regime and the new life springing up within it was most striking. History was not only happening before one's very eyes like a film put on by a celestial projector, it could be captured by the camera in a single image. Crawford took a photograph of a lawn in front of what had once been the royal palace, where the washing from the sanatorium was hung out beside a decaying baroque statue. The poor were inheriting the earth, just as it was said that they would.

Except, of course, that the poor were not inheriting the earth. In the Ukraine they were already starving; and it got worse after the summer of 1932 when Stalin ordered impossible grain targets. Anyone defined as a *kulak* – and it could mean little more than owning a cow and a bit of land – had their property removed, was forbidden to join a collective farm, and could be deported. It was the forced labour of so-called *kulaks* that helped to build up industry in places like Magnitogorsk, and thousands died in the process. What we know now is that Stalin's push to industrialize, the miracle of forced evolution lauded by Westerners like Crawford, came at an intolerably high price.

Crawford wrote up 'A Tour in Bolshevy' at high speed; by October he'd sent it to the publisher Victor Gollancz. His object in writing the book was, he said, to 'hasten the downfall of capitalism'; and, meanwhile, to 'make as much money as possible' out of capitalists. But Gollancz rejected his typescript, and he decided against printing it at his own expense. He was disappointed, but told a friend that 'on the whole I think I can do more good without putting all my cards on the table'. Instead of publishing the book he distributed copies to his friends, including the one he gave to Stanley Casson 'as an incitement to sedition' in November 1934, which ended up, along with Casson's papers, in the Sackler Library.

By 1934, despite Soviet attempts to cover it up, the Ukrainian famine of 1932–3 had come to the attention of the Western press. Malcolm Muggeridge reported on the unfolding disaster in the

*Manchester Guardian* in March 1933. Still, it was easy enough for Soviet sympathizers to dismiss the reports, or diminish their significance. The newspapers were always trying to undermine Soviet achievements. Vested interests were involved; and they were bound to seize on any bad news and exaggerate it. And so on. As Muggeridge found out, it was almost impossible to present the believers with any contrary evidence that would weaken their faith. The blindness of fellow-travelling visitors to Russia in the early 1930s was, he said, 'one of the wonders of our age'. 'There were earnest advocates of the humane killing of cattle,' he wrote,

> who looked up at the massive headquarters of the Ogpu with tears of gratitude in their eyes, earnest advocates of propor- tional representation who eagerly assented when the necessity for a Dictatorship of the Proletariat was explained to them, earnest clergymen who walked reverently through anti-God museums and reverently turned the pages of athe- istic literature, earnest pacifists who watched delightedly tanks rattle across the Red Square and bombing planes darken the sky, earnest town-planning specialists who stood outside overcrowded ramshackle tenements and muttered: 'If only we had something like this in England!'

So powerfully did the will-to-deceive and the will-to-believe coin- cide, that the evidence of their own eyes and ears would always only reinforce their pre-convictions.

Muggeridge, too, had been convinced, on first going to Russia in 1932, that 'what was happening in Moscow must happen everywhere', as he remembered it in his memoirs. He and his wife had no plans ever to return to Britain, a country that was in their view moribund. But Muggeridge was one of the few Soviet sympathizers to change his mind after visiting Russia. As a correspondent for a foreign newspaper Muggeridge reported on a number of carefully orchestrated events. Early in 1933 he went to the ceremonial opening of the Dneprostroi Dam, a showpiece of Soviet engineering, along with other journalists in a specially arranged train. The journalists spent the journey drinking vodka and eating. At one point a German journalist casually threw a leg of chicken he'd been gnawing out of the window, and outside in the fields, a peasant dived for it. 'The gesture and response,' wrote Muggeridge, 'have stayed with me through the intervening years like stigmata.'

As a journalist who lived in Russia, Muggeridge saw many things that tourists who were just visiting would not. Would Crawford's mind have been changed by the sight of a hungry man diving on a bone discarded by a well-fed journalist? It is impossible to say. But he would not, I think, have allowed a world view to be brought down by a single bone. For Crawford and others like him, within the Soviet Union poverty, oppression, hunger, poor plumbing and all the rest of it were not *really* those things at all. Seen as part of a broader picture, a picture of World History, they were just teething troubles in an inevitable historical shift that was bigger than all of us, and that would surely deliver us up to sunlit plains of human happiness. This is a military commander's view, the corpses on the battlefield of history an unfortunate price to be paid for victory. One could not afford to be sentimental about it. A similar view was, in fact, held by Beatrice Webb, who knew far more than she said in her books. Muggeridge and his wife visited the Webbs at their Camden home before they went to Russia in 1932. 'It's true,' Beatrice said, warming her hands at the fire, and showing her teeth with the final word, 'that in the USSR people *disappear*.' For these true believers it was a question of where one's loyalties lay; with individuals, with nations, or with mankind as a whole. It was a question of valuing the future over the present. One had to keep one's gaze fixed on the distant horizon. One had to stand back, as Crawford wrote, and not be distracted by details.

# CHAPTER 6

Between the end of the First World War and his 1932 trip to Russia, Crawford took hardly any photographs. He had given up photography after the war, he said, on account of the great expense involved; and also because it was apt to become a kind of 'slavery'. But on a holiday to Germany and Austria in the summer of 1931, he was persuaded to buy a Voigtländer – a medium-format camera – and immediately started to use it. With this camera, and with the Rolleiflex he replaced it with some years later, Crawford went on to take around 10,000 photographs in the remaining twenty-five years of his life.

It was surely not a coincidence that it should have been at this time and in this place that Crawford took up photography again. Nowhere was photographic technology more advanced in the late 1920s and early 1930s than in Germany; and nowhere was the idea that the camera could reveal the true nature of the world more developed. Photography of the *Neue Sachlichkeit* (or 'New Objectivity') school sought to depict the objective reality of things, stripped of sentiment and the subjectivity of the photographer. Favoured subjects were ordinary, everyday things like apartment blocks, machinery, the human body, ship funnels or plants – like the close-ups of ferns by Karl Blossfeldt. But more important than subject matter was a clarity that was often described as 'scientific' in its precision, revealing to the viewer things about the world that were obvious enough but usually ignored or passed over, like the structure of a lift shaft, or the lines on a peasant's face. It involved a stance, on the part of the photographer, of an intense engagement with the world, but also a curious estrangement from it, as seen in the deadpan portraits of August Sander, for example, or – much later, but working in the same tradition – the photographs of cooling towers and silos taken by Bernd and Hilla Becher. Through cropping, close-ups and unusual angles, the new photography in Germany (and also in Russia) startled the viewer into seeing ordinary things in a new way. It was claimed that the camera could picture the world as it really was. It inspected, dissected and presented; it refused to deceive the viewer – as bourgeois or picturesque photography did – with misty dreams.

This clarity of vision, this photographic unveiling of the world had political aspirations which were all too soon, alas, subsumed into commercial art and the visual culture of Nazism. As it turned out, 'clear vision' and 'objectivity' could serve more than one master. But in the late 1920s and early 30s, the 'New Objectivity' was part of a broad Utopianism of the socialist Weimar Republic that had its sights set on a shimmering future in which technology would serve society and guarantee its happiness. New modernist architecture was part of the same vision, with designs for life in a new world available, in principle, to all citizens. These were the years in which the Bauhaus and the Deutsche Werkbund flourished, mounting exhibitions of modernist style, and designing furniture, new typographies and ambitious housing projects. 'New Objectivity' photography was showcased by the Deutsche Werkbund in 1929 in what was later seen as a landmark exhibition called *Film Und Foto*; it included Russian films, images by known photographers like Moholy-Nagy and Man Ray, and also anonymous documentary and scientific photographs including botanical images and aerial photographs. Boundaries between 'art', 'technology' and 'science' were deemed to have been dissolved, and everybody was encouraged to become an amateur photographer, since to be an *amateur* was to be 'one who loves' – and to love the world was a better prerequisite for good photography than the petrified conventions of art and professional practice. Photography could show beauty and interest in the smallest and apparently least significant detail; it could show, as one of the slogans of the New Objectivity had it, that 'The World Is Beautiful'. And there was a sense, at least in some quarters, that this kind of clear vision could turn photography into a political weapon, revealing not only the beauty of the world, but also the truth about modern life in every facet, exposing and enlarging to the eye every element, a photographic anatomy of reality that would surely transform the sensibility of its viewers.

Crawford was on holiday in Germany in 1931 with a leftish friend named Dr Simmons. Simmons lived near Newbury in a remarkable house he had designed himself, all concrete, glass and metal. Both men clearly shared an interest in modernist design (as well as certain political tendencies), for together they visited the Building Exhibition in Berlin, which included avant-garde designs by the modernist architects Mies van der Rohe and Josef Albers, and they toured the progressive housing settlement at Siemenstadt. Crawford viewed the modernist architecture he saw in Germany as the 'application of science to building'. As such, he wrote, it foreshadowed a new era, symbolizing 'the spirit of an age which has cast off authority and outworn traditions', a new spirit 'that is expressing itself unmistakably in science and politics'. Such architecture was a taste of things to come; clean, scientific, well-ordered. Crawford approved. And he would also have approved of the photographs he must surely have seen in Germany, with their cool and clear apprehension of the visible world. Certainly this was the style that he adopted in his own photographic endeavours. Like photographers of the New Objectivity, clarity was his goal. Like them, he favoured stark contrasts, with no blurring or mistiness. His focus, like theirs, was on the object or the scene in front of him, which it was his aim to illuminate as clearly as he could. He homed in, like they did, on particular details, winkling them from their hiding places and enlarging them to elucidate their nature, their 'thing-ness'.

He became, over the years, a very good technician, and published notes on photography from time to time in the pages of *Antiquity*. He made it his business to discover under which conditions, precisely, and from which angle a particular scene or object was seen to its best – that is, its clearest – advantage. You can't take too much trouble when taking a picture, he told the listeners of a 1955 broadcast called 'Reminiscences of a Field Archaeologist'. He walked around each site 'like a dog', he said, looking at it from every angle, seeing how the light falls on it. Inscriptions on a stone slab, the gouged-out outline of a boat on a shore, or the miniature craters made in sand by insects – these were best seen when light crossed them sideways, like the ramparts of a hill fort seen from the air at dusk. On a clear day a low sun could, as he knew, throw the world into stark relief; it was the best possible time for archaeological photography, as sharp shadows showed the exact way in which stones tessellated in a dry-stone wall, or how ancient tools have left their lasting marks on boulders and abandoned monuments. It was light – the position of the sun in the sky, the amount of cloud cover, and the qualities of the air – that made things clear to the eye, and therefore to the camera. What the photographer had to do was to be in the right place at the right time, camera in hand. Crawford knew all of this well, and kept scrupulous notes on each exposure – the place, date and precise time at which it was taken, the light conditions, and the direction in which the camera was pointing, as well as the shutter speed, and other technical data.

But if he was a good photographer – and he really was, or could be – it was not just a matter of technique. It was because he could *see*; and he believed what he saw to have significance.

It was commitment that lit up his photographs; and it is no coincidence that he should have taken up photography again in the year in which he wrote with such enthusiasm about the vast carpet of history and the coming of the World State, the year before he made the trip to Russia. There is a light of absolute certainty in his photographs that it is impossible to fake; they have something of the clarity of purpose of early modernist architecture. Conviction drove them both, and made them beautiful.

At times Crawford certainly took photographs as a tourist might, snaps of notable buildings, friends relaxing, comic animals or picturesque scenery to remind him of the view. Ever the entrepreneur, he even made some scenic shots into postcards to earn money. But most of his pictures were taken as if they – and the things they represented – might one day be evidence in some kind of post-historical tribunal. They were all, in one sense or another, *proof*.

His interests – in terms of photographic subjects – were both vast and specific. It was the way in which the great universal needs of human existence in this world – shelter, food production, disposal of the dead, and so on – took different material forms in different environments. It was a scientific maxim that uniform causes produce uniform reactions: the need for shelter causes dwellings to be built, the fear of unknown forces causes charms to be created and monuments erected, the existence of fish causes fish hooks to be made. The material nature of those dwellings, those charms, or those fish hooks are bound to be determined by the tools and materials available. And as tools, technologies and trade develop, these things will – so the story goes – evolve in accordance with more-or-less predictable laws. So it was that Crawford photographed the ways in which crops were laid out to dry in different places, the rounded forms of haycocks in Iona, hemp drying out in bunches in Transylvania, and – a formal parallel – the peat stacks he saw on the Isle of Lewis amusingly similar to the shapes of dolmens. He collected images

of grave monuments, scarecrows and types of cart; and he photographed dwellings of all kinds, from Sudanese huts, their doors
fashioned from flattened-out Shell oil cans, to the collective housing settlements of Weimar Germany.

Many of Crawford's photographs could have illustrated that
slogan of New Objectivity, 'The World Is Beautiful'; looking at
his photographs of dry-stone walls in Dorset and Cornwall, for
example, it is hard to deny that it is so. Such photographs suggest a love of the world that was almost mystical in its intensity
(ironic, perhaps, for a misanthrope). But like aerial archaeology
their beauty is inextricable from their purpose. All of these photographs were tokens of his belief that history was knowable, and
that its course – from the misty past to a rational future – could
be plotted out through haystooks and burial practices, through
the rise and fall of the use of charms, or the evolution of agricultural tools.

He built up a large collection of photographs and arranged
them – along with other collected images – in albums. So important to him were his photographic negatives and his albums that
he stowed them carefully and sent some away for safety during
the war. It's not easy to reconstruct his albums, now, after they
were disassembled by a so-called conservator. But evidently their
arrangement was a deliberate classification, sometimes geographical, sometimes typological. There are sequences of images
of gravestones and grave markers, sequences of beast-driven
carts, sequences of waves crashing on seashores, of animal tracks,
funghi, cobwebs and trees. In places the typological arrangement – a standard way of organizing anthropological material
in the nineteenth century, as in the Pitt Rivers Museum – was
turned to comic effect, like the photographs of sleeping archaeologists he collected and arranged, titled 'horizontal excavators'.
And everywhere – assisted, perhaps, by the archive's ruina-
tion – there are visual correspondences, like the photograph
of lightning over Southampton, echoing the zigzag lines of

trenches in an aerial photograph, or the photograph of a U-shaped German housing settlement, its form repeated in the earthen labia of the fort of Maumbury seen from the air.

Archaeologists at Oxford's Institute of Archaeology still occasionally delve into Crawford's collection, especially when they are looking for an image of a site that has since changed or disappeared. They turn up one of Allen's aerial views, or one of Crawford's photographs from a field trip, before a road was built, a quarry dug, or a town expanded. Crawford's photographs of ancient sites and monuments are now doubly framed; once by the moment in which they were taken, and again by the moment in which we look at them now. They are images both of ancient monuments, and of the landscapes in which they are situated as they once were. In some cases landscape or monument, or both, have changed almost beyond recognition. There's an image in the archive, for example, of the so-called 'Cat Stane', west of Edinburgh, taken in the late summer of 1935. Carved with an inscription in Latin, it is thought to mark the grave of an ancient personage. It's a beautiful photograph, taken on the kind of clear bright day Crawford favoured; the stone sits apparently undisturbed in a field of illuminated cornstooks. Type 'Cat Stane' and 'Edinburgh' into a search engine and it turns out that it now sits beside the runway of Edinburgh airport.

Archaeologists at the Institute have apparently tended to find less use for the other, rather more curious, sequences of photographs held in the Crawford archive, most of them dating from the 1930s soon after he returned from Russia; and as a result these seem to have retained more of their original order. There are the photographs of buildings in London associated with Marx, Engels and Lenin; the photographs of roadside advertisements; the images of anti-fascist graffiti, in London and in Berlin; the photographs of so-called 'wayside pulpits' outside churches. It is startling to come across such things among the standing stones and the ancient inscriptions; but they have something of the same

quality. It is as if the photographer is viewing the world around him from a great height, as if he had been propelled into the clean air of the future, like the saints you sometimes see in churches, raised up from the earth on winged feet. A church hall in suburban Southampton is viewed with the same kind of detachment as a Roman barrow. The whole world, past, present and future seems to be here laid out for inspection, in this museum without walls. The pictures and their presence here are a puzzle. But the vertiginous feeling they convey is real; and it has, I think, a real enough cause.

# CHAPTER 7

The capitalist world looked different to those returning from the Soviet Union. 'A new optics is the most undoubted gain from a stay in Russia,' wrote Walter Benjamin in 1927, coming back to Berlin after nearly two months in Moscow. Britain after Russia looked different to Crawford. The defamiliarization was as much a matter of the senses – optics – as politics. Seen from the vantage-point of the future represented by the Soviet Union, Britain as it was in 1932 looked like a civilization on the point of extinction; a soon-to-be-olde worlde – with any luck. After the Revolution Britain would reclassify its own capitalist past as the bad old days, just as Russia had reclassified its own Tsarist history. There would be no place in such a country for religion, for example. All of Britain's parish churches, the Anglicans, the Congregationals and the Christadelphians would go, their buildings turned to rubble, their paraphernalia preserved as exhibits in anti-religious museums like the ones in Russia. Private property would be abolished, and slum dwellings and unsanitary housing would be replaced by Constructivist architecture and communal housing. Agriculture would be collectivized. Advertising would go. Come the Revolution just about every aspect of British society and culture, all of its half-timbered cottages, inner-city slums and checkerboard fields, all of its adverts for Sunlight Soap, Krusto pastry and Whiteways Cyder, its flag-flying fêtes, private land, stately homes, bowler hats, exclusive golf courses and gentlemen's clubs – all of these would become, in an instant, the artefacts, rituals and remains of a superseded culture. They would not simply become part of history – the word implies some continuity with the present. They would become the prehistory of an Internationalist Socialist Republic of Britain, as alien to it as lynchets, querns and burial mounds were to Britain in the twentieth century. The whole 'archaeological cul-ture' – to borrow a contemporary term – of capitalist Britain would be relegated to museum display.

At the same time – in this new Socialist Republic – the history of the British Revolution, and the role that the British Isles had in the development of international communism, would be resurrected and celebrated. Socialist history would become mainstream. Heritage sites would be memorials to the Tolpuddle Martyrs or the Peasants' Revolt, not the palaces of the aristoc-racy. Statues would be erected, one might think, to Wat Tyler, Keir Hardie, and Thomas Paine, to Darwin, perhaps, and Newton. And all of the homes and haunts of the founding fathers of com-munism, Marx, Engels and later, Lenin, when they lived and worked in London and Manchester, would become national shrines. Britain was, after all, the very birthplace of communism – *Das Kapital* was researched in the Reading Room of the British Museum, and *The Communist Manifesto* was the outcome of a congress held in rooms above a Soho pub. This half-hidden his-tory would one day become the official history of the British Socialist Republic, taught in schools and promoted in museums. On that day, Westminster Abbey and Buckingham Palace would become relics of the past, kept open – like the palaces of Catherine the Great in Russia – as lessons about the superstitions and decadence of our ancestors. And Number 41, Maitland Park Road, near Chalk Farm, would be preserved as the house where Karl Marx died; the carpet he wore out in a line as he paced from desk to window, window to desk, would – if it were still there – be cordoned off, the traces of the great man's feet pointed out to coachloads of visitors, the physical residue of a man having world-changing thoughts.

In Russia the Revolution had brought with it its own reshuf-fling of history, bringing sidelined events and unsung heroes from the past out of the shadows, rewriting Tsarist historiography and relegating feudal and class society to the glass cases of museo-logical display. The Russian Revolution itself was given a history and endowed with roots almost immediately, even while it was still being played out. The Museum of the Revolution in Moscow was begun in 1917; it was housed in a grand neoclassical build-ing that had once been the English Club. Its displays endowed a history to an event – the October Revolution – that was not to be seen as sudden, or without precedent, but as the inevitable out-come of a revolutionary history going back to opposition to Napoleon, and still further back, to the peasants' rebellions of the Middle Ages. It offered, in effect, a history of Russia that was the history of the Revolution. And this, thought Crawford, who vis-ited it in 1932, was only proper. Was not history as told in British schools and museums the history of the emergence of Britain's own present ruling class, the bourgeoisie? And now that class and its culture was in decline, and so the days of nationalist, Whiggish history were numbered. 'A proletariat that has captured power', he wrote in 'A Tour in Bolshevy', 'and whose culture is on the up-grade will be interested in the steps by which it has achieved power. It will demand a historical background, a his-torical explanation of the present. But that present still lies in the future. We have not yet got a British museum of the Revolution.' *Not yet.* It's a startling thought. But one day, maybe soon, we would. And that museum could make good use of photographs of Marx's signature in the ledger of the British Museum Reading Room, or Lenin's (signing under the assumed name of Jacob Richter), both of them promising to abide by the library rules; or

↑
3|0                    3|

30  HOLFORD SQUARE,  where Lenin lived

photographs of the house in Holford Square, near King's Cross, where Lenin stayed with his wife, Krupskaya, from 1902 to 1903 (later destroyed in the Blitz); or of the Brotherhood Church on Southgate Road in Islington, where the London Congress of the Bolshevik Party was held a decade before the Russian Revolution. Photographs like these would have to be collected, in preparation; they would be the building blocks of a new history, giving the British Revolution retrospective roots, reinforcing an understanding of its inevitability. And this was surely the reason why Crawford took them with such fervour; he was not looking backwards, but ahead.

Crawford was clearly impressed by Soviet museums in general. Unlike museums in the West, they seemed to him to be active places, laboratories orientated towards the present and the future, not bunkers gloating over the hoarded spoils of the past. Soon after returning from Russia he wrote an article for *Russia Today*, entitled 'Putting the Past in its Place', firmly expressing this view. 'Soviet archaeologists,' ran the opening to this article, 'link up the past with the present in order best to understand to-day and the future. In capitalist countries the museums *dare not* do this. They prefer to glorify the past and maintain a discreet ambiguity about the present and the future.' Museums in Russia, he wrote, preserved the past with no display of 'sentimental regret'. 'There is here no reactionary zeal for the good old times and places where a man was a man and a peasant wasn't.'

Crawford's visit to Russia in fact coincided with what turned out to be a rather brief period in which Soviet museums were organized along lines that were both experimental and aggressively Marxist. This was part of the ideological front of the Five-Year Plan. Museums of all kinds were on the front line of the revolution in consciousness that the Bolsheviks were trying to effect; and for visitors from the West, the perspective on the world they offered could be weirdly disorientating. After 1930 it was the task of specially trained curators and particular party cells devoted to methodology and propaganda techniques to devise ways of using objects, wall texts and graphic design to mould – almost viscerally – the perspective of the museum-goer. The so-called 'Experimental Marxist Exhibition' was flourishing in 1932. Its task was to release the revolutionary energy ossified within objects from the past, by re-contextualizing them in new historical narratives, known as 'talking' museums. Techniques of montage and defamiliarization borrowed from the artistic avant-garde were used to impress on the museum visitor the dynamic nature of historical materialism. This took different forms in different kinds of museum. In museums of art, 'high' and 'low' forms were mixed together, and exhibits could combine architecture, photographs, maps, easel paintings, folkloric objects, painted slogans and wall texts, to create multimedia 'environments'. These were meant to connect past to present, and at the same time were supposed to make bourgeois 'art appreciation' or object fetishism quite impossible.

Thus it was, for example, that a visitor to the Hermitage in 1932 expecting to see Catherine the Great's art collection would

have found not so much a series of paintings to be admired, but specimens of a bourgeois category hitherto known as 'art', exemplifying stages of socio-economic history, from feudalism to late bourgeois capitalism. The collections in Russia's big art museums (amassed under the Tsars and preserved by Lenin, though he never knew quite what to do with them) were rearranged, under Stalin, to provide an explication of Marxist historiography. At the State Museum of Modern Western Art, for example (later closed as dangerously bourgeois), the Tahitian paintings of Gauguin were exhibited alongside a tract by Lenin on Imperialism. Again, Crawford was impressed. He had never had much time for art (although he was interested in architecture), but at the Hermitage he found his tour guide's explanations most illuminating. It was, he thought, only natural that the collections should have been rearranged to illustrate the Marxist point of view that art is 'a portion of the superstructure based upon material foundations', and that it therefore is 'subservient to the dominant class'. But he was even more pleased by what he found in Russia's other museums, especially in the areas in which he felt qualified to judge.

There had been a similar sort of rearrangement of material in museums of anthropology, archaeology and folklore as had taken place in art museums. Existing collections of anthropological or archaeological material from pre-revolutionary museums were re-ordered to display the history and aspirations of State communism. A hand-woven fish basket from Kazakhstan, for example, that before Stalin might have been displayed in a provincial museum as an example of peasant craft, of antiquarian or general interest, would now have been redeployed in a diorama showing a continuum of the history of food production stretching from the past to the present. Hunting and gathering would be shown to have given way to small-scale agriculture, which in turn would cede through the will of the people to the collective farm of the present. Thus Crawford was very impressed by a display he saw at the museum at Tiflis which juxtaposed a heavy wooden plough of a type used by the local Hefsurian peasants (presumably the Khevsur people, thought by some to be descended from the Crusaders) with a photograph of a tractor, the very symbol of collectivization. The everyday objects and tools of these Caucasians, that were still being used, were deliberately represented as evolutionarily retarded. This included their religious practices, to Crawford's evident approval. In Soviet museums in general, anything to do with religion or superstition – and in archaeological or ethnographic museums, this could cover a great deal – was deliberately framed as part of a pre-revolutionary past, the persistent remnants of which in the Soviet present had to be rooted out as an unfortunate, if picturesque, Tylorian 'survival'. In this way Stalin made efficient, if brutal, use of the same anthropological perspective that informed museums like Oxford's Pitt Rivers Museum.

Anti-religious displays were taken further in dedicated anti-religious museums, such as the Leningrad Museum of the History of Religion and Atheism, overseen by the increasingly powerful League of the Militant Godless. Objects and rites of the pre-Revolutionary Russian church were exhibited at these anti-religious museums alongside those of other faiths (Islam, Judaism, Catholicism, Buddhism), and superstitious practices from around the world. Practices like Holy Communion or the veneration of relics were depicted as if they were all primitive superstitions peddled by religious authorities and a priestly caste who stood to gain wealth and power from the credulity of the people. Parallels were drawn between ancient beliefs and those still current, and between 'civilized' and 'primitive' cultures, in what was described by a foreign visitor as 'comparative idolatry'. Totems from the South Seas were juxtaposed with Christian crucifixes, altars alongside sacrificial stones; imagery of Christ's resurrection was rhymed with the Ancient Egyptian myth of the rebirth of Osiris; all nonsense, of course; fairy tales to keep the people dreaming rather than

acting, to keep them waiting patiently for their rewards in heaven
rather than demanding them now. And to ram this home, photographs, statistics and other exhibited documents professed to
reveal the close connections that existed in non-communist countries between the Church, the State, the Royal Family and the
military.

Again, Crawford was thrilled, not least because the cultures of
Western capitalism were no longer the 'norm' against which
others were measured, and Christianity was represented as a faith
as irrational and fetishistic as the animistic and superstitious
beliefs of primitive peoples. At an anti-religious display housed
in a House of Culture in Leningrad he saw exhibits showing the
close association of the Church with the army in capitalist countries: photographs of bishops blessing regimental colours, for
example, and quotations from speeches made by priests during
the First World War. Statistics of the profits made by the Church
and the Salvation Army were pinned up as evidence of the empty

pretence of Christian 'otherworldliness'. It must have been gratifying to Crawford to see his own anti-religious stance reflected
in state institutions. But he was also excited by the *method* of
such exhibitions, and the way in which they effectively rela-
tivized capitalist modernity. 'The Museum technique,' he wrote
in 'Tour in Bolshevy', 'is here applied to the primitive rites and
customs of modern Europe. The method is strictly objective, con-
sisting of a display of facts. It is an example of practical Marxian
anthropology, which attracts no attention when it is applied to
some remote community in the heart of Africa or Australia.' It
was surely this kind of 'practical Marxian anthropology' that
Crawford himself began to practise, using his camera, after he
returned home to Britain.

Soviet museums in the early 1930s could be defamiliarizing
and disorientating for visitors from the West. Back home in
Europe or America museums were not really expected to *do*
anything with anything like this amount of energy – although,
of course, they did uphold, apparently effortlessly, an image of
national sovereignty and national history; and they did the job
of defining 'other' cultures while their own culture – that of bourgeois capitalism – remained unrepresented, ground zero. What
was perhaps most estranging (quite literally) for Western visitors
like Crawford was that among the exhibits in Soviet museums,
the culture of capitalism – their culture – was put in the spotlight
too, subjected to the sort of scrutiny usually reserved for other
cultures safely distant in time and space. Capitalism was not so
much the *enemy* – this was before the Cold War – but a form of
life, like feudalism, or primitive polytheism, that had been superseded. So, for example, a visitor to the Ethnographic Museum in
Leningrad in 1932 would have seen not only such things as the
cloaks of Siberian shamans, dioramas of the 'primitive' dwellings
of the Samoeds and their like, but also images of the increasingly
opulent furnishings of the homes of bourgeois landowners and
manufacturers – the flock wallpapers, the gilt mirrors, ruched

curtains, potted ferns, stuffed birds and cluttered ornaments – in the period leading up to their downfall. The culture of capitalism – its art, artefacts, political organization, interior decor and its religious beliefs – had been officially consigned to the glass cases of museological display. Western visitors – especially Christian ones – were effectively presented with an image of themselves as primitives, not yet fully modern, still mired in superstition and myth. Few avant-garde artists in Paris, London or Berlin could have delivered such a bracing visual shock.

Much of this Soviet *détournement* of capitalist culture and religion was admittedly crude. The defamations of the anti-religious displays were, in the words of the writer (and sometime communist) André Gide, 'monstrous, abject, and ridiculous'. In art museums, art pooh-poohed as 'bourgeois' increasingly included almost anything – including early Soviet works – that was not realist in style and proletarian in subject matter. It was ironic, as the art historian Adam Jolles points out, that avant-garde museum display techniques were used to degrade experimental artists who were now becoming the victims of Stalin's clampdown. But Crawford, by his own admission, knew little about art, and cared even less for religion. He did not have time, moreover, to study Soviet museums in detail, or he might have noticed certain casualties of truth there, evidence of the difficulty of imposing the party line on the vast range of cultures and objects even within the Soviet Union, let alone outside it, as historian Francine Hirsch has pointed out. In their anxiety to establish the existence of social class among the peasantry, for example, museum officials in the Ethnographic Department of the Russian Museum in Leningrad labelled Ukrainian festival costumes as the clothing of the *kulaks*, or land-owning peasants, and ordinary everyday peasant garments as the clothing of the less well-off; whereas, in fact, both costumes were worn by the same people on different days. *Kulaks* had to be represented as different from the *bedniaks* and *seredniaks* (poor and middling peasants) in order to establish their supposed identity as capitalist enemies of the people. Museum displays effectively had to support and justify policies of eradication – with the goal of liquidating avant-garde art, popular religion, and the smallholding peasantry. But to Crawford in 1932 what was exciting was the shift of consciousness, and the confidence with which it was applied. It was a perspective shift, enthroned in museum policy, that implied the completion of an evolutionary movement – and with it, a sense that at last the whole was swinging into view, the nirvana for which Crawford had been seeking at least since writing *Man and His Past*. Part of this new perspective was the re-positioning of bourgeois imperialism as a superseded evolutionary stage – which is how Crawford, at least in his 1931 article 'Historical Cycles', saw it himself.

The museums Crawford saw in Russia surely gave him an idea as to what museums might be like in a post-Revolutionary Britain. It was not just his musings on a future 'British Museum of the Revolution' in 'A Tour in Bolshevy'. His papers show that in May 1932 he was already drawing up plans for a 'Museum of Human Evolution' that could only come into existence in a post-capitalist society that had expunged religion of all kinds. It is not clear, from the notes, where this ambitious 'Museum of Human Evolution' might be built; perhaps in the USSR, but each world region, wrote Crawford, would probably have to have one of its own. The aim of this museum, wrote Crawford, would be to show what the human race has accomplished, 'without "divine aid" or "divine intervention", from the stone axe to the Five-Year Plan'. The Museum would have its own Plan of Scientific Research, coordinating scientific work throughout the region. And it would include a sideshow for 'Human Folly throughout the Ages'. This would include such things as the Pyramids, the 'cult of the dead' in prehistoric Western Europe, and 'priest-craft religion generally'. The idea for this 'Museum of Human Folly', as explained in a note by Crawford's friend Hunter, was that such

mistakes should never be repeated. It would, then, be very like
the anti-religious museums of Soviet Russia. Crawford must have
enjoyed fantasizing about how existing British museums and collections (including London's own British Museum) might be
re-ordered without the deadening hand of vested interests. He
would in fact have shared this fantasy – applied to a different
field – with the art historian Anthony Blunt, later surveyor of the
Queen's pictures and a Soviet spy. 'What a field day the Minister
of Fine Arts will have,' wrote Blunt in 1937, 'when, the day after
the revolution, the State takes over all privately-owned paintings
and collects the best in a central museum!'

Perhaps, then, it was in preparation for a British Museum of
Human Folly that not long after returning from Russia, Crawford
started to take photographs of the activities and material culture
of Church organizations in Britain. It was certainly an exercise of
what he called 'Marxian anthropology', which for Crawford had
considerable satirical potential in the interim. In the suburbs of
Southampton he photographed the wayside pulpits and other
signs and posters pasted outside churches and church halls. He

photographed the placard outside the Christadelphian Hall in Shirley which listed its articles of faith in large black capitals, including the assertion that the Bible is the Word of God, that Jesus Christ is the Son of God, that there will be an Earthly Kingdom of God, that Jerusalem has been chosen by God, and so on. In July 1934 the same church was advertising a talk entitled 'Hell – Its locality & use'. 'Christadelphians are rather credulous about certain things, such as hell, god, man, Jerusalem, the Bible and the future,' wrote Crawford on the back of one of these photographs. In October of the same year, the Hall was hosting a lecture considering the relative merits of Creationism and Evolution. But as Crawford noted in another scribbled remark, the Christadelphians seemed to be quite sure about the future. The main placard outside the pebble-dashed building proclaimed that 'Jesus Christ Is Coming to Establish His Kingdom'.

Crawford returned to the wayside pulpits of his local churches in much the same way as Major Allen returned again and again to crop sites in the fields of the Thames valley, spotting new signs and recording them with his camera. These signs were evidence of the stubborn survival of superstition and primitive thought. For what else did inscriptions like 'HELL – Its locality & use' or THE LORD IS RISEN INDEED indicate, seen in the great historico-evolutionary march towards rationalism, science and socialism? No, the days of such beliefs and proclamations were numbered; and in time the church buildings they adorned would – like those in Russia – be turned into rubble, their bricks retrieved, cleaned and sorted, and used to build communal apartment blocks. A most worthy transformation. And then people would visit anti-religious museums, just as they did in Russia, and stare in disbelief at the evidence of the things their ancestors once believed. In the meantime, Crawford would gather data, like the 'Christian publicity' painted on the roof of a building in Bath, its letters spelling out a message ('Christ died for our Sins') that was meant to be as visible from passing traffic as the White Horse of

Uffington was by distant travellers, the icon, perhaps, of a more ancient faith.

It was doubtless in a similar spirit of a satirical anthropology of the present, with an eye to the future, that Crawford took other sets of photographs of contemporary Britain after he came back from Russia. There were, for example, the photographs he took of landowners' signs, like the sign on the golf course near Bamburgh Castle forbidding access to members of the public at all times on pain of prosecution, and restricting Club members' access on Sundays. The rules and regulations laid down by property owners were apparently at this time one of Crawford's bugbears; so, too, was the way in which the whole country – apart from its churches – shut up shop on a Sunday. Another bugbear – one of his biggest – was the omnipresence of adverts, everywhere from roadsides and railway carriages to table mats. These he documented, too, capturing them with his camera, as they came and went on the roadside hoardings of the Southampton Poster Service. There was nothing like this in the USSR, where public space was used for public information and celebration of collective action. There, there had been placards advising workers of the dangers of alcohol and the shame of drunkenness – here, there were adverts associating beer with athleticism and strength. In Southampton – as in every other town in Britain – you could hardly escape from a papered dreamworld of consumption, promising health, joy and prosperity through processed foodstuffs, motoring and cinematic fantasies. Products and their consumers were infused with an almost holy glow, Friary Ales the way and the light, a smoker of Gold Flake turning her kohl-eyes heavenward in ecstasy like St Teresa of Avila, a similarly ecstatic telephone operator, her head thrown back in joy. One day all such things would be turned to dust. In the meantime, the turnover on the neo-classically framed Poster Service hoardings was fast, and as he documented them, Crawford classified their promotion of products and events according to the primitive instincts they appealed to: militarism

SOUTHAMPTON
ENGLAND
—

Militarism          Beer

('the famous Tidworth Tattoo'), sex appeal (Gold Flake), nationalism ('Be British Buy British Beer'). His photographs would form a catalogue of pre-revolutionary ephemera, documents of a culture as barbaric, in its way, as any to be found in the pages of *Antiquity*.

Some of these photographs have Crawford's name and address on the back, and pinholes in their four corners, suggesting that they may have been exhibited; he was certainly invited to show some work at a photographic exhibition at Marx House in 1940. But the degree to which Crawford was putting his skills to use as a service to organized revolutionary communism, present or future, is far from clear; and it is just as likely that he had his own, and only partially knowable, purpose. His papers from the years in which he was most active, politically and photographically, were largely destroyed in the war; and he himself destroyed other papers. The remaining evidence does not suggest an enormous amount of participation in organized political activity. He was not, apparently, a member of the Communist Party at any point. But he was in touch with some of its key figures: with Robin Page Arnot, who was a founder of the Marx Memorial Library and Workers' School; and with Ralph Fox, who before he died in the Spanish Civil War spent nearly three years at the Marx-Engels Institute in Moscow. He had dealings with the organ of the Communist Party of Great Britain (CPGB), the *Daily Worker*, making the odd submission, donating to its bazaar fund, and planning selling campaigns for the paper – or at least talking about it – on the streets of Southampton. He was clearly involved with the Friends of the Soviet Union, contributing at least once to its paper, *Russia Today*, and donating the profits of his lecture on Russia at the Basingstoke Rotary Club to the local branch of the FSU. He implied in a letter that the lecture had got him into trouble, perhaps with his employer; and it may be that his status as a civil servant made it difficult for him to be more politically active, or more openly active than he was. But it may also have been a preference (whether or not it was a necessity) for subterfuge; and a residual discomfort with group activities, dating back to his public school days, that was only temporarily (if exhilaratingly) lifted on the foreign soil of Russia. Back in Britain he liked the frisson of believing himself to be, as it were, the only Marxist at the Ordnance Survey – or, for that matter, the only Marxist at the Athenaeum Club (he almost certainly was not, of course). And it was a *frisson* that was particularly gratifying when he believed himself about to be proved right by history, regardless of the input from him. Revolutionary change was for Crawford largely a matter of faith, not works.

One or two of Crawford's friends were more openly and actively political than he was. His companion on the trip to Russia, Neil Hunter, was for a time Secretary of the British Anti-War Movement, set up in 1932 with Comintern support to campaign for mass resistance to any war preparations made by a capitalist government. Crawford was a close friend, too, of the openly Marxist archaeologist Gordon Childe, whom he met in 1925, and whose work he promoted in *Antiquity*. It may well have been this friendship more than anything else that helped form Crawford's political outlook. Childe was surely the intellectual, the internationalist, the synthesizer and illuminator of archaeological data that Crawford would have liked to be himself. Childe, like Crawford, had emerged from a strictly religious upbringing as an anti-clerical rationalist (in the words of his biographer, Sally Green). Both had connections to Scotland; Crawford, thinking perhaps of his roots, was increasingly drawn to fieldwork there, and Childe was Professor of Prehistory at Edinburgh University. Like Crawford, Childe thought big, disregarding the artificial disciplinary boundaries that divided 'prehistory' from 'history', and the artificial national boundaries that so often restricted conceptions of geographical space. But unlike Crawford, he was able not only to conceive of a big picture, but to fill it out convincingly. He spoke many different languages, and had by all accounts a phenomenal memory for sites and artefacts, coupled with a great ability for synthesis. In works like *The Dawn of European Civilization* (1925) and *Man Makes Himself* (1936) he mapped out the vast ages of human history as a complex mosaic of interacting archaeological cultures; a complexity through which progress was discernible even at times of crisis like the 1930s. Like Crawford, Childe believed in the necessity of broadcasting archaeological knowledge to the broadest possible public, and he wrote a number of books specifically for a popular audience, including *What Happened in History*, a broadly Marxist synthesis which sold hundreds of thousands of copies after its publication in 1942. The two men got on well, and were clearly bonded by their political as well as their archaeological interests (Childe liked to sign off his letters to Crawford in Cyrillic letters), as well as by a shared tendency, perhaps, to melancholia. But Childe was far more active politically; indeed he had followed a political career in his native Australia before he became an archaeologist. The British Security Service had kept him under surveillance since 1917, when, as a student in Oxford, he was believed to have been keen to undermine the war effort. His activities were followed and his mail intercepted throughout the 1930s and beyond, resulting in two fat files in the Public Record Office, retained until 2006. His trips abroad were noted, and the meetings he addressed were attended by plain-clothes police officers, who dutifully reported back his discussions of archaeological matters. He continued to be under observation until he died, although the Scottish Regional Security Officer reported in 1941 that he was 'inclined to think that he is of the progressive, intellectual type and is not likely to be dangerous'.

It seems to have been primarily through archaeological interests that Crawford was connected to communist circles, including those that centred on the Marx Memorial Library. Robin Page Arnot contributed at least once to *Antiquity*, and before he died Ralph Fox – who was the author of a book on

Genghis Khan – was talking to Crawford about the possibility of a joint trip to Armenia to look at prehistoric remains. Prehistory and antiquity were in fact subjects of some currency among communist circles around the 1930s. Towards the end of his life Marx had got interested in the idea of primitive communism, an interest that was picked up and developed by Engels in his book *The Origin of the Family, Private Property and the State*. Archaeology could be mined for evidence that private property and so on were not necessarily 'natural', and that mankind had once lived without restrictions of class or authority. By tracing a time before the existence of social classes and the State, Engels could imagine their disintegration, with all the weight of history behind him. Production could once again be reorganized more equably; and, he wrote, the machinery of State would be put 'into the museum of antiquity, by the side of the spinning wheel and the bronze axe'.

Engels was writing in 1884. By the 1930s there was a feeling (shared by Crawford, of course, with his carpet metaphors) that so much new material about prehistory had been revealed, that sense needed to be made of it. This was where Gordon Childe came in. According to Crawford, writing in *Antiquity* in 1936, Childe's *Man Makes Himself* was the book Marx would have written had he had access to all of the knowledge discovered in the fifty years since his death. Childe's model of world history was one in which technology – broadly conceived – was the motor of human progress. Man was a tool-making animal, and society could only progress when the political and economic system allowed technology, science and invention to develop. Progress could be retarded when the system inhibited technological development, like the decline of medicine in Ancient Greece when an aristocratic disdain for manual labour stopped physicians from carrying out dissections. These sorts of issues were very much on the agenda of the Communist Party in the 1930s. A CPGB manifesto from 1935, entitled 'For Soviet Britain', drew its readers' attention to the recent address given to the British Association for the Advancement of Science by Sir Josiah Stamp, 'the leading railway capitalist'. Science, said Stamp, was going too fast for economics; an adjustment would have to be made. Capitalists might take this to mean that science would have to be curbed, which was doubtless Stamp's intention. But scientists were beginning to see that capitalism was holding science back, ran the Party manifesto. Stamp was quite right in his diagnosis, but not in his proposed cure; progress could only be made in a socialist society.

Robin Page Arnot certainly knew about the photographic survey Crawford was doing of the homes and haunts of Marx. 'It's good you have been getting so many data on Marx-sites in London,' he told him in a letter from 1934, 'before every trace has vanished.' He asked him whether he was intending to 'do the same for Engels' in Manchester, because he knew a man who could give him full particulars. Crawford wrote, too, to the Marx-Engels-Lenin Institute in Moscow to ask for details about sites, and he was supplied with a full list of Lenin's residences not only in London but in Geneva, Paris, and other European cities. He left no stone unturned when it came to identifying the precise buildings in which the prophets of revolution lived, stayed, or held their meetings; he was very thorough. After compiling lists of buildings, he checked in nineteenth-century post office directories to make sure that house-numbers had not changed, or to discover at what point named buildings had been demolished, and what had taken their place. Marx's home in the spring of 1864, for example, was given as '1 Modena Villas, Maitland Park, Haverstock Hill', an address confirmed – as Crawford found out – by the London post office directory for 1866. By 1934, though, the villas, and the address no longer existed; the site seemed to be occupied by a block of flats called The Grange, a fact apparently confirmed after correspondence with a local Congregational Church, the St Pancras Borough Library and owners of the site.

He had to be sure that he had photographed the correct site, even
if – as in this case – there was no trace left of the original building. And he aimed to apply the same sort of thoroughness to
many other sites he photographed, mainly between May 1934
and May 1936; all of the unprepossessing façades of terraced
houses that were the homes of Marx, Lenin and Engels, or the
buildings that were the sites of their activities. Even those buildings through which these figures passed briefly were documented,
like the bed and breakfast on the Isle of Wight where, plagued by
ill health after the death of his wife, Marx took a holiday in the
early 1880s.

One of the texts Crawford used as a guide on his photographic expeditions round London was a memoir of Marx by his friend and drinking companion Wilhelm Liebknecht, published in 1901. Liebknecht was one of many European radicals who ended up as émigrés in London in the 1850s, where he met Marx and Engels. The house of the Marx family, according to Liebknecht, was 'a pigeon-loft, where a multitude of various Bohemian, fugitive and refugee folk went in and out, little, great and greatest animals'. Liebknecht was one of these animals; for twelve years, he says, he was practically a daily visitor to Marx's house, in Dean Street in Soho (Liebknecht himself lived in nearby Church Street) and later in Grafton Terrace, and Maitland Park Road, where Marx ended his days. After thirty years spent mostly abroad, when he came to write his memoir, Liebknecht went on what he called 'a voyage of discovery' back into these streets, 'to search for the apartments of the family of Marx'. Marx himself was long since dead. London had changed so much in the time that Liebknecht had been away that he compared his investigation of the city to Schliemann's excavation of Troy. In the company of Marx's daughter Tussy and her common-law husband Edward Aveling, Liebknecht wandered around the side streets of Soho Square, where, in Old Compton Street, they found the 'old model lodging house' where Liebknecht had first stayed, remarkably unchanged. It was like opening a pharaoh's tomb, wrote Liebknecht; time had made a halt here, and he was transported back to the boisterous and hilarious years of his youth. On they went, to the 'three-story, grey-black house' in Church Street where Liebknecht later had lodgings. The house in Macclesfield Street where Engels once lived was no longer there, and the pub opposite had been turned into a gin palace; but they did find the Dean Street rooms where Marx had written the *Eighteenth Brumaire* and where he and his wife lost two infants to bronchitis. The explorers then took a bus up Tottenham Court Road (past the tabernacle where three of

Marx's small children were buried) to Kentish Town, where they found Marx's homes in Grafton Terrace and, nearby, in Maitland Park Road.

Liebknecht's 'archaeological' expedition was one of the sources for Crawford's own, forty years later, when he, too, sought out the buildings occupied by Liebknecht, Marx and Engels, and the pubs they frequented, like the Mother Shipton – named after the Yorkshire prophetess – in Kentish Town. But unlike Liebknecht Crawford really was, of course, an archaeologist; and his eye for sites, traces and inscriptions lent a particularly convincing quality to the photographs he took. More used to documenting Roman or prehistoric sites, he photographed these homes and haunts, however humble, as if they were of no less importance than Hadrian's Wall or the Rollright Stones; all were the abandoned sites of historical action, whose significance, clear enough to the photographer, would one day become clear to all.

The sense of abandonment is underlined, in fact, by the depressed economic circumstances of the mid-1930s. Marx's Soho, in 1934, is a sea of 'To Let' signs, with many windows blank or boarded up. But there are other signs of the times, too, scratched or scrawled or posted on the sooty buildings, and Crawford, with his archaeologist's eye, was alert to these accretions. At 41 Maitland Park Road the blue plaque – only recently put up to commemorate Marx's residence there – had been damaged by fascists, whose black-shirted forces were gathering at their headquarters at 33 King's Road, under the leadership of Oswald Mosley. Crawford photographed both the damaged plaque, and the King's Road HQ, papered with publicity for the fascist cause. But there were plenty of signs of resistance to the gathering forces of fascism at home and abroad, and it was these that Crawford seems to have made a particular point of seeking out. In the window of a Jewish butcher in Charlotte Street in Soho, there was a notice advertising a 'mass protest demonstration against

Nazi persecution' in Hyde Park on 27 October 1935. This apparently unprepossessing photograph is, in fact, an extraordinarily
layered image, as Crawford – thanks to his exhaustive
researches – knew well. The post office directory from 1875
showed that the shop had been the site, in the nineteenth century, of Lassassie's hairdressing shop and French newspaper
agency. Lassassie was a council member of the First International,
and his shop was the place, apparently, where revolutionists came
to have their hair cut. The fact that the revolutionary hairdresser's
was now a Jewish butcher's, advertising an anti-Nazi protest
clearly appealed to Crawford's archaeological eye. And so, too,
did the chalked inscriptions that he found in the streets of central London where Marx and Lenin and the rest once lived. Near
Lenin's erstwhile quarters in Regent Square, Crawford documented graffiti reading 'Mosley and Musso means mass-murder'
and 'Close the Suez'. And all round Chalk Farm and Kentish
Town there were chalked anti-fascist graffiti, the reaction to the
rising tide of fascism in Europe and the threat from Mosley's

blackshirts at home. These were anonymous, transient inscriptions; the chalk that was used for graffiti in an age before spray cans could be washed off in a rainstorm. Crawford photographed them when they were fresh; evidence, surely, in some impending tribunal.

Crawford himself witnessed state fascism first-hand when he visited Berlin in 1934, on his way to Warsaw for an International Congress of Geography. He was in Berlin in August, when Hitler held the plebiscite that would have his power as president and Führer sanctioned by popular vote. Crawford photographed the posters hastily stuck up around the city urging Berliners to vote 'Ja' to Hitler. On the day of the plebiscite he counted the number of swastika flags displayed from the balconies of apartment buildings in different areas (42 – nearly one per balcony – in one prosperous-looking street in Wedding, known as a working class district; rather fewer in a tenement block in the same

area), in a kind of impromptu sociological survey; and he photographed the entrance to one of the polling booths, flanked
intimidatingly by Hitler's storm-troopers from the SA wearing 'Ja'
posters.

He also started, on the day of the plebiscite, to create a quite
extraordinary archive of photographs. All around Berlin, on
palings, fences, walls and bridges, Crawford saw the fugitive
slogans of anti-Nazi and pro-communist graffiti. Some of the
graffiti was barely legible, or almost invisible, since it had been
painted over, rubbed or scratched out by Nazi recruits in the
run-up to voting day. In some cases, as Crawford noted, the
paint was still wet. Sometimes it looked as though those doing
the covering up were in as much of a hurry as those who had
left the graffiti, barely bothering to remove the slogans altogether from sight. In other cases it took a trained eye, an eye
trained like Crawford's to notice and decipher inscriptions, to
make out the words underneath the paint. It certainly took a
rare eye to notice and document such things for posterity.
Some of the graffiti dated since before Hitler, supporting the
communist Ernst Thälmann who by 1934 had been impris-
oned. Others were more recent, like the slogan *Tod den Nazis*
(Death to the Nazis) that Crawford found, half-scratched out,
on a canal bridge. Such things were traces of resistance, vestiges
of dissent that had been defaced, or papered over with posters
saying 'Ja'.

There were other instances, too, where – as Crawford noted –
the Nazi Party had superimposed itself upon the city. Crawford
photographed the former Headquarters of the Communist
Party in Berlin, Karl Liebknecht Haus, which had recently been
renamed Horst Wessel Haus, after a Nazi hero. Crawford considered the study of place names – an important aspect of local
history – to be one of his specialities; and here was an instance
in which change was so sudden, so deliberate, it could be
charted. The renaming seems as crude as the obliteration of the

graffiti; a banner stretched across a window, and a placard stuck above the door. Similarly crude was the way in which the Nazis – like the Soviets – made their own museums as they came to power. Crawford visited a makeshift 'Revolutions Museum', organized by a unit of the SA, that had set up shop in Neue Friedrichstrasse. Souvenir postcards collected by Crawford from this museum show weapons apparently confiscated from Communists, the trophies of street fighting, alongside other German Communist Party items like banners and collection tins. A poster advertising the Museum – the subject of one of Crawford's photographs – declared that it showed the symbols of an era that had now been superseded. Fascists could play the evolution game, too.

Crawford, like certain other intellectuals including his one-time hero H. G. Wells, did not believe that fascism could possibly survive, let alone triumph. Wells, as George Orwell wrote, saw Hitler as a kind of witch doctor, a ghost from the past, appealing to the most primitive loyalties of clan and nation; as such he was

doomed to disappear. The idea that fascism would win out was
an impossibility, evolutionarily speaking, a historical reversal as
unlikely – as Orwell wrote – as a Jacobite restoration. This seems
to have been Crawford's view, too. 'The vision of triumphant
Fascism is not,' he wrote in 'A Tour in Bolshevy',

> like that of Russia, the vision of a new world that is coming
> into being; it is the old world of capitalism we know so
> well at its cruellest and most efficient point. Its pace is
> more rapid than that of socialism in Russia, but that does
> not mean that its triumph is more assured, rather the
> reverse – cabbages grow quicker than oaks, but they only
> last a year.

Crawford, like Wells, clearly conceived of the hold that
Nazism had over people as primitive, a throwback to barbaric
religions of old. Crawford mounted in his album a postcard
showing Hitler and Mussolini shaking hands; 'Note expressions
of wrapt ecstacy, religious AWE on faces of satellites,' he wrote.
Such a phenomenon could only be a temporary reversion (an
'evanescent phenomenon' as Crawford put it), that would be
proved as such after a worldwide socialist revolution. His photographs were a preparation, of the most material kind surely, for
that day.

If Crawford was gathering photographs of the world around
him in preparation for a post-revolutionary future, it is no
wonder that we feel a sense of vertigo looking at them. It is as
if we have been propelled into a future that might have been,
and never was. He photographed the world as though he was
seeing it from a vantage point outside history, *after* history, after
the revolution. The future he was preparing for never came; the
post-Revolutionary British Museum was never built. The
archive we are looking at is the ruin of an imaginary museum.
And it is the ruin, too, of a particular and visionary kind of

faith; a faith that history is knowable in its entirety, that it obeys certain laws, leads inexorably towards something, and that everything makes perfect sense. It would not last very much longer.

# CHAPTER 8

Britain was supposed to have been the first country to have a proletarian revolution. It had, after all, been the first to industrialize; as a result it had the biggest and most self-conscious working class. That was why Marx and Engels went there in the 1850s. It made sense for communism to be invented in the industrial 'workshop of the world'. But revolution did not happen in Britain; it happened in Russia, a country that was essentially pre-industrial, a country full of peasants, not factory workers. Lenin, and later Stalin, may have liked to see themselves as heading up an expeditionary force into the future; but how it was that they were leading a country that had hitherto – in evolutionary terms – been bringing up the rear remained something of a mystery. And how it remained the case that the British had still not had a revolution was a question that every visitor to Russia in the 1920s and 30s – including Crawford – was asked.

The reluctance of the British proletariat to recognize and act out its historic role was something that exasperated the authors of *The Communist Manifesto* back in the nineteenth century. Britain might have been the country in which class difference was most extreme, class contradictions most shameless; but somehow, despite a number of false starts, this never resulted in the mass rising up that had been foretold. In a letter of 1858 Engels told Marx that in Britain he feared the proletariat was 'actually becoming more and more bourgeois, so that this most bourgeois of all nations is apparently aiming ultimately at the possession of a bourgeois aristocracy and a bourgeois proletariat *as well as* a bourgeoisie'. This wasn't how it was supposed to go. But as George Orwell suggested more than eighty years later, the British on the whole had always seemed more interested in gardening, dog racing or pigeon fancying than radical activism, whether it was their historical destiny or no.

As the 1930s drew to a close, Crawford started to work in his spare time on a book he called 'Bloody Old Britain'. Generically the book is hard to place. It was, he said, 'an attempt to apply archaeological methods to the study of contemporary society' at the end of what he called 'the first inter-war period'; but it wasn't just this – remarkable enough in itself. It was archaeology in the service of social satire, a piece of political propaganda, and a parody, too, of a tourist guidebook of the 'Come to Britain' type popular at the time. But most of all, it was a rant against a society that did not know how to do anything properly, which persisted in being irrational, and which refused to realize its own ridiculousness and futility. Britain is depicted as a place of sham gentility and appalling snobbery, a place where the food is terrible, women are vain and undiscriminating, where the antique architecture of class distinction warps all human interactions; where everything is badly made, nothing works, and yet nobody seems to notice or care that things might be organized differently – indeed, nobody seems to think that things might be organized at all.

The book was never published, even under its censored title 'Bunk of England'. It was too angry, too unpatriotic, particularly for wartime, which was when Crawford submitted his manuscript to Methuen. In March 1943 the publisher told him that while he had 'never read anything like this book, nor quite so

whole-hearted', Crawford's 'political outlook' was 'quite unnec-
essarily bitter', and that publishing this book at this point 'would
be like hitting a man when he is down'. Crawford contented himself with circulating copies to a few friends, which may in any
case have been his original expectation. The typescript – which
languishes in the archives of the Bodleian Library – is a one-hun-
dred-and-eighty-pages-long howl of indignant rage barely
contained by the distanced tone of the scientist-observer in satirical mode. It is appallingly misanthropic and misogynistic; often
contradictory, rambling, and uneven, alternating between bitter
comedy and tedious polemic. But it is also, at times, hysterically
funny. It is funny in the way that Basil Fawlty is; you fear for the
man as you laugh. He is so very angry.

The idea of the book, as announced in the Foreword, was to
examine the material culture of Britain in the 1930s as though it
were one of the prehistoric or ancient civilizations more com-
monly studied by archaeologists. Just as an archaeologist might
examine the potsherds, the tools and the remains of any
dwellings of a primitive settlement for clues to the nature of a
long-vanished culture, Crawford set out to look at the utensils,
homes and consumer durables of modern Britain. Archaeologists
proceed from a study of material objects and their remains. But
the investigator of a modern culture, he noted, had access to a far
broader range of evidence. He could observe 'the quality of the
food, the temperature of the bath-water, the functions of the hotel
porter'. And so, in 'Bloody Old Britain', he did. He noted the smell
of railway carriages, and the way in which sheets and blankets are
tucked in around beds (so tightly that it is impossible to get into
bed without untucking them). He recorded how butter is served
in small round balls; and how, in certain low-grade but preten-
tious restaurants butter balls are simulated by thin shavings
curled round to look as if they were solid. He observed the usage
of the ubiquitous doily in the domestic interior, where – as he
remarked – it seemed no object was permitted to come into

contact with the 'sacred surfaces' of household furniture. In some cases, he wrote, it seemed as though even food were not permitted to come into contact with plates; a small piece of paper was often inserted between a portion of fish and its dish. Such phenomena would require further research (perhaps psychological) as to their significance; so, too, would the display of dead flowers in a vase from which all water had long since evaporated, to be found on every table setting in cafés and restaurants, regardless of the size of the table.

If it is the archaeologist's task to deduce things about a society from a study of its material culture, what, asked Crawford, can be deduced about the culture of contemporary Britain from such things as these? To judge by the evidence, he wrote, this is a culture in which – rather bizarrely – appearances take precedence over use value. So important are appearances to this society that it is more important that a knife look 'stainless', for example, than that it should be able to cut with ease. It is more important that a blind look 'cheerful' than that it should keep out the light. Human comfort is deemed to be worth sacrificing so long as things *look* respectable, expensive or just 'pretty'. This accounts for certain rather bizarre habits and living arrangements. Regardless of its size, for example, the bourgeois British home dedicates an entire room to appearances, explains Crawford; it is called the Parlour. The Parlour is not to be used (it is too cluttered up by pot plants, cut glass and china ornaments); neither is anything in it made to be used. Crawford dedicates five pages to a lengthy analysis of the Parlour fire irons – the tongs, poker and shovel that are designed to look elegant rather than perform their function of feeding and maintaining a fire. They are 'for Appearance', he writes, 'not use, which they regard as degrading to their bourgeois dignity'. That is why the tongs do not open wide enough to grip a lump of coal, why the copper knob on the end of the poker (put there to beautify it) is affixed in such a way that it falls off when held, why the stand on which the fire irons are delicately hung collapses in a heap as soon as one of the tools is removed. They may look like the tools required to create and maintain warmth, an essential component of all human life; but in the British Parlour they perform only a symbolic function in the maintenance of the appearance of respectability and good taste.

Crawford pauses to imagine a research topic of the future: 'Pre-revolutionary Fire-irons as Cult-objects.' It's the sort of thing Soviet museums might have displayed for real. And indeed Crawford's experience of Russia underpins 'Bloody Old Britain'. Communist Russia for him was a place where Use, and Human Comfort, had priority over Appearances – at least in principle. Things might be dirty, but at least you could stretch out your legs in the cinema. Chairs were made to be sat on in Russia; and it was more important that the cinema-goer should have legroom, than that an extra line of seats be jammed in to increase profits. No, Russia was a civilization precisely in which appearances counted for very little; that was why the Soviets had no time for evening dress. Nobody was offended there, as they were in Britain, by the tools and accoutrements of labour, like the shorts that Crawford liked to wear on digs, or the knapsack he liked to carry his clothes in on a weekend away. How deeply rooted it was in Bloody Old Britain, this eminently bourgeois game of keeping up appearances. It was just as Engels feared; British society was sticking like glue to the shrine of respectability, whatever the cost. It was so irrational of them.

Capitalism, though, fed on this irrationality. It fed in particular on the irrationality of women, Crawford maintained. After all, if women – in their stupidity – could be persuaded, for Appearances' sake, to buy pretty ornaments or useless fire irons, there was a lot of money to be made out of them. Things did not have to last; they did not have to be well made; they did not have to do their job particularly well; in many cases they did not have to do any job at all. They just had to look right. There was a profitable congruity between the consumer's shallow desire for prettiness and the manufacturers' goal of economy of material, in Crawford's view, and the result was shoddiness. Manufacturers could produce ever more remarkable fancy goods, novelty items like square teapots. Female consumers, blinded by the ingenuity of the design, would not notice the shoddy workmanship; and they would not care much if the teapot would not pour, or if its lid fell off when you tried. The main thing – and there was clearly a lot at stake here, for use value to be so summarily abandoned – was that it should look nice on the table.

Such things, wrote Crawford, were unique in the history of the world; and they were evolutionary abominations. Take spoons for instance. 'Spoons,' he wrote,

> from neolithic times down to the twentieth century, have naturally accommodated themselves to the shape and size of the human mouth, neither of which have altered appreciably since then; if anything the mouths have become smaller. Suddenly, however, the bowls of soup-spoons have altered their shape and become *round* and inconveniently wide. This . . . has the effect of making the process of ladling up the soup become more difficult and take longer.

Evolution was a process of adaptation, not mal-adaptation. Something was going wrong here. The housewife's desire for prettiness and the manufacturer's privileging of profit over use were the wrong principles of selection. And the world that was being created out of these principles was one in which the basic, everyday tools of human beings, evolved over centuries – the spoon that fits the mouth, the knife that cuts the meat – were being wilfully discarded in favour of new, badly designed or unnecessary products. To judge by its material culture, this was a society that in evolutionary terms was surely in sharp decline.

In Crawford's analysis in 'Bloody Old Britain', it was capitalism

that both created this culture and profited from it. He read this
back from material objects which, to his archaeologist's eye,
spoke volumes. Take the humble glass tumbler, for example. A
vessel for holding liquid; just the sort of thing archaeologists are
used to looking at. Classifications of entire cultures have been
based on the remains of pots and other vessels. In the case of the
Beaker people (much discussed by Crawford's friend Gordon
Childe) it was a particular pottery style, found over great swathes
of Western Europe, that gave a prehistoric culture its name. Pots
and vessels (or the broken remains of them) endure long after
other artefacts have rotted away; in some cases they alone remain
as witnesses to the culture that produced them. Read in a certain
way, they bear the imprint of social relations, cultural exchange,
production methods, use patterns, value systems. And here's
Crawford on the twentieth-century British tumbler:

> The chief function of a modern capitalist tumbler is not to
> hold liquid but to appear to hold more than it does. There are
> many ways of achieving this deception – 'waisting' it, splay-
> ing out the mouth so that it cannot be filled, increasing the
> thickness (but *not* the internal width) of the base, 'ribbing' it,
> so that each incurvation 'saves' a little liquid, making it
> unduly tall (and narrow) and often conical in shape, etc. One
> of the effects of some of those artifices is to deprive the tum-
> bler of stability (hence perhaps its name) and thereby
> increase breakages and consequent sales.

The tumbler is not, in this analysis, designed for durability
or use. It is not really designed to serve its user at all. It is a servant, effectively, of capitalism, the system that made it. Through
various devices (sold to the customer as style) it tricks its user
into thinking it holds more than it does. Elegance is a pretext
for profit. And for the first time in human history apparently utilitarian things are made precisely in order to break easily. This

would later be widely known as planned obsolescence; it helps keep the wheels of capital turning.

Consumerism, in 'Bloody Old Britain', is a big confidence trick. In Crawford's analysis it is in the nature of capitalism to devise ever more ingenious ways of giving people as little as possible for their money. Capitalism always promises more than it delivers, like those curls of butter that are made to look like solid balls. Bread is invariably made with adulterated flour, biscuits puffed up with air so that they reduce to nothing in the mouth, bottles of lozenges half packed out with cotton wool. You never get what you pay for, and you can never quite find what you want. Despite the promises made by the ubiquitous adverts spewed out by the system, choice, ease and 'value for money' are an illusion. Through an astonishing sleight of hand which most people are unable or unwilling to see through, we are being sold a big lie. The reality of life under capitalism is very different from the dream world of advertising that it pastes over every available surface. The happiness, fulfilment and comfort that are promised are simply never delivered.

Much of the comedy of 'Bloody Old Britain' derives from the nightmarish vision it creates of a world in which objects conspire against the human being that they ought to serve. Chairs are so narrow that they stick to the author's behind when he stands up, dressing-table mirrors refuse to stay at the angle required for shaving, towels will not absorb water, glass tumblers fall over and break as soon as you look at them. Faced with these delicate objects upon which it is dependent for sustenance or repose, the human body suddenly seems grotesque, of truly Brobdingnagian proportions. Fingers are too big to grasp the handles of tiny cups, forks are too small to convey sufficient portions of food to the mouth, feet hang through necessity over the ends of beds. Tools in many cases just refuse to do their job. The chapter on 'Dining-room furniture' begins, like all of the other chapters, with some doggerel verses, penned by Crawford. It describes a mealtime in

SOUTHAMPTON
ENGLAND

Faked food & drink

a British hotel, a scene of human degradation and inadequate utensils:

> I hear the clash of stainless steel,
> > The never-ending strife,
> As skids upon the greasy plate
> > The blunt unbending knife.
>
> The waiters watch the struggle
> > With listless hungry eyes:
> The knives are surely winning
> > But the forks are under size . . .
>
> The tiny tables tremble,
> > The jugs refuse to pour.
> The tumblers tumble over
> > And spoil the lovely floor.
>
> The paper napkins rustle,
> > The cuplets leap with glee:
> The coffee is so bloody
> > That they're going to have some tea.
>
> Bring forth the arty tea-pot,
> > All square, with broken spout –
> ('Quick, hold the lid – it nearly did')
> > And pour the poison out.

Quite a lot of 'Bloody Old Britain', as it happens, is about hotels and guest houses. It is hotel beds that are the most uncomfortable, hotel food the most unpleasant, parlours in guest houses the most unaccommodating. Much attention is paid to the mysterious function of the hotel porter, his sole purpose to carry out tasks for hotel guests which they are quite capable of doing for themselves (such as carrying a bag a few feet) and then to claim money for the privilege. A fiction is maintained that this is 'service'. Crawford is particularly agitated by this '"service" humbug'; it is, he suggests, profit-seeking thinly disguised as courtesy, and its only service is to itself.

If Crawford was so sensitive to the bogus hospitality of hotels and guest houses it may be partly because he spent so much time in them, like the many weeks he spent investigating the field archaeology of Scotland around this time. When out doing field-work he was at the mercy of the hospitality trade, and he was obviously not impressed. He admits, in the Foreword to 'Bloody Old Britain', that it was 'written in hotels during the winter of 1938–9, and is therefore strongly biased'. Hotels, pubs and guest houses were just not very hospitable, despite appearances; and he was letting off steam. Some of his rage is vented in verse, like these lines (to be sung to the tune of 'Once with gladness men of old'), at the beginning of the chapter on Hotels: 'Holy Moses, every day/ Now I bend my knees and pray/ By my bed so rude and bare/ (Stuffed with mangy horses' hair)/ That the staff of this hotel/ May be burned alive in HELL.'

H. V. Morton's best-selling travel book of 1927, *In Search of England*, was also framed as a narrative composed on the hop as the author travelled around the country. According to the author's introduction, it was written 'without deliberation by the roadside, on farmyard walls, in cathedrals, in little churchyards, on the washstands of country inns'. But whereas Morton found charm in those inns, Crawford found a living nightmare. 'Bloody Old Britain' is a riposte to the benign vision of the country and its amenities as found in Morton's books, and the many, many others that followed in the 1920s and 30s, encouraging motor tourism along the highways and byways of the British countryside. Crawford's book was written as a counterblast to the tourist literature and advertising imagery promising cosy inns with – as he put it – Falstaffian landlords, and elegant restaurants staffed by attractive and attentive film stars disguised as waiting staff. Tourists really ought to be warned of the grim reception they will get in British hotels and restaurants, suggested Crawford. '"See Britain next", the slogan says:/ Spend your summer holidays/ In our nasty new hotels,/ Sample their disgusting smells,/ Lousy service, tariffs dear./ Filthy food, hard beds, warm beer.' Don't bother coming to Britain, suggests Crawford, unless you want to be abused in pubs if you ask for food outside certain limited hours, or if you dare to ask for a cup of tea. You won't find in these islands any of those charming provincial restaurants you get on the Continent with their local speciality dishes and business-like patrons. You'll be ripped off at every stage in just about every place you go. And there's no point in complaining; it will get you nowhere. British hotels, writes Crawford, really ought to exhibit a list of disclaimers and warnings, one of which would be: 'Considerable misunderstanding will be avoided if it is realized that the hotel is run solely as a profit-making concern, and that the comfort and convenience of guests is a secondary consideration.'

Why can't the British manage to do things better? This is the cry that resounds throughout 'Bloody Old Britain'; and it's not just about grim hotels, 'fake' or adulterated food, and poorly designed teapots. It extends to the design of houses, town planning, the preservation of archaeological sites, the conservation of the countryside, the placement of roadside advertisements, the running of museums, road safety, the unregulated noise of car engines and the commercialization of sport. The sections of the book that discuss these things are not always as entertaining as the chapters on hotels and dining-room furniture, but they are no less heartfelt. Predictably it is issues to do with the countryside, archaeological fieldwork, and museums – things that affected Crawford's professional work – that receive the most attention.

'The English countryside,' he writes with heavy irony, 'is that part of England which lies in between the motor-roads.' And the countryside has, he continues, been grotesquely degraded and

vandalized by the civilization represented by those roads; not just
the roads themselves, but all of the ribbon developments they
give rise to for miles along their length, the unchecked and
unregulated lines of new villas, fringed by ugly roadside advertisements. This was an urban, car-based civilization which saw
the countryside simply as a resource to be plundered. Thus it
was, for example, that the ancient turf of Butser on the South
Downs had been stripped to supply suburban gardens and cricket
fields with nice neat lawns. In many places, wrote Crawford,
especially around the Thames valley, the countryside had been
cannibalized to feed the roads themselves, as landlords received
more income for allowing their land to be dug up for gravel des-
tined for road building, leaving slimy pools fit only for weeds and
mosquitoes. What is lost in the process, complains Crawford, is
valuable archaeological information, accessible from the air.
Buried relics may be dug up by mechanical excavators, and some
of them might, if their finders are public-spirited, find their way
to museums – but as for the landscape itself, the process is
destructive and irreversible. The whole business is unregulated,

making it largely a matter of chance what gets recorded, and what gets preserved.

It may be that Crawford was thinking, here, of Major Allen, for the family business that funded his aerial explorations of the Thames valley had diversified from its original manufacture of agricultural machinery, and was now effectively making money from road-building and its need for gravel. Quarrying for gravel in the Thames valley began in earnest in the 1920s and 30s to make concrete, and to surface the many roads that were being built and reinforced. Deep excavation of this kind is one of the few human processes that will remove all trace of ancient remains from the landscape for ever. And there were plenty of them. As Crawford told Allen in 1932, 'the gravel flats by the Middle Thames were inhabited in every period, prehistoric and historic, and the inhabitants have left traces of themselves, which come out in the crops every year'. It was these crop sites that Allen photographed. John Allen and Sons made and serviced the machines that were involved in the excavation of gravel pits, and the steam-rollers that were used in road-building. The company also owned a number of gravel pits in the area over which Major Allen took his spectacular photographs. When one of these pits, near Dorchester, was dug, the crouching skeleton of a man who had been there for thousands of years was uncovered. Allen made it his business to preserve fragments that were found, and sent at least some of them to museums, but it was nobody's business to make sure that he did. And in the meantime, ancient landscapes were being irrevocably hollowed out and removed from sight for ever.

The State, too, played its role in the destruction of the British landscape, according to Crawford. He describes how, in the name of something (misleadingly in his opinion) called Defence, aerodromes, barracks and other buildings pepper the countryside, including areas of great archaeological interest like Salisbury Plain (saved in part in 1927), Lulworth Cove in Dorset, and the

Pembrokeshire coast. Other historic landscapes such as that surrounding Grimes' Graves near Thetford in Norfolk had been
effectively removed from view by afforestation by the Forestry
Commission in the 1920s. Forests like the one at Thetford were
planted after domestic timber resources struggled to meet the
needs of trench warfare in the First World War; they had their
roots in a military economy. Crawford's objection was that the
ancient landscape covered up by Thetford Forest, and others like
it, ought to remain visible; to be allowed to excavate once before
the planting commenced was equivalent, in his view, 'to telling a
Christian that he might consult the Bible once in his life in a
public library, and his children and their descendants never at all'.
Doubtless his frustration was exacerbated by the fact that he was
employed by one arm of the Government to record sites which
another arm was in the process of defacing. There was no regu-
lating body with the power to protect ancient sites if they
happened to occur in State-owned land, which would include by
default any land earmarked for aerodromes or Forestry
Commission planting. The destruction was not purposeful,
Crawford allowed, it was generally just ignorant; but surely, he
thought, if things were better organized, and government departments communicated more effectively between themselves, it
could be avoided.

Things were done much better abroad in Crawford's view. The
Germans, for example, were a model of organization. Fascism
might have been a misguided and evanescent phenomenon, but
it certainly seemed to value its archaeologists. Domestic prehistoric archaeology was particularly well funded and well
coordinated in Germany, as Crawford enviously noted. In other
ways, too, the Germans had the right idea. Their efficient system
of Youth Hostels, for example – well organized, basically furnished – meant that one need not suffer the faux hospitality of
the Guest House when travelling. It wasn't just Germany, though,
that provided a foil for the appalling ways of the British in

'Bloody Old Britain'. Just about any country had better food, including decent bread. You could buy a pair of shoes that would last you longer in Egypt. The irritation of car hooting had been abolished in Mussolini's Italy. Roadside advertisements were sensibly marshalled into neat dedicated areas in Switzerland. And absolutely nowhere did you find the kind of cringing (if not hostile) cack-handedness you got in shops, hotels and restaurants in Britain.

Laissez-faire capitalism was the problem in Crawford's Bloody Old Britain. That was why advertisements, shoddy goods, jerry-built villas and adulterated food were ubiquitous and unstoppable; they made money, and it seemed to be nobody's business to control them, just as it seemed to be nobody's business to stop a developer from building over heathland. It was capitalism, too, that was behind the low standards of British food and hospitality. Things had not always been this bad, wrote Crawford. Old travel diaries showed that the food and hotels of these isles were once as good as anywhere else. But early industrialization in Britain meant that a system that produces for profit, not use, had reached its most advanced stage of development in Britain. Other countries – France, for instance – had a less highly developed form of capitalism, and still had a peasant culture. Perhaps that was why French food was so much better. But things were also better in France because they at least had got rid of their aristocracy. The British, however, still cringe at the yoke; with a number of far-reaching consequences. Snobbery remains the 'chief characteristic' of the British, and a crippling consciousness of status is evident in everything from architecture to attitudes towards luggage, manual labour, and dress. Compare a group of French artisans, unselfconscious in dirty overalls at a public bar, with the 'pitiful spectacle of an Englishman apologising for not wearing evening dress at a dinner party', Crawford suggests. 'The French gained their self-respect once and for all at the Revolution. The English, not having had the guts to do this yet, still retain the slave-mentality of feudalism

in a bourgeois world.' That, too, is presumably why British service is so bad; servility is a sore point.

A civil servant such as himself, as Crawford noted in 'Bloody
Old Britain', was not supposed to take sides politically. Servility
was a sore point for Crawford, too, not least in his dealings with
his employer. But the official ruling need not stop *him*, he
thought, since he considered his stance to be scientific, not ideological. As the 'orderly application of intelligence to the human
environment', he wrote, science was universal, not national or
partisan. Science was the 'Supreme Value' to which Crawford
offered his allegiance as a scientific worker. If he supported
socialism, it was because he considered it to be 'the natural corol-
lary of science in the regulation of human affairs'. This was more
or less the view of a number of British scientists at the time. J. D.
Bernal, for example, made an explicit equation between science
and communism in his 1939 book *The Social Function of Science*.
Both he and a number of others held that the advancement of science would bring about the downfall of capitalism more surely
than class war. And for Crawford change could not happen too
soon. Socialism, he wrote in 'Bloody Old Britain', 'will be the only
remedy of a half-ruined world'.

'Bloody Old Britain' is in many ways a project absolutely typical
of the 1930s. As the literary critic Valentine Cunningham has
shown, it was a decade in which many British writers and commentators explored their own country as though it were a strange
land; and they often had a broadly leftist agenda. In his *English
Journey* of 1934, for example, J. B. Priestley travelled all over the
country in the wake of the Depression to see for himself what kind
of people, industries and towns made up the nation. George Orwell
went north to Wigan to investigate the living conditions of the
inhabitants of this mining town. Bill Brandt documented with
the eyes of an outsider 'The English at Home', the title of a book
of his photos that was published in 1936. And in 1937, the same

year as Orwell's *Road to Wigan Pier* was published, the extraordinary project of Mass Observation was announced in the pages of the *New Statesman*. The brainchild of a surrealist poet (Charles Madge) and an anthropologist (Tom Harrisson), Mass Observation applied ethnographic methods – including photography – to the everyday life of the people of the nation. It called for special 'participant observers' to keep notebooks in which they would jot down things like the gestures of motorists, the sorts of ornaments people were likely to put on their mantelpieces, and the temperature at which tea was served. Such things were meant to give an insight into the 'national unconscience' (with a nod to Freud). Mass Observation was an attempt to investigate the British with the same sort of objectivity as its co-founder, Tom Harrisson, had attempted among the headhunting Orang Ulu and the Dayaks of Borneo. It was an 'anthropology of ourselves'.

'Bloody Old Britain' was begun not long after Mass Observation, and was in some ways a similar – if not derivative – idea. Both applied the methods of social science to contemporary culture, although the emphasis in Mass Observation was on participant observation (as you might expect from a project that was essentially anthropological), whereas 'Bloody Old Britain' preserved the distanced kind of observation familiar to archaeologists, more used to dealing with things than with people. But the purpose of 'Bloody Old Britain', unlike Mass Observation, was satirical. It used the language of social science to carp about the culture of capitalism. Sometimes this degenerates into little more than a moan – quite literally – about the price of fish. But at other times it is very successful. Where Crawford's book works best is in the set-pieces where he puts his archaeological training to satirical use, like this passage on the 'whiskey-and-splash':

With . . . whiskey (in England) water is drunk, either plain or mixed with soda. The latter is supplied in minute bottles;

and the combined result is called 'a whiskey and splash.' The bottles are now so small that any further reduction in width will cause their sides to coalesce. The next development to be anticipated is that they will be sold solid, and their use become a mere ritual. The bottle will have to be bought as before of course, and the magic ceremony of inverting it over the whiskey will still be performed; but now the effects will not be immediately visible. The soda-water makers will then turn *all* their receipts into profits (instead of only 90%), for they will not need any soda at all. The bottle-makers will have only to replace lost and broken bottles (and being solid there will be few breakages). The publican will be able to sell the same bottles over and over again – indeed he will only need a permanent stock of some half-a-dozen or dozen bottles in all, instead of hundreds weekly. The consumer will be able to get drunk quicker for the same price.

Crawford's bitterness about the way things were going was not unique – far from it. Much of 'Bloody Old Britain' would have been very familiar territory for middle-class readers in the 1930s, particularly the horror voiced at the desecration of the British landscape, and at the degeneration of standards of workmanship, service and taste. Publishing Crawford's book in 1943 might have been 'like hitting a man when he was down', but Methuen assured him 'it would have sold very well indeed before the war, when no-one could de-bunk England and English ways with sufficient savagery to get the public's goat'. A visceral distaste for the debasements of life in modern Britain was commonplace in the literary culture of the decade, as the critic John Carey has pointed out. The adulterated or 'fake' food, for example, that so enraged Crawford also disgusted George Bowling, the hero of George Orwell's 1939 novel *Coming Up for Air*, who bites into a frankfurter and discovers it to be made of fish. 'That's the way we're going nowadays,' he muses. 'Everything made out of something else.' F. R. Leavis was one of many intellectuals – including H. G. Wells – who was appalled by advertising and the culture of consumption it represented. E. M. Forster's despair about the growth of urban sprawl, and his disdain for the social class that lived there, was similarly representative. Many writers lumped humanity in with the mix, often to horrifying effect. Few writers found poetry in suburbia, and suburban life seems to have been almost universally pilloried (Stevie Smith's poetry was a noble exception). This, after all, was the decade in which it was acceptable to say, as John Betjeman did in 1937, 'Come, friendly bombs, and fall on Slough/ It isn't fit for humans now.'

Neither was Crawford the only one who thought modern design, whether of utensils, homes or town planning, needed taking in hand in Britain. The Design Industries Association (DIA) was founded in 1915 to 'improve the standard of design in everyday things of life'. The DIA proclaimed a revolt against the sham and the shoddy, deploring the public desire for the 'artistic touch' – frills, fussy decoration, imitation mildew. In the 1920s and 30s it organized trips to Germany and Scandinavia so that the British could see good design in architecture, furniture and everyday objects. Like Crawford, associates of the DIA often complained about how depressing it was to return to Britain after a trip abroad. There were some beacons of hope: the DIA vigorously promoted the sort of good modernist design embodied by the map and stations of the London Underground, by Crittalls' metal-framed windows, or by Silver End, the extraordinary Essex village designed around the Crittalls' factory. But there was still a great deal of work to be done in naming and shaming crimes against good design. In 1929 the DIA was railing against the British housewife's preference for such atrocities as fluted, serrated and decorated cutlery, and the Manchester branch was collecting and exhibiting ashtrays, vases and other vessels that were decorated with adverts – just the sort of thing that comes under Crawford's critical eye in 'Bloody Old Britain'.

One of the aspects of bad design singled out by the DIA in the late 1920s as particularly offensive was the unchecked spread of advertising hoardings, especially along main roads and railway lines, and the enamel signs or advertising effigies that littered roadside verges right across the countryside. The DIA came to share with the Campaign for the Preservation of Rural England a concern with what was often referred to as *amenity*, concerning visual aspects of the British landscape, or 'the face of the land'. Particularly singled out were suburban bungalows, the design of roads, the proliferation of roadside cafés and the design of petrol stations. As part of a concerted 'Countryside Campaign' the DIA and the CPRE collected photographs of atrocities (and, rather less often, examples of good design or roadside management), and exhibited them in a series of regional exhibitions (including one that visited Southampton in September 1929). These were photographs very much like those by Crawford, showing huge billboards smothering old buildings or blotting out views. Some of the photographs collected by the CPRE were published as

'Cautionary Guides' to particular cities – Carlisle, St Albans and Oxford. These were guidebooks to a city's worst sins against good taste. In addition to the main offender of advertising, there were also images of shopfronts, café signs or wall-mounted typography (extraordinarily mild by modern standards) that were deemed to be indiscreet, or in poor taste.

The CPRE's Clough Williams-Ellis offered a prolonged diagnosis of the problems facing the British landscape in *England and the Octopus* (1928) and *Britain and the Beast* (1937). These books examined the country as though it were a patient suffering from an uncontrolled rash, with great eruptions of spots and sores across its body. This was very much the language used in this kind of literature for the unplanned developments of roadbuilders, landlords and entrepreneurs. There was an 'epidemic' of bungalows, for example, from which few areas were 'immune'. Williams-Ellis's tone was alarmist, its rich but unpleasant metaphors betraying an equally unpleasant fastidiousness. The buildings that lined new roads – ribbon development – 'grow up and multiply like nettles along a drain, like lice upon a tape-worm'. Britain was under threat from the 'beast' of development, an 'octopus' whose tentacles – roads and all that came with them – were strangling it.

What was to be done? While many middle-class commentators agreed on the seriousness of the problem, most of them were rather more coy about the solution. Better education, definitely – and this was where the 'Countryside Campaign' came in, as well as books like *Culture and Environment* (1933) by F. R. Leavis and Denys Thompson, which encouraged readers to engage in their own 'fieldwork' to promote awareness of their environment, and the ugliness of modern design and advertising. More planning, surely; some sort of centralized control and strong leadership would have to intervene if the country was not going to go to the dogs – or the octopus. But there was little consensus over any political solution. Many of those attracted to the CPRE were

naturally conservative, resenting any changes made to the countryside. Some, like Crawford, advocated socialism. In a 1937
review of Williams-Ellis's book, the poet Cecil Day Lewis wrote
that only socialism could deliver Britain from the Beast. Williams-
Ellis himself visited Russia in the same year as Crawford, and was
most impressed by its town-planning achievements. The
Russians might not have perfected their plumbing and so on, but
they certainly – unlike the British – had the right idea. As he told
the readers of *England and the Octopus*, the Russians had shown
in Baku on the Black Sea that every town could be like Welwyn
Garden City, no matter how remote. But the politics of the CPRE
were far from clear-cut, as the geographer David Matless has
pointed out. Williams-Ellis criticized all political parties in
*England and the Octopus*. And such was the regard that the British
Union of Fascists had for the CPRE that it instructed its members
to desist from chalking graffiti. Visual hygiene was on the agenda
of both fascists and socialists. Neither did socialists have a
monopoly when it came to their distaste for advertising.
Wyndham Lewis hoped that fascism would put an end to 'the
sickly rage of advertisement', instigating instead a single state
brand of soap.

Others had less interest in *changing* Britain, and more in just
getting away from it. Crawford was certainly not the only one
who professed to prefer abroad. The writer Cyril Connolly
described Britain in 1929 as a dying civilization, 'decadent, but
in such a damned dull way – going stuffy and comatose instead
of collapsing beautifully like France'. The idea that there was a
Better Place somewhere else – whether it was Moscow, Berlin,
France or Morocco – was, according to Paul Fussell, almost
endemic among writers at this time. And if you couldn't go
abroad, you might seek out some pocket of the British Isles that
was not yet infected by the mess of power stations, chicken
coops, bungalows and arterial roads that was modernity's excuse
for a civilization. In 1935 after he inherited some money,

Crawford himself bought a piece of land in Cyprus where he had a house built; and as the decade progressed, he was clearly looking for somewhere far from urban centres – Taransay or Canna in the Outer Hebrides, for example – where he could sit out the war that he was sure was inevitable. In the meantime on trips abroad Crawford made it his business to avoid his fellow countrymen. 'If ever a people wanted a sound thrashing it's the English,' he told a friend in a particularly nasty letter of 1938 after coming across a crowd of them in uniform in Le Havre. 'They are too stupid to realize what horrors they really are.' And he sought out any negative accounts of visits to Britain written by foreigners, like Henry Miller's 1938 *Max and the White Phagocytes*, or Margaret Halsey's 1938 *With Malice Toward Some*, a book which included such observations as 'Englishwomen's shoes look as though they had been made by someone who had often heard shoes described, but had never seen any'.

Crawford seems to have worn his lack of patriotism like a badge, at least among his friends. Ostensibly, at least, it was his view that patriotism was (or ought to be) redundant. Nations should not even still exist, and they should certainly not elicit the sort of primitive loyalty that they did. The very idea of 'Britain', like the idea of 'Germany', and other countries, was – or ought to be – irrelevant. Only Science commanded his loyalty. Science, pure and supremely rational, which transcended the petty and the partisan, rendering clan loyalty and religion alike unnecessary. 'If war comes,' wrote Crawford in 'Bloody Old Britain' – and in the winter of 1938–9 it was more than a looming possibility – 'I shall remain neutral.' What would be the point, he asked, in waging another war between nations? It would be nothing more than 'a clash of imperialisms, a gangsters' feud'; and he had no interest in the winning of it. It wasn't that he sought a fascist victory. The point, he wrote, was that any war between Britain and Germany was irrelevant in the bigger scheme of things, since it would soon enough be rendered unimportant by the socialist revolution that would surely succeed it. One had to take the big view. As for defending the nation and its values in the meantime, Crawford suggested in the pages of 'Bloody Old Britain' that the famous 'liberties' of the British were so degraded that they were not worth fighting for.

Crawford's view of the impending war between Britain and Germany was echoed in some small quarters of a divided left that sought to resist fascism, but did not want to fight for the 'banks', as Crawford put it, or risk repeating the inconclusive carnage of the First World War. After the Nazi–Soviet non-aggression pact in August 1939, the official party line of the CPGB (once prodded by the Russians) was to view any conflict between Britain and Germany as an imperialist war. This was an unpopular ruling, however, that caused many Marxists, and most fellow travellers who were militantly anti-fascist, to find themselves outside the fold; party membership plummeted, and others on the left lost respect for it. Only after Hitler invaded Russia in June 1941 could the battle lines be drawn clearly between fascism on the one side, and the combined forces of liberal democracy and communism on the other. But Crawford does not seem to have changed his mind much about the war even then, and could never muster up the kind of patriotic feeling that was necessarily invoked by the War Office and other government bodies in order to win the war. Apparently he still had his sights on a future World State, that would come into being, presumably, through socialist revolution in one country after another.

Crawford was not the only left-leaning intellectual to disparage patriotism and underestimate – in effect – its persistence and its power, both at home, and abroad in the totalitarian regimes of Europe. But as George Orwell pointed out in his 1941 essay on H. G. Wells, millions in Germany were willing to fight for Hitler, whereas 'hardly a human creature' would 'shed a pint of blood' for the creation of a peaceful World State as proposed by Wells. Even the Russians were fighting for an idea of 'Holy Russia', wrote Orwell, as much as for socialism. A World State, Orwell wrote, might be eminently sensible and desirable. But 'the energy that actually shapes the world springs from emotions – racial pride, leader-worship, religious belief, love of war – which liberal intellectuals mechanically write off as anachronisms'. Orwell, of course, turned out to be right. 'Nationalism, religious bigotry, and feudal loyalty' were far more powerful than what Wells – and Crawford – considered sanity.

# CHAPTER 9

Crawford wrote 'Bloody Old Britain' in the winter after the Munich Agreement. It was in September 1938 that Neville Chamberlain returned from talks with Hitler with his 'piece of paper' promising peace in exchange for parts of Czechoslovakia. At the same time as Chamberlain was negotiating with Hitler, as Crawford recounts in his autobiography, the north sheet of his Map of Britain in the Dark Ages was being printed. From the window of his Southampton office he could see it being turned out on a printing machine in the building opposite. There were, he recalls, seven printings; in each a different colour was added to the sheet, blue, brown, and so on; and as the map got progressively darker, day by day, Crawford felt more and more hopeful that it would be finished and swept to safety before war broke out. One of the annoyances of the growing tension in Europe was that it threatened to put an end to such projects, if it should develop into war. And the tension certainly got in the way of the sort of international collaboration that was needed to carry out big projects like the International Map of the Roman Empire. The only policy one could adopt under such circumstances, thought Crawford, was to 'make no distinctions between Nazis, Fascists, Communists or Democrats' when dealing with archaeologists abroad. How else could the important work of international co-operation and synthesis embodied by *Antiquity* and the Roman Map be continued?

Thus it was that Crawford visited Nazi Germany on archaeological business several times in 1938–9. The first of these visits was in connection with an exhibition of aerial photographs held in Berlin in the spring of 1938. Crawford was asked to give a lecture on aerial archaeology at the Air Ministry. 'It is not often that one can teach the Germans a new technique, particularly in photography,' he wrote later, 'and I felt rather proud to be asked to do so.' His lecture, translated into German, was published by Lufthansa in a handsomely produced volume called *Luftbild und Vorgeschichte*. He was very pleased with it – and equally annoyed that the Ordnance Survey had not jumped at the chance of publishing something similar. 'If the State which employed me did not want it the loss was theirs,' he wrote later. 'It was very disheartening but I was getting used to that.' After Berlin, Crawford was due to go to Athens to discuss business connected to the Map of the Roman Empire. On the way to Greece he stopped in Vienna, where he met up with Oswald Menghin, an archaeologist and friend who had just been made Minister of Culture in the new Nazi government of Austria. Menghin took him to an event celebrating the recent *Anschluss*, where they watched a march past by Nazis apparently just let out of prison, and Crawford was introduced to Burckel, Hitler's new Reich Commissioner for Austria. Later that evening Menghin and Crawford went on to a concert; and the next day Crawford flew on to Athens and, a few days later, back home to Southampton.

Not long after this, in April 1938, Crawford returned to Germany for a holiday in Schleswig-Holstein. He wanted, he said, to visit the Dannewerk, a long defensive earthwork running across the Danish peninsula just inside the German border. It was so warm, he remembered later, on the day he walked along the site, that snakes were coming out of their holes in the bank. German archaeologists were themselves investigating this area at the same time, and Crawford was taken about by them in their cars to see the various sites. Herbert Jankuhn, the archaeologist who was excavating the Viking settlement of Haithabu, showed him round the province of Angeln. This, he told Crawford, was the homeland of the Angles who came to the British Isles many centuries ago. The two men stood on a hill outside the town of Süderbrarup where Jankuhn suggested the Angles might have discussed their forthcoming invasion of the country over the sea; an ironic conversation to be having under the circumstances. Crawford thought this might make a nice topic for *Antiquity*; but as he wrote later, it had to wait. 'Other events supervened, and this earlier invasion receded into the background.'

Crawford was apparently very impressed by what he saw of German archaeology during these and other visits. His editorial in the June issue of *Antiquity* praised the organization and methods of museums in Germany, where posters encouraged members of the public to turn in finds, and pamphlets explained how sites could be identified, and how they ought to be respected. In 'Bloody Old Britain', too, he reserved high words of praise for the seriousness with which the Germans approached their prehistory.

Museum staff had cars at their disposal to take archaeologists to excavations, or to visit construction sites like the new *Reichsautobahns* whenever finds had been made. A new body, the Landesanstalt für Volkheitskunde, was being formed, wrote Crawford. Organized on a regional basis, it was concerned, he wrote, with the survey, recording and preservation of German prehistoric archaeology. Crawford was clearly envious of the high status archaeology enjoyed in Germany in the 1930s due to state support; what a contrast to Bloody Old Britain, where so much was left to chance.

The Nazis certainly funded prehistoric research well, as the archaeologist Bettina Arnold has shown. Eight new chairs of German prehistory were endowed between 1933 and 1935, and by 1939 prehistory was taught in more than twenty-five universities. There was an unprecedented amount of funding available for excavations across Germany and Eastern Europe. A host of new institutes, museums and journals was established. Prehistoric artefacts in museums came out of storage, were dusted off and exhibited. Neither was the subject's renaissance confined to specialists. As Crawford perceived, the education of the German people about their own prehistory was taken very seriously, as was their active participation in a variety of contexts. Films about the ancient German past were made and widely shown; open-air museums displayed reconstructions of prehistoric settlements; citizens were encouraged to educate themselves and make their own discoveries. A 1938 membership flyer from the Reichsbund für Deutsche Vorgeschichte (Confederation for German Prehistory) captures the prevailing tone: 'Responsibility with respect to our indigenous prehistory must again fill every German with pride!'

It doesn't seem to have occurred to Crawford that there might have been a price for state support of prehistoric archaeology in Germany – or if it did, he preferred to keep quiet about it in order to facilitate international co-operation; or simply in order to complain about the relatively low level of official support that by contrast was received by archaeologists in Britain. For the fact is, as Arnold and others have pointed out, German prehistoric archaeologists effectively struck a Faustian bargain with the Nazi regime in exchange for the funding and prestige they received. It's not difficult to see the attraction, for a group of scholars who felt themselves to have been under-funded and undervalued for years, their status – in the highly status-conscious universities of Germany – well below that enjoyed by classical or Near Eastern archaeologists. The new regime offered them unprecedented opportunities. But the Nazi Party, or certain parts of it – notably Himmler, who headed up his own research organization, the SS-Ahnenerbe which oversaw a large number of excavations – had its own reasons for doing so. If German prehistory was promoted over classical archaeology, it was in order to raise up the status of the former at the expense of the latter, a policy which at its most extreme had archaeologists attempt to show that the Ancient Greeks were really German. The Ahnenerbe and other Nazi research organizations supported the excavation of sites specifically connected with Nordic peoples – like the Viking sites of Schleswig – with the aim of entrenching nationalist pride in the deepest possible soil. You might think that under these circumstances, the German sheets of Crawford's Map of the Roman Empire were bound to be something of a non-starter.

Hitler apparently privately wondered whether Himmler's prehistoric researches really served the nationalist cause. 'It's bad enough,' Hitler's architect Albert Speer reports him as saying, 'that the Romans were erecting great buildings when our forefathers were still living in mud huts; now Himmler is starting to dig up these villages of mud huts and enthusing over every potsherd and stone axe he finds.' Invidious comparisons aside, however, prehistoric archaeology was bound to be a discipline of interest and potential use for the Nazis, obsessed as they were by roots, by blood, and by soil. The interest that the public was encouraged to

take in the dwellings and material culture of their distant ancestors was indivisible from a broader context in which the
superiority of the German people – from the roots up – was at the
very core of Nazi ideology. This was the real purpose of the
Landesanstalt für Volkheitskunde, which was not – as Crawford
seemed to think – a benign organization that would simply record
and preserve regional archaeology; its main priority was to define
and celebrate a bogus essence of the German 'folk'.

The Nazis were bound, too, to take a keen and rather practical interest in a subject that claimed, as the pre-Nazi German
prehistorian Gustaf Kossinna did, that it could discover the geographical extent of a particular culture or ethnic group through
the distribution of artefacts. Hitler's territorial claims for a
'Greater Germany' were based on exactly this kind of 'evidence'.
Those excavations throughout Germany and its neighbouring
countries that were so handsomely funded had as at least one of
their goals the discovery of artefacts that would establish a precedence for German occupation over a broad territorial area.
Prehistoric archaeology worked hard for its money, and its high
status; it offered a 'scientific' justification for the racist ideology
and the expansionist foreign policy of the state that supported it.

At its worst the Nazi agenda had archaeologists seeking prehistoric 'evidence' to support National Socialism and authenticate
its origins, like those who spent their time tracking down runic
markings on potsherds that looked a bit like the 'SS' symbol,
designed in fact by an out-of-work illustrator in 1929. At its best
it can only ever have been an uneasy alliance. Herbert Jankuhn
was funded by the Ahnenerbe; he later bragged that the Haithabu
excavations that Crawford visited were Himmler's favourite dig.
But no doubt he and the other archaeologists Crawford met in
1938 told him that they could turn the situation – with all of its
compromises – to their own advantage and to the advantage of
their discipline. They could pay lip service to the Nazis, and take
the money; they could utilize the prevailing nationalist fervour,

and at the same time hone their skills, train a new generation of fieldworkers, and advance archaeological knowledge through an excavation programme that they never dreamed they would have. And they might even have believed that this was possible.

Other archaeologists, though, were not given the same opportunity. After the Nuremberg Laws of 1935 the eminent prehistorian Gerhard Bersu was effectively forced to retire from his academic position, since his father had been Jewish. Crawford had known Bersu for some years – they collaborated on the Map of the Roman Empire – and was anxious to help. Bersu was an expert excavator, and in 1937 Crawford persuaded the Prehistoric Society to fund a dig that would be overseen by him. The excavation was at the smaller of two Iron Age sites at Woodbury, near Salisbury, that had turned up by chance in an aerial photograph taken by the RAF in 1929. Ironically enough, Bersu was appointed to the task at a point when the President of the Prehistoric Society was the German archaeologist Adolf Mahr, who as well as being the Director of the National Museum of Ireland turned out to be the leader of the Irish branch of the Nazi Party. But it was under Crawford's presidency of the Society that Bersu carried out the first season of work at Woodbury in 1938, where he uncovered the complex layout of a large Iron Age farmstead, utilizing the much-admired German techniques of settlement archaeology, and setting a standard for subsequent work of its type in Britain. When war broke out, Bersu and his wife stayed in Britain, financially supported by Crawford and Gordon Childe (among others) who knew, presumably, that they could not return home.

The fact that Crawford could support Bersu in his plight as a refugee at the same time as he was praising the State funding of archaeology in Germany is just one of many paradoxes of the time. But for him there does not seem to have been any conception of inconsistency. In both cases with a curious kind of pragmatism he took the part of science. How could it be bad for prehistoric archaeology that it was being funded and supported so wholeheartedly? If important finds were made, the source of the funding was inconsequential in the bigger scheme of things. The most important thing was for scholars and scientists to continue to work together across international boundaries. Nationalism and science would not coexist for long in any case. The latter would inevitably triumph over the former. As for Bersu, finding him work was surely as much about utilizing the skills of an expert excavator, made wastefully redundant (and at the same time getting an interesting site investigated), as it was about humanitarianism; although it was doubtless that, too. It was the same when Crawford wrote a testimonial for the Nazi Oswald Menghin, stranded in an American internment camp after the war: 'Archaeology needs everyone nowadays,' he told him, 'and I do hope that you will be set at liberty soon to go on with your fine archaeological work.'

In Crawford's eyes, science and technology were *inherently* progressive, for all that particular nations or partisan groups sought to turn them to non-progressive ends, like war. It was inconceivable to Crawford – as it was to H. G. Wells – that science could be put to use in the service of ideas, as Orwell wrote, more appropriate to the Stone Age. And yet this – although Crawford could not see it – was the case in Nazi Germany, a technologically advanced society in which science effectively served superstition. Science for Crawford, as for Wells, was an objective thing that could only be good; scientists could be good or bad at their job, correct or incorrect at interpreting the evidence; but Science was Science, and the contingent position of the scientist made no difference to the objective reality and neutrality of any discoveries they might make.

But there is something else, too. Crawford had the broadest possible view of history, a conception of vast time within which empires and nations, still less individuals, are less significant than they think they are. And he was in a hurry to build up a picture of the patterns of world history, the construction of which was more important, and more urgent than any petty concerns over how it was built, or by whom. He was surely not an unfeeling man. And yet in his Presidential Address to the Prehistoric Society of December 1938, after Germany had invaded both Austria and – with Chamberlain's consent – the Sudetenland, Crawford told his listeners, 'The Germans have already begun a campaign of air-research in Germany, and one hopes that there too the eastward drive, already begun in other spheres, may be accompanied by archaeological activities.' Nations were doomed anyway, and so if Hitler was riding roughshod over their borders in the name of a people which happened to have a very high degree of technological and photographic expertise, then let us at least hope that some excellent aerial photographs would result.

In August 1939, a fortnight before war broke out, Crawford was again on his way with a colleague to Germany for a congress, still hoping to make progress with the Map of the Roman Empire. It had been a particularly fruitful summer for British archaeology. Bersu had continued his expert work plotting out the settlement at Woodbury. And in July, the excavation of a mound near Woodbridge in Suffolk had turned up not just the extraordinary imprint of a vast ship that had been dragged there and buried in the Dark Ages, but also a great hoard of gold jewellery, a pile of silver bowls, a jewel-encrusted helmet, a sword studded with garnets and a long ceremonial whetstone with faces carved into each end. It looked as though these and other treasures had been put there to accompany an Anglo-Saxon king to the afterworld. Crawford, together with his new assistant W. F. Grimes, visited the site known as Sutton Hoo, and photographed the finds as they emerged from the sandy earth for the first time in nearly a thousand years. Moss from nearby woodland was used to pack around the delicate objects as they came out. As Charles Phillips, the archaeologist in charge remembered, it was something of a

race against time, for war was brewing; but luckily the weather remained fair (they had no cover), and policemen were installed to guard the site against journalists and robbers, both of whom would have retarded progress. The site's owner, a spiritualist widow named Mrs Pretty, delighted everybody by donating the treasures to the British Museum. The press called it 'the English Tutankhamun'. Even Crawford came over almost patriotic in the editorial of the special issue of *Antiquity* devoted to the discoveries: 'We felt that we were present at the unveiling of history, and that the history of our own country.'

War, though, when it came in September, put an end to archaeology for the time being. The finds at Sutton Hoo, some of them with earth still clinging to them, were sent to a place of safety. Excavations were largely postponed, with the exception of a number of 'rescue sites' on land that was earmarked for development in connection with the war effort. Crawford attempted to carry on with his programme of fieldwork, but it was not easy, especially when he was suspected of being a parachutist or spy as he went about his business. Archaeology is a good cover for espionage, as certain police informants seemed to think. Bersu, too, came under suspicion, as any German wandering around with maps and plans might have done at this time, let alone one who was an associate of the ideologically suspect Gordon Childe. 'It is suggested,' Major General Sir Vernon Kell informed the Chief Constable at Cupar in Fife, 'that, although he was professing to be an antiquarian, he was in fact indulging in improper activities.' In May 1940 Bersu and his wife were sent as 'enemy aliens' to an intern camp on the Isle of Man. There they made themselves useful throughout the war by carrying out more excavations (under armed guard), using volunteers from the internment camps. The Security Service apparently continued to monitor the correspondence between Childe and the Bersus, but found little more than gifts of food and archaeological information pass between them.

As Britain prepared for aerial attack or invasion, the Ordnance Survey offices – despite their vulnerable position in a target town, and despite a request from the Director General – were instructed to stay put. Crawford made it his business to send copies of valuable maps and other documents to places of greater safety, in case their original plates should be destroyed. He sent copies of the Period Maps, for example, to Harvard for safe keeping. In private, as he told his friend Harold Edwards – a conscientious objector – he was making his own secret preparations for a German invasion. He was going to get rid of what he called his 'library of red literature', for a start; he didn't want the Nazis to find certain books on his shelves when they reached Nursling. Not that a German victory would be much worse for him than a British one. If the British won, he wrote, he would be 'quietly victimized for not volunteering'. If the Germans won it would be bad for everyone, but he would at least have the satisfaction of the 'discomfiture of the sorry and complacent godly'. 'Better destroy this letter,' he told his friend (he didn't), 'and don't have any others of mine lying around.'

Crawford made more preparations as things hotted up. When the bombs started to fall in June and July of 1940, he took a tip from the ancients, and buried hoards of money – and, later, tins of food – in his garden. 'It was the solution of the Britons in the period of Roman domination, when they were threatened by Scots or Picts raiding,' he told Edwards. 'It shd. be proof against most dangers, excepting only currency devaluation.' He sent Edwards a secret map, showing where the treasure was buried – £40 of silver in paper bags, interred beneath some red rambler roses – so that he could come and dig it up if necessary, and dispose of his effects without them falling into the hands of the enemy (you'd better do it at night, he wrote). Churchill's speeches during the Blitz apparently roused no patriotic feeling in him, although he admired his use of language, and paused to discuss with Edwards the philological source of its power. 'Have you noticed,' Edwards asked Crawford in July, how Churchill 'uses nearly always short words of Anglo-Saxon origin and how effective they sound?' 'The Saxon words are always the most expressive,' Crawford replied. 'Note how the circumlocution office prefers Local Defence Volunteers (all romance words) to C.'s far better Home Guard (both Anglo-Saxon). It wd. no doubt refer to "sexual intercourse" if obliged to, rather than say "fuck" as Churchill would.' Despite such amusements Britain's darkest hour was felt by Crawford to be dark indeed. As the bombs continued to fall into the autumn, he dreamed of escape. 'My God,' he wrote, 'I'd give £50 for a way out and a living in some other country.'

In November the bombing campaign on Southampton stepped up. The dockyards were the main target, but the whole city and its suburbs were affected, and so, too, were outlying areas like Nursling, where there were military hutments. Night after night bombs fell on the city. By 27 November Hope Villa was housing not only Crawford and his housekeeper, but also a Belgian sea captain, and a greengrocer and his family, who had come from Southampton for a rest. Crawford lay in bed at nights, listening out for the drone of overhead bombers. By now like others he was getting rather trembly, mistaking indigestion for distant bombs, wondering where the next one would fall. On the night of the 30 November, clearly terrified, he sat down to write a letter to Edwards, describing events as they happened. The household (the sea captain, the greengrocer family, the housekeeper and him) had been having a game of darts, when they looked out to see Southampton in flames. Pieces of shrapnel were falling with dull thuds in the garden. 'The sky was lit up with white starlike flares slowly sinking and then breaking out afresh . . . up at them ran streams of red lights . . . and all round the stars of shells bursting – all this against a background of lurid red revealing dense masses of smoke, the town burning.' At least one bomb fell quite nearby. The all-clear came at 2.30 a.m.; in the meantime they finished their game of darts, ate an uncomfortable dinner, and then the sea captain told everybody stories. A shaky Crawford asked Edwards if he could come and stay with him and his wife for a few days for a rest. 'It's just plain HELL.'

It was one of Southampton's worst two bombing raids; the other one came the following night. The government worried about morale levels in the city. Even in the midst of this, out in Nursling Crawford was thinking of the Ordnance Survey offices. Some days earlier, anxious about safety in the face of the renewed bombing campaign, he had, he said, urged the Director General to allow him to remove important documents from the building. He, however – in Crawford's words – preferred to 'act correctly.' Despite this, Crawford managed to move much of his own office to new quarters he had secured in Nursling, where he planned to work. He was very glad, he told Edwards on the night of 30 November as he watched the city burn, that he had managed to save something. 'It seems hardly likely that the O. S. can last much longer,' he wrote; 'indeed it is very likely to be a smouldering ruin at this moment.' He was right. What he discovered the next day when he went into the city ('just a ruin . . . it is indescribable') was that the Ordnance Survey office had been almost completely destroyed. 'I feel a bit upset,' he told Edwards, and went to stay with him the following day.

The Ordnance Survey buildings on London Road suffered direct hits on the night of 30 November, and again the following night. Fires followed the explosions, and could not be controlled since the city's water mains had been damaged in an earlier raid. Nobody was badly hurt. But entire departments and most of their records were destroyed, including the Library, the Manuscript Store, the Large-scale Negative Store, the Map Store and the Drawing Office. What was lost included map stocks and plates, glass negatives, original plans and drawings, administrative records, a valuable collection of books on local history that had been amassed in the nineteenth century, and nearly all of the Name Books for England and Wales. The actual business of printing maps – the Survey's main wartime activity – was able to carry on, since printing works had been commandeered as reserve headquarters, and most of the necessary duplicate printing plates and so on had been taken there. But the losses of historic material were immense. And despite his unilateral attempts to clear out his things, it turned out that Crawford lost a lot that night, too. It had taken a number of vanloads to transport the Archaeology Office to Nursling; and many things were saved, including the plates for the maps of Britain in the Dark Ages and Roman Britain, and all of Crawford's collection of 6-inch maps with their field notes, made by himself and his correspondents. Much of the Archaeology Office had been saved. But on 30 November the last two vans stood loaded and ready to go when their sapper drivers were apparently summonsed to a 'dental parade', whatever that might be. Somehow they were delayed; and the vans and their contents, including Crawford's own

personal library, papers and other archaeological records, were
destroyed along with everything else that night. Crawford was
struck with fury and grief; and he never quite got over it.

The story of how Crawford saved the old maps of the
Ordnance Survey became part of archaeological folklore. One
version recalled how Crawford, exasperated by the refusal of the
Director General to make proper preparations, flung his cap onto
the floor (a characteristic gesture, apparently), and threatened to
write to *The Times* to rouse public opinion. He was told that if he
was that bothered, he should take his 'precious maps' home to
Nursling; and so he and Grimes stored them in his garage at
Hope Villa, where they – unlike the Ordnance Survey offices –
survived the war. Crawford himself considered the event to be
not only a significant chapter of his life, but a historically important story of institutional incompetence that ought one day to be
made public. He wrote up his own account of the events leading
to the night of 30 November, which was to be released after all of
the officials involved at the time were dead. In 1957 he suggested
to the executors of his will that it would be a good idea to make
several copies of this document, and place them in different
places for safe keeping. When he was putting his papers in order
he had temporarily mislaid it, but was sure that it would turn up;
it didn't, and until it does the story he recorded may not be told.
Such is history, as Crawford knew well; only that which is found
can go forth.

The destruction of November 1940 was a real body blow to
Crawford. So much information, accumulated over generations,
had been lost, despite his tireless attempts, over the years, to
guard against entropy and catastrophe. All of his work was an
attempt to protect the records of an ever-retreating past against
the ravages and indifference of the present. All of it was a great
gathering in, as if in preparation for some future redemption. He
was always doubling, copying, saving, so that a record would
be kept and go forth to the future, where it might one day make

perfect sense. That was surely why he so embraced – almost identified with – photography, a technology which duplicates ephemeral,
evanescent reality and thereby makes it into a record of itself,
sends it forth into the future. And the records had to be kept, since
they were the pieces that would surely accumulate to reveal to us
the meaning of history, the pattern on the carpet. Hence Crawford's
collecting activities: his gathering of images of field sites and monuments before they were destroyed or altered; his accumulating
of aerial photographs from military bases before the sites they
show were built over with villas or runways, or made invisible by
the wrong type of crop; his amassing of photostats of cadastral
plans of private estates before the originals disintegrated into dust or
were lost. And now great portions of these archives, painstakingly
built up, ordered and preserved, parts of the carpet of history, were
gone. He surrounded himself quite literally with accumulated
records, as a surviving photograph of his office from 1936 shows;
everything in the picture apart from the framed maps and a single
file-box, he said, went that November night. What made it worse
was that the tragedy was avoidable.

Crawford's irritation with the intransigence of the Ordnance
Survey had been building up for years. He had long been infu-
riated by the way he felt his work was undervalued, and his
entrepreneurialism repeatedly blocked by red tape and protocol.
His autobiography is littered with stories of how most of his initiatives, including the Period Maps and aerial investigations,
met with incomprehension, bureaucratic intractability or simple
refusal. There were those, for example, who even in the late
1930s seemed to believe that Crawford liked to use an aeroplane
for fieldwork as a way of getting around the country, and asked
him – when he applied for funding for an aerial survey of
Roman Scotland – how much it would cost to do the same trips
by taxi. 'Trying to get a move on in the Civil Service,' he wrote,
'was like trying to swim in a lake of glue.' Even before the Blitz
on Southampton he was angry that his work was not properly

understood or decently remunerated, and he was threatening to look for work elsewhere, preferably abroad. Wartime conditions seem to have made him grumpier, more eager to leave. In May 1940 he was reported for refusing to show his pass at the gate of the Survey offices, and then – when the request was repeated – abusing the porter, threatening to report him, and using 'improper and obscene language'. The destruction wreaked by the Blitz came as the final straw to an already angry man. It was final, devastating and almost allegorical evidence of the inflexibility of officialdom (how urgent could a dental parade be?). And it also seemed to indicate just how unimportant the powers-that-be considered the historic resources of the Survey that they had not – despite warnings – taken more steps to preserve them.

After the November raids Crawford's anger seems to have tipped over into serious depression. On Christmas Eve and Christmas Day he wrote a whole series of resignation letters to various societies: the Norfolk Research Committee, the Oxford Architectural and Historical Society, the Wiltshire Archaeological and Natural History Society, the Spelaeological Society. He ended his subscription to *Notes and Queries* for Somerset and Dorset. He had gone to ground; and it was not at all clear what he should do. He made arrangements for his will; but assured a clearly concerned Edwards that he was not suicidal. He involved himself with his garden. He clearly could not muster much enthusiasm for *Antiquity*, or for archaeology, although he continued to send copies of maps, photographs and other documents to places of greater safety, and he was always urging others to do the same. He apparently enquired about early retirement, but discovered that since he was not yet sixty and still medically fit, this could only happen if his post were abolished during the war period, in which case his pension would be intolerably low. He felt his time was over at the Ordnance Survey, but apparently had little interest in making himself useful by doing war work. He was sure, as he told his friend in March 1941, that his future was being discussed behind the scenes; and so it was.

Some archaeologists were already putting their skills to work in connection with the war. Crawford's assistant, Grimes, had been sent by the Ministry of Works to excavate defence sites, like the Neolithic pits and other earthworks at the hamlet of Heathrow in Middlesex, that were to be removed from sight with the building of the new London airport. Other archaeologists, used by now (in large part thanks to Crawford) to interpreting aerial photographs, went to work at the Central Air Photograph Interpretation Unit at Medmenham, near Marlow in Buckinghamshire. Here they studied RAF shots taken over enemy territory, looking out for camouflaged runways, or for signs of activity: disturbed earth around an aerodrome, the movement of barges along canals, the extension of railway lines. The young archaeologist Glyn Daniel wrote to Crawford in March 1941 to tell him about the work: 'A very suitable job for archaeologists as you will agree: I feel that in a very minor way I am carrying on your traditions in the last war.' Before long, according to Charles Phillips (who would later become Crawford's successor at the Ordnance Survey), Medmenham was 'the strongest concentration possible of practical archaeologists on this side of the Channel'. As well as Daniel and Phillips, Dorothy Garrod (the Disney Professor of Archaeology at Cambridge), Grahame Clark and Stuart Piggott and others were all employed there. It would, you might think, have been ideal work for Crawford at a point at which he was underemployed, the Archaeological Branch of the Ordnance Survey having been effectively closed down for the duration of the war. But he does not seem to have shown any interest in joining up. He was still looking for work abroad. The Survey and the Treasury discussed his future. And as a result, in the summer of 1941 arrangements were made for him to be seconded to the Royal Commission on Historical Monuments of England 'for special duties during war time'.

These special duties were the photographic documentation of Southampton for the National Buildings Record (NBR), a task which occupied Crawford for the rest of the war. The NBR was begun in the wake of the Blitz as an attempt to collate a record of the nation's architecture. It sent off photographers – including Crawford – to photograph buildings that were at risk of being destroyed, and those that had already been bomb-damaged. The aim was to create a comprehensive inventory of Britain's built environment, including buildings of all ages and types, from churches and monuments by celebrated architects to vernacular tithe barns, public houses and common-or-garden terraces. The work gave Crawford a new lease of life – and, as he wrote in his autobiography, he needed one. Over the next five years he took over 5000 photographs of bomb-damaged Southampton. Working for the NBR gave him a licence – quite literally – to snoop around in a way that would otherwise have been impossible under the circumstances, in which anyone inspecting bomb damage could be regarded with suspicion. It was a unique opportunity to study the anatomy of the city, and create a photographic archive of its parts. Crawford effectively turned his war duty into an exercise in urban archaeology. Apart from anything else, in Southampton – as in the City of London – the bombs had revealed remnants of an older city. Nineteenth-century cement was shaken off the ancient city walls under the pressure of bombardment. Medieval cellars appeared amongst the blasted ruins of the old town; fragments of ancient walls and fireplaces poked out from beneath later additions.

Crawford's task, as set out in the NBR's 'Notes for Photographers' suited him very well. He was to photograph external views of the façades of churches and other buildings, and separate views of doorways, gates, piers, balconies, arches, effigies, carvings and any other notable details. Picturesqueness was frowned upon, as it was by Crawford. It was records, not 'pictures' that were required. The focus was to be exact and sharp, elevational views to be supplemented by views taken at an angle to show recessed or projecting architectural features. This was exactly the sort of hard documentary role that Crawford – ever since his German holiday of 1931 – believed to be photography's highest calling.

Crawford's photographs of a blitzed Southampton are among his best and most beautiful. They are the products of a quest for civic intimacy, an intense investigation of streets and back streets, shopfronts, wharves, and forgotten corners of the city that had been blasted into the sunlight. There is a perfect fit between the poignancy of the subject matter – those empty streets, deserted buildings, shattered windows – and the melancholy of the photographer, his presence only ever betokened by the shadow of his head, or the toes of his shoes as he frames a vertical shot. They are images in which the shock of destruction is met by the repetitive, obsessive cataloguing of details. And everywhere there is the sense that never before had the city revealed itself in this way, and never again would it look quite like this, never would the light shine in just this way through these new spaces blasted between things. It was as if in one traumatic moment the whole city had been laid bare, its historical layers spewed forth, before some final, imminent apocalypse on the Last Day that would turn even these ruins to dust.

Crawford photographed the accumulations of brick and masonry that hovered on this brink, like the façade – all that was left – of a chapel, or the abandoned and derelict offices of the old dock-house, its front window bricked up. The signage of these buildings, announcing their collapsed business – CANADIAN PACIFIC, PORTLAND BAPTIST CHURCH – were empty signifiers now, as they might be after a revolution. Crawford documented a whole series of horizontal gravestones from above, as though it were a matter of some importance that the inscription on each of them was a record that had to be kept; he photographed text and graffiti engraved into stone everywhere, even though it was no longer

obvious from whom these messages were issued, or to whom they might be addressed: *Lord Help Me*, *Lord Help Me*. And wherever he went, Crawford followed the pattern of a lifetime by finding more material among the rubble than anyone had expected; more, in some cases, than was required. He homed in on iron-work features that would doubtless soon be melted down as salvage: a gatepost feature at the Ministry of Food in the shape of a cup of tea, a poppy-head finial on a railing. And on a bricked-in doorway in the south wall of St Michael's Church in the winter of 1941 after Russia entered the war, the chalked words 'Help the Soviet Union'. Just as he had surprised his wing commander in the First World War by his observational skills on reconnaissance missions, and the Director General of the Ordnance Survey by his additions to the map, he impressed the director of the NBR by what he found in Southampton. 'What a wealth of stuff you dis-cover,' he told him, as he looked through his prints.

Working for the NBR, wrote Crawford later, taught him how to 'look at a street . . . analytically', and how to 'look at a wall and read its history'. His photographs show the makeshift way in which the city's inhabitants over the centuries had cannibalized ancient and medieval remains, incorporating them into walls, leaning their sheds and pigsties against them; Southampton turned out to be a palimpsest of settlement as interesting, in its way, as Athens or Rome. Crawford sought out the sutures, the seams between old brickwork and older masonry, the places where cracked flints had been sandwiched between stones, where an air-raid shelter has been built into an ancient stone vault under a grain store. Anywhere where his eye found evidence of the work of tools, he homed in with his camera to picture the tessellation of flints, the roughly painted sign, the figures scratched into masonry. Seen through his eyes every wall, fireplace or roof had been *made*. Nor was he able to stop himself from playing the old archaeologist's game of follow-ing the Ariadne's thread that led back from every lost monument, every old stone that had been washed up in a new place, made to form

part of a new construction. The statues he photographed outside a house in Lawn Road, for example, were not just statues; they were identified as coming from an eighteenth-century house nearby that had been pulled down in 1852. A record had to be kept; old habits died hard.

Crawford's work for the NBR far exceeded his brief. It turned, eventually, into an obsessive interest in reconstructing a map of Old Southampton, piecing together its street plan building by building, quite literally, like the crossword puzzles he enjoyed doing. It was, he told Edwards in March 1942, 'the most fascinating piece of research I have tackled for years and the only anchor left me'. If it looked suspiciously like local antiquarianism – the sort of thing Crawford was rather scathing about before the war – there were reasons for his intense and methodical application to the task. Crawford continued to be depressed, apparently, throughout the rest of the war. His correspondence with Gordon Childe indicates that both men considered the world to be plunging into another Dark Age in which life would hardly be worth living. Childe was perhaps even more pessimistic than Crawford, holding out little hope either for state communism as it existed under Stalin or for the rationality of the human race. 'I suspect,' he wrote, 'history has been moving too *fast*. A tiny minority thinking we live rationally has provided the vast mass with equipment ill adapted to this epipalaeolithic mentality but has on the whole grievously (and I think culpably) failed to sell as Yanks would say a rational mode of life.' Civilization was collapsing all around them; the future looked bleak. Suicide was a possibility, and they discussed it – but it was not a solution. 'Let us turn our eyes from this disordered present,' Childe wrote to Crawford in 1943, 'to the past where from our high ivory towers we may discern an order.' Crawford himself thought that in the midst of so much destruction 'the only remedy is to become completely introverted and concentrate on work at home and try to forget it'. And so, the plan of Old Southampton.

The future might be uncertain, but there were still patterns to be discerned in the past. It was a radical lowering of ambitions; a hugely reduced field of vision. 'I like the work,' he told H. G. Wells in a letter of 1942 as he approached his two-thousandth photograph of the city, 'and have no further ambitions.'

Old Southampton, then, was something of a consolation. For a while, it seems that he had lost interest in just about everything else, although he managed a series of lectures on Roman Scotland in 1943 (described privately by him as 'the most outstandingly dull that even the Society of Antiquaries ever experienced'). *Antiquity* suffered. It visibly shrank in size during the war years, mainly due to paper shortages, but also due to lack of copy; the width of the volumes when seen all together is the index of the times, and of Crawford's mood, like the rings in a tree. Roland Austin maintained the production schedule, although he received little of the praise heaped on Crawford for keeping the journal

going through difficult times. There were no editorials; a fact that Crawford later ascribed to the fact that they would have been inappropriate in wartime, but which was surely due more to his own temporary disassociation. As for his working life, Crawford never returned to the Ordnance Survey. He retired at the first possible opportunity, which came in 1946. When Charles Phillips, who took over as Archaeology Officer, tried to discuss the new arrangements he was making for the continuation of Crawford's work, he 'blankly refused to discuss the Ordnance Survey or any of its affairs'. This, wrote Phillips, was 'an index of how thoroughly the iron had entered into his soul.'

# CHAPTER 10

The war began in 1940, and it lasted for more than twenty-five years. The warring nations used all of the modern technology at their disposal; tanks, warships, aerial bombardment; they fought on land, on sea, and in the air to deadly effect. There was, however, no conclusive victory. A great Pestilence came in the wake of the conflict, and an epidemic of a deadly disease they called the Wandering Sickness. The whole of the civilized world – including Britain – was in ruins. There was a return to the barbarism of another age, with ragged and ill-fed peasants ruled over by primitive and bloodthirsty warlords. There was little fuel and few spare parts; motorcars left over from the 1930s had to be pulled along by horses. But a new world was being planned by the Air-men, the engineers and the technicians, from their base at Basra, where in 1965 they held a Peace Conference. They called themselves 'the Brotherhood of Efficiency'; 'the Freemasonry of Science'; 'Wings over the world'. They were 'the last trustees of civilisation when everything else has failed'. The world they were planning would have no nations, no clans and no wars; it would be, in effect, a world state. They alone possessed the technical know-how to create this new world, exploiting all of the 'giant possibilities of science that have been squandered hitherto upon war and senseless competition'. In time – and with the help of 'Peace Gas', useful for putting disruptive elements to sleep – they succeeded. By 2036 they had mastered the earth's resources, built vast underground cities (leaving untouched England's green and pleasant land), and were pioneering space travel. Human beings were healthier, better educated, more attractive. Their potential for development as a race was unbounded.

This was the vision of the future presented in 1936 to cinema audiences who had come to see Alexander Korda's new film *Things to Come*. The film script was written by H. G. Wells, who based it on his 1933 book *The Shape of Things to Come*. Wells's book is an imagined history textbook from the year 2106, as revealed in a dream to an employee of the League of Nations. Parts of it are uncannily accurate in its predictions. It is only one year out for the outbreak of the Second World War. Its vision of the future effects of concentrated aerial bombardment were so vivid that apparently when the film was reissued in 1940 after the Blitz had begun, cinema audiences fell weirdly silent during those scenes. But the idea that the world – guided by the Air-men of Basra, of all places – would eventually turn its technological capabilities to positive peacetime ends under the munificent umbrella of a World State has so far turned out to be way off the mark. And even Wells, it seems, was becoming increasingly pessimistic by the end of the war. 'There is no Pattern of Things to Come,' he announced in 1945 in his final book, *Mind at the End of its Tether*. On his deathbed in 1946 he was apparently planning a gloomier sequel to the film *Things to Come* in the light of the atomic bomb. After the cataclysm of the Second World War the great march of time no longer made sense in the way that it had done to Wells, the author of *The Outline of History*. History no longer appeared to obey any kinds of law. 'Events now follow one another in an entirely untrustworthy sequence,' he wrote. And, stark and inescapable, there was the 'hard harsh conviction of the near conclusive end of all life', a grim fact from which there could be no satisfactory deliverance.

On the whole, wrote Wells in 1945, 'we do not apprehend the fact that we are "spinning more and more swiftly into the vortex of extinction".' Even the man who does realize it is not overly affected by it in his day-to-day life. It does not prevent him from having likes and dislikes, affections and irritations. 'He is framed,' he wrote, 'of a clay that likes life, that is quite prepared to risk it rather than give way to the antagonistic forces that would break it down to suicide. He was begotten by the will to live, and he will die fighting for life.' Life, after all, goes on – until it no longer does, of course – even when the long perspectives that made sense of it turn out to be illusory, and like everything else, they crumble into dust.

*

Gradually, it seems, the politico-evolutionary perspective that had sustained Crawford's outlook crumbled away. In his autobiography he wrote that it was the happy influence of Harold Edwards that disillusioned him about Soviet communism. The two men had met on the boat to Leningrad in 1932. Edwards was a bookseller, who as a young anarchist had set up and run the Progressive Bookshop in Red Lion Street in London between 1918 and 1921. He later moved to Ashmore Green, near Newbury, keeping for a time another shop in the capital where he specialized in antiquarian books. After their 1932 meeting the two men stayed in touch; Crawford became a regular visitor to the home of Harold and his wife Olive, including during the time that Southampton was blitzed. They got on very well: the free-thinking Edwardses were very fond of Crawford, and by the last decade of his life he seems to have almost become part of the family. It was a relationship both personal and professional; when Crawford turned *Antiquity* into a private company in 1948 after Roland Austin retired (or was evicted), Harold and Olive became its directors, with Crawford as chairman. Edwards became *Antiquity*'s publisher, and he and his wife managed its business side.

Large parts of the correspondence between Crawford and Edwards are preserved in the Bodleian Library. Edwards's letters to Crawford date from 1940; but since Harold himself donated his side of the correspondence to the Bodleian, Crawford's letters go back to the 1930s, giving an insight into years of his life from which there is little surviving material. In their letters they talked about current affairs, news from Moscow, Bloody Old Britain, gardening and the petty irritations of modern life. And they discussed the many books that they passed between them; Edwards informed Crawford about new titles, and supplied him with copies on request. Edwards, for example, recommended in 1941 that Crawford read Arthur Koestler's *Darkness at Noon*, a book about Stalin's purges and the Moscow show trials. Koestler's book did not, though, altogether put Crawford off the Soviet

Union. Late in 1943 he told Edwards that amidst the nightmare of destruction wreaked by the governments of the United Nations, he 'still believe[d] the USSR to be sound'. Edwards, meantime, by his own admission was 'hardening . . . into a reactionary'. In November 1944 Crawford was asking his friend for a copy of a book called *The Age of Enterprise*, a 'devastating critique of Big Business in USA', recommended by Gordon Childe as a valuable contrast to the achievements of planning in Russia. 'But I forgot,' wrote Crawford; 'you are now of course a renegade! But business is business, isn't it?' In 1945 and 1946 it seems that Crawford was involved with the Labour Party – evidence, perhaps, of a shift of focus in line with the desire for change that brought in Attlee's Labour government after the war. There is a sense, in his letters to Edwards, that he was beginning to become disillusioned about Russia by 1947 at least. But a more decisive change – according to the correspondence, at least – can be charted in 1949. In June Edwards lent Crawford a book by George Orwell – surely his dystopian novel *1984*, published that very month. 'Sorry about Orwell,' Edwards wrote a week later, 'but the fact is that Communism does lead to this sort of thing.' Worse was to come. In September Edwards wrote again. 'I am lending you a little book on the Lysenko controversy,' he wrote. 'It is v. readable, and is a warning to us all.'

Trofim Denisovich Lysenko was a Soviet agronomist and biologist. His theories of heredity ran counter to received scientific wisdom, but by 1949 they had nevertheless come to dominate the field in Russia thanks to Stalin's support. The key difference was that Lysenko maintained that characteristics that had been acquired by an organism due to its environment could be passed on. His experiments in the late 1920s with so-called 'vernalization' – the acceleration of grain germination through a reduction in temperature – were reported by an excited Russian press as he suggested the possibility of turning winter wheat into spring wheat, and promised hugely increased yields. Lysenko was given his own laboratory at the Odessa Institute of Plant Breeding and Genetics. From here he encouraged collective farms to sow vernalized seeds – this meant sprouting them, leaving them in a cold place, and planting them in the spring rather than the winter. The farms were meant to report their yields back to him, thus enabling him to claim his results as due to the experiments of the people. His vastly exaggerated and unchecked reports of these and other 'experiments' endeared him to Soviet officials at a time when drought and collectivization had resulted in catastrophic harvests and reduction of seed stock.

In this climate, too, it was a priority to develop seed that was resistant to cold, drought and disease as quickly as possible. Speed was of the essence; but plant breeding takes time. Lysenko seems to have taken this as an opportunity to denounce classical genetics. Instead he claimed that vernalization and other kinds of engineering could improve not just one yield, but future generations of the same stock. Mendelian genetics held that characteristics acquired in the lifetime of an organism could not be inherited; but, argued Lysenko, this was the line you might expect a bourgeois science to claim. What practical use was a theory of heredity that saw change occur over many thousands of generations? The socialist state needed results much more quickly than that. By 1935 he had won the support of Stalin, and orders were made for vernalized wheat to be planted over vast areas of the Soviet Union. The poor success of this scheme did not deter Lysenko from pursuing it. Where it failed it was dressed up as success, or blamed on saboteurs in the field. This was a strategy bound to appeal to Stalin, for – as Lysenko had surely noticed – it was the same as his own.

Lysenko continued to attack genetics on a number of fronts. He was expert at engineering his own rise in the Academy and the Party through self-publicity and a keen sense of the prevailing political winds. It was not just that he promised miracle crops and unimaginably increased yields. His fervent insistence on the essential malleability of heredity was bound to make him popular with a regime which was attempting to build a state of supermen and women out of ethnically and physically mixed peasant stock. As Lysenko surely realized, his 'new biology' was ideologically congruent with Stalinism. It could be opposed with powerful effect to the kinds of ideas promoted by fascism. The Nazis, after all, believed superiority to be innate, and 'poor' stock effectively irredeemable, something which simply had to be eradicated. Lysenko's line was very useful to communist ideologues, for it effectively championed nurture over nature. If inherited characteristics could so rapidly be moulded, then the future could be engineered, and the past need not hold us back. Science and belief became blurred; it was claimed by Lysenko and his followers that dissenters were bourgeois or reactionary for adhering to Mendelian genetics. The new Soviet Union, it was argued, called for a new 'socialist' science. To this end much was made of the fact that Lysenko himself was from a peasant background. As if to accentuate his identity as a worker in the field rather than a laboratory-based theorist, he always appeared in the clothes of an ordinary collective farmer, and took care to get himself photographed advising other similarly attired workers about their crops.

Lysenko was clearly an effective (if crude) manipulater of evidence. It wasn't just the staged photo opportunities. He faked data, falsified reports and suppressed information. When it came to impressing Stalin, the simplest methods of the showman seem to have been enough. Summoned to account for Moscow's poor potato supply in 1937, Lysenko produced a handful of small potatoes from one of his pockets, claiming to have dug them up at the Potato Farming Institute where one of his fellow scientists (also present at the meeting) worked. From his other pocket he then produced three large potatoes which, he told Stalin, were typical of those he was growing in Odessa. Stalin was apparently so convinced by this display that he ordered the other scientists present to follow Lysenko's methods.

It was after a conference of the Lenin All-Union Academy of Agricultural Sciences in July and August 1948 that Lysenko, and the implications of his success, were widely discussed outside Russia. With Stalin's support, this meeting effectively established Lysenko's stance against genetics as official Soviet policy. Biologists who supported genetics were forced to confess to their bourgeois shortcomings in what amounted to a purge of the entire discipline. If they refused to recognize the error of their ways they were removed from their posts, and risked imprisonment or execution. The persecution of dissenters from Lysenko's line within the field of plant breeding had in fact been going on for some time. The biologist Nikolai Vavilov, who had so wowed his Kensington audience in 1931, was in 1941 sentenced to death by firing squad for counter-revolutionary activity, espionage and sabotage; he died two years later. With Vavilov and others out of the way (and made an example of), it was easier for genetics to be officially vilified as bourgeois mysticism in the summer of 1948.

Western scientists were shocked by the outcome of the 1948 meeting. Those with socialist sympathies – some of whom had tried to defend Lysenko in earlier days – were embarrassed. They had hoped that Lysenko's wilder schemes and ideas would be kept in check by his opponents. Now it appeared that those opponents were being silenced, their research in genetics officially branded 'pseudo-scientific' and brought to an end. A few, reluctant to play into the hands of anti-communists, continued to defend Lysenko. But for most, the spectacle of scientists being persecuted for pursuing their research was grim indeed. And all this under the guiding eye of a Soviet state that was supposed to be based on science, a state that was supposed to be planning its future according to scientific findings. Instead it seemed to be spawning its own atavistic metaphysic, based on an ossified

understanding of the writings of a handful of social prophets, as
dictated by an intransigent and paranoid leader. A flurry of books
on the so-called 'Lysenko affair' appeared, including one by Julian
Huxley, and a slim volume entitled *Russia Puts the Clock Back*,
produced by the left-wing publisher Victor Gollancz. This was
possibly the book Edwards sent to Crawford to read. Russia was
not supposed to be putting the clock back; quite the contrary. It
was supposed to be speeding up evolution, towards a world state
as Crawford hoped; but how could it when it retreated into
dogma and insular suspicion of the findings of international science? The Soviet Union seemed to have taken a very wrong turn.
Edwards commiserated with Crawford a month after sending
him the book. 'I quite agree with all you say,' he wrote. 'It is quite
incredible the manner in which these Soviet people write, quite
oblivious of anything outside their own little dung-heap. I sup-
pose it is not their fault, after all the crime of "Cosmopolitanism"
is a v. serious one and may well mean the labour camp.'

It wasn't just the Lysenko affair that put the kibosh on dreams
of a future world state planned by scientists, with the Soviet
Union as its forerunner. The late 1940s were a period in which,
far from socialism making the world safe for science, science and
technology were increasingly being used as weapons by communists and anti-communists alike in the opening years of the
Cold War. Fearful of the threat from Russia, and eager to hold its
own alongside America, Britain embarked on a nuclear programme in 1947. The American B-29s that arrived in England in
the summer of 1948 – the year of the Berlin blockade – were
meant to put Moscow within striking distance of American
atomic weapons. In August 1949 the Soviet Union tested its first
atomic bomb. The horrific effects of an atomic explosion had
been demonstrated at Hiroshima and Nagasaki; and now vast
resources were being poured into research that had as its goal the
efficient destruction of mankind. And all this in the context of a
stand-off which threatened to ignite with devastating effect at any

moment: over Berlin in 1948, Korea in 1950. For many, including Crawford, it was well nigh impossible to believe either in God or socialism in such a world. Crawford turned to doggerel verse: 'Let us now stand up and praise/ God Almighty Cosmic Rays/ who created life on earth/ and, for what it may be worth, /thus evolved a Cosmic Plan/ for eliminating Man.' The Second World War had been destructive enough, as Crawford had seen in Southampton. But with these weapons in the hands of such rivals, it would hardly be desirable – or possible – to survive another war.

The spectre of another war looms large in Crawford's correspondence with his friends. In 1946 he was wondering whether the Vatican City might be a safe place to base himself in such an event. He was thinking of settling in Ireland, but, as he joked to Edwards, it 'will probably be annexed (after the destruction of England) by the USA, as an aerodrome'. Switzerland was another possibility; but when he went there in the spring of 1947, he confessed – in an unusually unguarded moment – that he would find it difficult to leave Nursling after so many years. It was surely also a factor that he disliked most other nationalities as much as he claimed to dislike his own countrymen; human beings the world over could be so disappointing. He knew he could not, in fact, leave Britain. But so seriously did he take the possibility of another, even grimmer, war, that it was the subject of an editorial of *Antiquity* in 1948. He urged the multiplication of copies of resources like the Reports of the Royal Commission on Ancient Monuments and the Corpus Scriptorum Orientalium lest they be destroyed in another war. This was after all – as he noted – nature's own practice; millions of eggs and seeds are produced to insure that life goes forth. And the preservation of ancient scripts and key documents was important enough; it was, he wrote, 'nothing less than the safeguarding for posterity of some of the best work of the pre-atomic age. It is the exact equivalent of that which was performed by the monasteries in the last Dark Age . . .' Another war, then; a war, perhaps, without a foreseeable end.

This was the vista Crawford was looking out at towards the end of the 1940s. Neither did he seem to be much more cheerful about the prospects of a Welfare State, for it would not stop many of the worst aspects of consumer capitalism, not to mention the fact that it paid for itself with crippling taxes. In 1951, gloomy again, he was reading a book about American advertising, the sort of thing that before the war he might have viewed with a horror attenuated by the belief in a socialist alternative. Now, though, it merely compounded his depression. 'Good God,' he wrote, 'what a society: and we've got to choose between that and the USSR and camps.' A book by Margarete Buber, describing her time in both a Nazi and a Soviet camp was, Crawford told Edwards in 1950, 'the last nail in my political coffin. I am now more fanatically anti-Soviet, anti-communist etc. than you are yourself.'

Political disillusionment is something like losing a faith, unintelligible to those who have not experienced it. In the case of British communists and fellow travellers in the 1940s and 50s, it seems often to have been experienced as a betrayal and a deep embarrassment. Some fell on their swords, like Douglas Hyde, the news editor of the *Daily Worker* who penned his own confession, tellingly entitled *I Believed*. Hyde's memoir came out in 1950, the same year as the testimonies of six ex-communists, including André Gide, Arthur Koestler and Stephen Spender, were published as *The God That Failed*. It may have been easier for others, who had never quite pinned their political colours to the mast, to ease their way out of private disappointment. Cynicism rushed in to disavow a hardly dared-for hope. As for Crawford, he must have been glad that his 'Tour in Bolshevy', like 'Bloody Old Britain', was never published. If it had been, he would have had to account for his wide-eyed optimism and his unfulfilled prophecies. As it was he could wipe them aside in a couple of sentences when it came to writing his autobiography in the early 1950s. But there was still surely a profound sadness for the man who had rejected the millenarianism of his upbringing, putting his faith instead in another kind of deliverance for the world; for it now looked as though that deliverance was not to be. Beliefs, like buildings, can become ruins; and when they crumble they surely take part of their human hosts with them.

All this time, in the years between 1945 and 1950 as he was readjusting to a new perspective of the world, Crawford was dividing his time between two main interests, one close at hand, the other as far away, almost, as could be imagined. The first, following his wartime work for the National Buildings Record, was medieval Southampton; it led to the Friends of Old Southampton being founded in 1946 in opposition to a post-war planning scheme for the city. The second interest pursued by Crawford in these years was the history and archaeology of the Sudan, which he worked at doggedly in Nursling, producing a fat book on the Fung (Funj) Kingdom of Sennar. This was a return to an interest that had begun more than thirty years previously, during Henry Wellcome's excavations at Abu Geili in the years before the First World War. In January 1950, Crawford returned in person to the Sudan, courtesy of the Sudanese government, on an archaeological reconnaissance trip; and he returned again the following year to the Middle Nile, where he made plans of the stone-built castles in the valley between Atbara and Abu Hamed.

As he worked in Nursling on his history of the Fungs, the Sudan had, he said, 'become an escape-land of the mind at a time when the island of Britain was an austere prison'. It was exhilarating to return in 1950 to a country that had lived in his imagination for so many years. It was delightful to be away from a sodden and grim post-war Britain, with its poor weather, its rationing and its escalating taxes. It was a relief to be in a place where conditions were refreshingly basic and the bread – like all peasant bread – was good. He claimed to have dwindling interest, these days, in the British archaeology for which he and *Antiquity* had become known. Too many places had been spoiled. 'It was devastating,' he wrote in his autobiography, 'to visit some old familiar spot and find it devastated by one or other of the many spoliators of the countryside.' What's more, he no longer had the Ordnance Survey paying his hotel bills when out on fieldwork, and had to fund his own – invariably grimly disappointing – accommodation. If readers complained – and they did – when after the war *Antiquity* stopped featuring British prehistory as much as it had done in the 1920s and 30s, Crawford defended himself. The 'blank periods' in British prehistory, he told his readers (rather prematurely), have now largely been filled in; but there was still ample to be done in Africa and Asia. No doubt he was justifying his own preference, at this time, for getting away from Britain. But there is a hint, too, in Crawford's writings, that perhaps the future might lie outside Europe. An *Antiquity* editorial from 1952 suggested that 'Europeans today, in the unhappy state of their continent, look more and more to other lands to carry on the struggle'. And in an imagined appraisal of his own work, dating from his bicentenary of 2086, he humorously predicted that in the twenty-first century it would be his book on the Fung Kingdom of Sennar that would be used in all of the universities. He had clearly not stopped thinking about the future, although in this post-nuclear age he was not so confident about what it might be like.

Crawford was in fact remarkably productive in the years following his retirement. Four publications came out of his Sudanese interests. He compiled a short history of Nursling. He wrote up the basics – as he saw them – of field archaeology, and published them as *Archaeology in the Field* in 1953. His autobiography, entitled *Said and Done*, was published two years later. He continued to edit *Antiquity*, reduced in size since the war, but still produced once a quarter. His papers include notes for a number of books, talks and articles which never materialized. He branched out entrepreneurially in a number of journalistic directions to supplement his pension (for smaller jobs he sometimes asked to be paid in cigars, presumably to avoid paying tax). He offered the *Bedford Transport Magazine* an article on the transport aspect of his Sudanese trip. *The Post Office Magazine* turned down his article entitled 'Embarrassing Postal Packets'. More successful was a broadcast he made for the BBC on 'The Language of Cats', in which Crawford interpreted and mimicked cat noises, with – by all accounts – uncanny accuracy. So popular, in fact, was this talk – the Bodleian holds a fat folder of letters he received from listeners – that it was reprinted in the *Listener* and a monthly called *Our Cats*, and repeated on air. Crawford was approached to write a book about cats by an American publisher, and he got as far as planning one. No doubt he realized there was a market for such things (he could hardly ignore all the fan mail) and he was happy to exploit it. But he resented the time this took from his other research. 'Hell!' he wrote in a letter to Edwards after the success of his first 'cats' broadcast, and another was suggested. 'Why the devil should I have to waste my time like this? There's not all that much left!'

The bigger project that the cats were taking him away from was his last book, *The Eye Goddess*. In 1953, after the archaeologist R. J. C. Atkinson discovered that there were tiny axes and a dagger carved into the stones of Stonehenge, Crawford began to develop an idea that an 'axe cult' signalled by Atkinson's discoveries might be connected to similar cults elsewhere. On New Year's Day, 1954, Crawford went to Stonehenge to investigate the carvings for himself. Windless and cloudless, it was a perfect day for inscriptions to reveal themselves to the eye; the low sun, he said, lit up the carvings beautifully, and he photographed all that he could find. He was sure at least one was a Mother Goddess symbol like others found in Brittany. Crawford became obsessed by what he called 'the Faces', symbols relating to the human face, especially the eyes, that could be found in cult-objects, or carved into rocks and tombstones all over Europe and into Africa. These, he thought, were evidence of what he rather grandly called the Archaic Religion of the Old World, which worshipped a Mother Goddess and which stretched from the Old Stone Age to the beginning of the Christian era, spreading westwards from Syria and Mesopotamia. Remnants of it, he noted, were still to be found in Catholic countries in the worship of the Virgin Mary, as well as in corn dollies; and the eye symbol lived on in the trinkets hung up in the cabs of lorries and taxis in Mediterranean countries. Crawford eagerly gathered evidence on trips to Brittany, Greece, Sicily and Ireland in the 1950s; he took some beautiful photographs of rock carvings and inscriptions. He was good at this, after all, this spotting of traces, marks and signs. He found vestiges of eyes and faces everywhere, he photographed them as well as other unrelated marvels he found, like the hundreds of snails crawling over the viaduct at Knossos, or the crescent shapes that appeared in the shadow of a tree during an eclipse of the sun. In many ways Crawford's final obsession with an 'eye goddess' was appropriate for a man whose

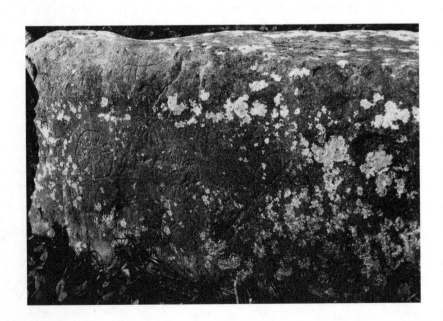

life's work was concerned with vision, and the attempt to view the world, as it were, from a great distance, like the all-seeing eye of world mythology. But the patterns that he claimed to find in 'the faces' and the information he gathered did not entirely convince his peers when the book was published in 1957. Glyn Daniel, by now lecturer in archaeology at Cambridge, owed Crawford a lot; *Antiquity* had published his first academic paper. But he was alarmed by the older man's latest book. He wrote to Crawford to say he had enjoyed *The Eye Goddess*, but how could he have made so many mistakes? 'Pure Bloody Ignorance,' replied Crawford on a postcard.

By the 1950s British archaeology was on a much firmer footing, mainly thanks to the efforts of Crawford and his generation. *Antiquity* may no longer have been quite as agenda-setting as it had been. Its editor's more recent research may not always have been brilliantly reviewed. But Crawford himself had acquired an almost mythical status among British archaeologists as the uncompromising – if eccentric – progenitor of them all. He used to appear at conferences in what Grahame Clark described as a 'greenish bowler hat' of uncertain age; and would turn up at excavations where he would question young archaeologists about their work. Archaeology had undoubtedly moved on; as Jacquetta Hawkes fondly wrote in 1952, readers of *Antiquity* were beginning to 'shake their heads tolerantly over the confident 19th-century rationalism' of the journal and its editor. But Crawford was still seen as something of an oracle when it came to British archaeology. His dedication to the discipline was legendary; his long bicycle trips in the field, his battles with authority and with the cranks, his rejuvenation of antiquarianism through flight, his almost unparalleled knowledge of the terrain. He had the habit, wrote Grahame Clark, 'disconcerting to some people, of judging others, however distinguished by rank, wealth, abilities, or official position, solely according to what they put into archaeology'. And as Hawkes remarked, for Crawford there were 'few indeed who have not failed in their duty' towards the subject.

Crawford was known for his eccentricities as well as his achievements: the 'ill-formed and ill-smelling' cigarettes he rolled himself, his violent antipathy to religion, his lack of patience, his self-imposed isolation out in Nursling in an apparently comfortless house he shared with a number of cats, and many spiders whose antics he studied. His socialism was common knowledge. Not everybody knew about the frequently foul-mouthed doggerel verse he wrote, often lampooning his fellow archaeologists, or the arguments he got into with everyone from his photographic developer to the company that made his favourite biscuits. But many – including a number of unfortunate subscribers to *Antiquity* – had experienced at first hand his opinionatedness, his dogmatism and his disdain for those who did not view the past through the same archaeological lens that he did. His editorials and the books he published in his last decade did little to dispel this reputation. When Charles Phillips, who knew Crawford well, reviewed his *Archaeology in the Field* in 1953 he chose his words carefully. There was, he said, a 'strong imprint of his personality on every page . . . Those blemishes which some of us have grown to appreciate can be sensed with just as much pungency as the general weight of learning, experience and common sense which inform these pages. Anyone in future years who wants to know what Crawford was like must read this book.'

Crawford's autobiography, too, is revealing, despite its reticence on emotional and political matters. It shows, unsurprisingly perhaps, that he had an eye to the judgement of posterity – it was for his contribution to archaeology that he wanted to be remembered, and he was careful to enunciate exactly what he thought that to be. Thus it was that 'Editor of *Antiquity*' was inscribed on his gravestone underneath his name at the request, apparently, of those who knew him best. But his autobiography is revealing in other ways. Apparently trifling events left an indelible mark on him,

especially misunderstandings concerning money, or odd remarks
impugning his rectitude. There was the time way back in 1910, for
example, when Professor Herbertson upbraided him for putting
a carpet bought at his own expense in his new office in the
Geography School. Crawford was clearly distressed about the
whole incident, with its implication that he had been extravagant.
As he wrote in his autobiography, 'It was a long time before I
forgot it.' The description of the event, more than forty years later,
suggests that he still had not forgotten it; it is one of many remembered slights, only half laughed off. Aerial archaeology reveals to
us 'how sensitive the soil is, how slowly nature heals the wounds
made by man'; so it was, too, with Crawford. And perhaps it was
this sensitivity that made him so observant, and such a good photographer. His own nature was reflected in the landscapes, scarred
by time, that he surveyed.

Towards the end of Crawford's life, some of his associates
were worried about his isolation. Since the deaths of his last
remaining aunts in the 1930s he had, as far as he knew, no
surviving family. A chance meeting on an overnight train to
Scotland in 1953 put him in touch with a long list of cousins he
did not know he had. But he continued to live on his own, with
no car and no telephone, with only his elderly housekeeper to
attend to his domestic needs. Was he lonely? No more, perhaps,
than he had always been. Back in 1940 he told Edwards that the
only time he ever felt part of a community was as a prisoner of
war, 'and it was a fine experience'. Part of the attraction of Soviet
communism for such a man was surely its promise of collectiv-
ity, communality. It was not something he ever quite managed to
create for himself. But if he was lonely, he was certainly not dis-
connected, as Mortimer Wheeler pointed out. 'If he joined a
committee or a sodality, he did so only to resign at the first
opportunity. He had other, more mysterious ways of keeping in
touch with the work of other men. It was a constant wonder to
me how, from his remote cottage at Nursling, he (and his cat)

surveyed a wider world than we at the busy centre found it easy to do.'

He certainly remained attuned to technological developments. At dinner at St John's College in Cambridge he heard about the invention of radiocarbon dating, developed by scientists at the University of Chicago, and described in a scientific journal in March 1949. Alert to the implications for archaeology, he announced it to his readers in September the same year. In the mid-1950s, as rockets were being tested on the island of South Uist (much to Crawford's distaste), he got interested in astronomy. He was still concerned by the big questions that had motivated him to begin *Antiquity* thirty years earlier, only now his horizons were, if anything, broader. He was still trying to push himself off to get a better view of an ever-expanding whole. 'What is it all leading up to?' he wrote in an apparently unpublished piece of writing called 'That far off . . . event'. 'Is it leading up to anything at all? Is it leading up or running down?' Magicians and priests have long offered their answers, but, wrote Crawford, 'nowadays we look rather more hopefully to cosmologists'. Crawford had been reading up on the rival concepts of the origin and destiny of the universe that were being debated at the time. He could not imagine the universe having either a beginning or an end, and so as far as he understood it, he took the side of the Cambridge astrophysicist Fred Hoyle, who held that the universe remains in a state of equilibrium as it expands, and has no beginning and no end. Mulling over the implications of such an idea, applied to 'our own terrestrial environment', Crawford wondered what light it might shed on the poet's concern with mortality. Individuals, like species, prosper and die, become extinct. The death of an individual, the extinction of a species is understood as 'the end', but the universe itself is engaged in a process that does not end. We conceive of 'ends' – the end of a life, the end of the earth, even. But seen from a bigger perspective, all is process; 'the essential activity of the universe'.

*

In October 1957 Crawford got news that his old friend Gordon Childe had fallen off a cliff in the Blue Mountains in New South Wales, and died. He had been staying at his favourite hotel in Katoomba, and had gone for a walk. His coat, compass, pipe and glasses were found near Govett's Leap, a thousand-foot drop. Some considered the fall to have been accidental. But Childe had quite clearly told a number of friends that he anticipated having an accident on a cliff walk. Others have since suggested that political disappointment (it was the year after Hungary) played a part in Childe's death. Crawford believed it was suicide. He had an inkling, he told Edwards, that Childe felt he had reached an end with his work, and that retirement held few attractions for him. Crawford was sad. But everyone, he wrote, has the right to end their lives if and when they want to.

Just over a month later Crawford died in the night. He had long since made preparations for his afterlife. He left instructions for a trunk of letters and books in his living room to be destroyed by the trustees of his will. He had already arranged for most of his papers to go to the Bodleian Library, some of them sealed until 2000. He wrote a warning to the reader of his papers to think before judging him, or his correspondents; he blessed the aunts who had brought him up. Right up till the end of his life he was still searching for the big picture; two days before he died he received a letter from the palaeontologist Kenneth Oakley at the Natural History Museum in answer to an enquiry he had made. He supposed it was conceivable, he told Crawford, that strategically placed atomic piles in the ground could stave off a fifth ice age. On a foggy day early in December Crawford was buried in the church graveyard in Nursling.

# NOTES ON THE IMAGES

Most but not all of the images reproduced in this book come from Crawford's collection of photographs, now in the Institute of Archaeology in Oxford. For a full list of image sources, see the acknowledgements on page 277.

p ii    O. G. S. Crawford, 'British and *miles* better': roadside advertisement for National Benzole Mixture (motor benzole blended with petrol), 4 September 1933. Crawford has written 'A blot on the (British) landscape' on the back.

p xi    O. G. S. Crawford, slogan on Berlin fence: 'Wählt Thälmann' ('Vote for Thälmann'), dating from before Hitler, obliterated by Nazis. Ernst Thälmann was the leader of the Communist Party in Germany (KPD), and stood against Hitler as presidential candidate in 1932. In 1933 he was arrested by the Gestapo. This photograph was taken in August 1934.

p xii    Aerial photograph of Worthy Down, near Winchester, taken by Major George Allen in the 1930s, showing traces of ancient settlement.

p xiii    Souvenir postcard of Hitler giving a speech, one of a series of four showing various gestures collected and mounted by Crawford.

p 7    'Dried-up dew-pond near Cissbury, fortified by a surrounding ditch and earthen wall', photograph from Arthur and George Hubbard's book, *Neolithic Dew-ponds and Cattle Ways* (London, 1905). Crawford later described the book as being 'full of the wildest ideas.'

p 19    Fossilized mammoth tooth, found in the gravel at the Bodleian site in Oxford's Broad Street in 1937. Photographed by H. J.

Hambidge. From W. J. Arkell, 'The Geology of the Site of the Bodleian Extension in Broad Street', *Oxoniensia* III (1938).

p 31    Panorama of unidentified stretch of front, taken by O. G. S. Crawford in 1915–16.

p 33    Photograph taken by Crawford of the mine exploding on Hawthorn Ridge at 7.20 a.m. on 1 July 1916, the opening day of the Battle of the Somme. The photograph, taken from the second line trench, was poor due to a defective plate. The blast left a crater that is still there, although it is overgrown.

p 35    Aerial photograph showing trench line, tracks, shell damage and the southern tip of Mametz wood, 14 January 1916. The wood was one of the objectives of the Battle of the Somme; it was taken by the 38th (Welsh) Division after casualties of nearly 4,000 men.

p 61    Crawford dressed for an Ordnance Survey fieldwork expedition, photographed in 1931 by his friend Air Commodore Masterman, at his home in Hook, near Basingstoke.

p 62    Bowl barrow (a type of round barrow) on Coombe Down, near Ogbourne St George, Wiltshire, photographed by L. V. Grinsell.

p 66    Field of oats on south slope of North Tyne valley near Falstone, Northumberland, showing 'corn shadows' caused by uneven ground. Photograph taken by Crawford at 7.55 p.m. on an evening of exceptionally clear air, 3 July 1934.

p 68    O. G. S. Crawford, photograph of earthwork on Southampton Common, 1941.

p 77    Celtic Fields on Windmill Hill, near Crawley, Hampshire. Photograph taken by the School of Army Co-operation at Old Sarum, 4 p.m., 8 May 1922 from a height of 10,000 feet. 'The system of Celtic fields shown on this plate', wrote Crawford, 'is one of the most complete hitherto revealed by air-photography.'

p 83    Aerial photograph showing Woodhenge, taken on 30 June 1926 by Squadron-Leader Insall. Woodhenge is the larger circular earthwork seen in the distance; the dark circle appears where once was a ditch, the dots inside the circle appear where there were post-holes. The field is full of wheat, the roots of which can only penetrate so far into the chalky ground. The soil is deeper and richer in decayed organic matter in those places where post-holes and ditches were once dug, and so the roots of the crop have penetrated more deeply here, resulting in plants which appear darker to the eye.

in 1932. Inside he noted an electrically operated bread-slicer, steam-cooking appliances, and plenty of butter.

p 122 Photograph taken by Crawford in Erivan, Armenia, 1932, showing a demolished church on the right, and on the left, new flats.

p 126 Anti-vodka advertisement in public gardens in Sukhum, Abkhasia, photographed by Crawford in 1932. 'These,' wrote Crawford, 'are intended by the state to reduce the amount of drunkenness which is still excessive.' He gives his own translation: 'Look! Whose names are on the board? Slackers and drunkards, opportunists, kulaks, hooligans and petty thieves. Such inhabitants of Sukhum will be considered as enemies. Please read, comrades, letter by letter. Do not find yourself on the board.'

p 138 A lawn in front of the Tsar's palace, Detskoe Selo, photographed by Crawford in 1932, showing the juxtaposition of a bronze statue from the old regime, and washing from the sanatorium that had been installed by the new regime in the palace. Crawford described this photograph as a good one, 'contrasting former splendour and present democracy'.

p 145 Field wall of Purbeck stone, Langton Matravers, Dorset, photographed by Crawford on 30 June 1943. An issue of *Antiquity* in 1936 included an article by Crawford called 'The Work of Giants', about the dry-stone field walls of the West Country, accompanied by a number of extraordinarily beautiful photographs taken by him.

p 145 Vertical view of insect-craters, taken by Crawford at 6 p.m., 16 March 1950 in Melit, Darfur. The evening sun has thrown the sand 'craters' into relief, the same principle that reveals ancient remains as 'shadow sites' to an aerial observer.

p 148 Haycocks on the Hebridean island of Iona, photographed by Crawford on 16 August 1933.

p 148 Peat stacked for drying in miniature dolmens, Carloway, Isle of Lewis, 6 June 1936, photographed by Crawford.

p 149 Sudanese hut, with doors made from petrol tins beaten flat, photographed by Crawford in 1950.

p 149 Housing at Römerstadt, Frankfurt-on-Main, November 1932, photographed by Crawford. Römerstadt was a Weimar housing estate planned by Ernst May. Crawford collected images of progressive housing projects like this one.

p 150   'Horizontal Excavators', a page from one of Crawford's albums, showing archaeologists resting or asleep.

p 152   The 'Cat Stane' near Edinburgh, photographed by Crawford in 1935.

p 152   'Cat Stane', near runway, Edinburgh airport, photographed by Julie Howden, January 2006.

p 157   30 Holford Square, London, photographed by Crawford in September 1934. Lenin and Krupskaya lived at this address, not far from King's Cross, in 1902–3. When the square was bombed in the war, a piece of wallpaper from number 30 was sent to the Central Lenin Museum in Moscow. A monument to Lenin, designed by the architect Berthold Lubetkin, was erected on the site in 1942. After being repeatedly vandalized, the monument was removed and buried. Lubetkin also designed a block of flats for the site, originally named Lenin Court but renamed Bevin Court; it is still there.

p 159   'French Art from the Era of the Decline of Feudalism and the Bourgeois Revolution', installation at the Hermitage Museum, Leningrad, 1931, taken from Aleksei Fedorov-Davydov, *The Soviet Art Museum* (Moscow, 1933).

p 162   Installation in anti-religious museum, Donskoy Monastery, Moscow, showing images of resurrection.

p 166   Christadelphian Hall, Shirley, Southampton, photographed by Crawford in the summer of 1934.

p 167   Christadelphian Hall, Shirley, Southampton, photographed by Crawford in September 1934. On the back of the photograph, Crawford has written 'Christadelphians of Southampton are still undecided about Evolution, but quite sure about Jesus Christ and the future'.

p 170   Advertisements, Southampton, 1932, photographed by Crawford and annotated. The Tidworth Tattoo advertised here took place every year at the Tidworth army base on the edge of Salisbury Plain; to Crawford's distaste the Plain, with its rich archaeological heritage, was increasingly used as a military training zone in the early decades of the twentieth century.

p 176   1 St Boniface Terrace, 4 August 1935, identified – possibly wrongly – by Crawford as the bed and breakfast in Ventnor on the Isle of Wight where Marx stayed. Number 1 is on the left.

p 179   41 Maitland Park Road, photographed by Crawford on 17 May 1936. Crawford notes that the plaque, recording Marx's residence and death at this address, was damaged not long after its installation by the London County Council, by fascists who came at 2 a.m. for the purpose. The house was badly damaged in the Blitz and pulled down.

p 180   Headquarters of the British Union of Fascists at 33 King's Road, Chelsea, photographed by Crawford on 21 July, 1934. The latest issue of the *Blackshirt*, the organ of the BUF, is being prominently advertised here, with its headlining article on 'Lord Rothermere and the Blackshirts.' Rothermere, the editor of the *Daily Mail*, had just withdrawn his support for Mosley's party after the BUF rally at Olympia in June.

p 181   Notice in the window of M. Raznick, the butcher's at 37 Charlotte Street, Soho, photographed by Crawford on 13 October 1935.

p 182   Slogan, King Henry's Road, near Chalk Farm, London. Photographed by Crawford on 17 May 1936.

p 183   A street in Wedding, Berlin, on plebiscite day, 19 August 1934. Crawford noted that forty-two flags could be counted here.

p 185   Half-obliterated slogan reading '*Tod den Nazis!*' on a canal bridge, Berlin, photographed by Crawford on plebiscite day, 19 August 1934.

p 196   Advertisements photographed by Crawford in Southampton, 1932. In an annotation in his photograph album, Crawford points out the adverts for 'faked food and drink', including here Krusto (a time-saving pastry mix) and Oxade (instant lemonade). There is also an advert for Pratts Motor Oil, promoting 'a British holiday this year'.

p 200   Sign advertising 'The Grandest Site in Sussex', photographed by Crawford in 1934. This is an example of the sort of 'ribbon development' so disapproved of by the CPRE, where lines of new houses, each with its own garden and garage, are built along main roads. Crawford has written on the back 'Ye olde England and how to improve it'.

p 208   Advertising hoardings, photographed by Crawford on 9 May 1934. On the back of the print Crawford has sarcastically identified the scene as 'View of old cottages and hedge near Southampton'.

p 216   The Dannewerk, at its junction with the rampart of Haithabu, photographed by Crawford in April 1938.

p 223   Some of the finds at Sutton Hoo, photographed by Crawford in the summer of 1939: a bronze cauldron, collapsed; the remains of iron tackle; and a large silver dish, bearing the stamp of the Byzantine emperor Anastasius I.

p 230   O. G. S. Crawford at his desk at the Ordnance Survey, September 1936. The door in the back wall is the 'battery-watch' described by Crawford through which the officer in the next room could communicate with his staff. Crawford's cap – like the one he wore to Russia – is hanging on the back wall.

p 235   Ruins of Portland Baptist Church (1840), Southampton, photographed by Crawford for the National Buildings Record, 1942.

p 236   Inscription found near the old theatre on the west side of French Street, Southampton, photographed by Crawford soon after its discovery for the National Buildings Record, October 1942.

p 236   Nineteenth-century rail-head at 7 Palmerston Road, Southampton, photographed by Crawford in 1942/3 for the National Buildings Record.

p 238   Ancient stone wall incorporated into the modern wall of a store opposite God's House, Southampton, photographed by Crawford in 1942 for the National Buildings Record. The large stone vault beneath the store is being used as a public shelter.

p 240   Volumes of *Antiquity* on the shelves of the library at the Institute of Archaeology, Oxford. Photographed by K. Hauser.

p 243   Everytown, 2036. Film still from H. G. Wells's *Things to Come* (1936). The modern city is built underground.

p 256   'Staring eyes' on kerbstone at passage-tomb, Dowth, Ireland, photographed by Crawford in July 1955 for his book *The Eye Goddess*.

# SOURCES AND SELECT BIBLIOGRAPHY

This book draws on many sources, published and unpublished: limitations of space make it impossible to list them all. What follows is a selective list of sources I have used, including those books to which I am particularly indebted.

**The main sources** used for this book are the archive of Crawford's papers at the Bodleian Library, University of Oxford (MSS. Crawford) and the archive of his photographs in Oxford's Institute of Archaeology. I have also drawn on Crawford's many publications, including *Man and his Past* (Oxford, 1921), *Said and Done: The Autobiography of an Archaeologist* (London, 1955), *Archaeology in the Field* (London, 1953) and many others, most of which are listed in W. F. Grimes, ed., *Aspects of Archaeology in Britain and Beyond: Essays Presented to O. G. S. Crawford* (London, 1951). There is correspondence between Crawford and Alexander Keiller at the Keiller Museum in Avebury. Correspondence with H. G. Wells is in the Rare Book and Special Collections Library at the University of Illinois. The Ordnance Survey personal file on Crawford is held by the National Archives (UK) in Kew, (OS 10/4). A bound typescript of 'A Tour in Bolshevy' is in the Sackler Library in Oxford. The typescript of 'Bloody Old Britain' is in the Bodleian (MS Crawford 109). It was never published, but was known to some of Crawford's associates, including John Betjeman. According to Bevis Hillier's biography, *John Betjeman: New Fame, New Love* (London, 2002), Crawford's book may have been a source for Betjeman's poem 'A Lincolnshire Church', which contains the line 'Dear old, bloody old England'.

**History of Archaeology**: publications from the period include the periodicals *The Antiquaries Journal*, *The Geographical Journal*, *Oxoniensia*, and *The Proceedings of the Field Club of Hampshire* as well as Crawford's own *Antiquity*. For contextualizing the archaeology of the 1920s and 30s among others I have found useful Bruce Trigger, *A History of Archaeological Thought* (Cambridge, 1989), Glyn Daniel, *100 Years of Archaeology* (London, 1950), Glyn Daniel and Christopher Chippindale, eds., *The Pastmasters: 11 Modern Pioneers of Archaeology* (London, 1989) and Richard Hayman, *Riddles in Stone: Myths, Archaeology and the Ancient Britons* (London, 1997). I have also benefited from reading Adam Stout's unpublished BA dissertation, 'What's Real, and What Is Not: Fixing the Boundary between Fringe and Mainstream Archaeology in Britain' (University of Wales, Lampeter), and his PhD thesis, 'Choosing a Past: The Politics of Prehistory in Pre-War Britain' (University of Wales, Lampeter), soon to be published as *Creating Prehistory: Druids, Ley Hunters and Archaeologists in Pre-War Britain*.

**Work about, or memoirs by particular archaeologists** include Glyn Daniel, *Some Small Harvest* (London, 1986); Charles Scott-Fox, *Cyril Fox: Archaeologist Extraordinary* (Oxford, 2002); Lynda J. Murray, *A Zest for Life: The Story of Alexander Keiller* (Wootton Bassett, 1999) and Charles W. Phillips, *My Life in Archaeology* (Gloucester, 1987). Gerhard Bersu's work is described in Christopher Evans, 'Archaeology and Modern Times: Bersu's Woodbury 1938 and 1939', *Antiquity* 63 (1989). Gordon Childe's life and work are outlined in Sally Green, *Prehistorian: A Biography of V. Gordon Childe* (Bradford-on-Avon, 1981) and David R. Harris, ed., *The Archaeology of V. Gordon Childe: Contemporary Perspectives* (London, 1994). The Security Service files on Childe are held by the National Archives (UK) at Kew (KV2/2148–9). These files also monitor Childe's relationship with Bersu and his wife. For Henry Wellcome see Ken Arnold and Danielle Olson, eds., *Medicine Man: The Forgotten Museum of Henry Wellcome* (London, 2003). Little has been written about Crawford himself, apart from J. L. Myres, 'The Man and his Past', in Grimes, ed., *Aspects of Archaeology in Britain and Beyond* (London, 1951) and Mark Bowden, 'Mapping the Past: O. G. S. Crawford and the Development of Landscape Studies', *Landscapes* (Autumn 2001). Geoffrey Grigson's description of Crawford and *Antiquity* is published as 'Reading "Antiquity"' in his book *Recollections: Mainly of Writers and Artists* (London, 1984).

**Aerial Archaeology**. Major Allen's own text on aerial archaeology was published as 'Discovery from the Air' in a special issue of *Aerial Archaeology* (1984); Crawford's 'Archaeology from the Air' appears in Margaret Wheeler, ed., *A Book of Archaeology* (London, 1957). Other works on the history of aerial archaeology include Leo Deuel, *Flights into Yesterday: The Story of Aerial Archaeology* (London, 1971) and Martyn Barber's forthcoming book, *Mata Hari's Glass Eye and Other Tales*. My own *Shadow Sites: Photography, Archaeology and the British Landscape 1927–1955* (Oxford, 2007) has a chapter on aerial archaeology, and a further chapter on Crawford and *Antiquity*.

Studies of **archaeology under the Nazis** include Bettina Arnold, 'The past as propaganda: totalitarian archaeology in Nazi Germany', *Antiquity* 64 (1990); Philip L. Kohl and Clare Fawcett, eds., *Nationalism, Politics, and the Practice of Archaeology* (Cambridge, 1995); and Martin Maischberger, 'German archaeology during the Third Reich, 1933–45: a case study based on archival evidence', *Antiquity* 76 (2002).

The **early twentieth-century folk revival** is analysed in Georgina Boyes' book *The Imagined Village: Culture, Ideology and the English Folk Revival* (Manchester, 1993). Mary Neal is discussed in Roy Judge, 'Mary Neal and the Espérance Morris', *Folk Music Journal* 5:5 (1989).

Works on the **First World War** I have drawn upon include Peter Chasseaud, *Topography of Armageddon: A British Trench Map Atlas of the Western Front 1914–1918* (Lewes, 1991) and *Artillery's Astrologers: A History of British Survey and Mapping on the Western Front 1914–1918* (Lewes, 1999); Lt.-Col. J. H. Lindsay, ed., *The London Scottish in the Great War* (London, 1925); Mark Lloyd, *The London Scottish in the Great War* (Barnsley, 2001); Lt.-Col. F. J. Salmon, 'With the Field Survey Units in France 1915–1919', *Empire Survey Review* (January 1934); and Paul Virilio, *War and Cinema: The Logistics of Perception* (London, 1989).

In addition to the Annual Reports and Professional Papers of the **Ordnance Survey**, I also consulted Roger Hellyer, 'The archaeological and historical maps of the Ordnance Survey', *The Cartographic Journal* (December 1989); Charles W. Phillips, *Archaeology in the Ordnance*

*Survey 1791–1965* (London, 1980) and W. A. Seymour, *A History of the Ordnance Survey* (Folkestone, 1980).

Among many general works on the **culture and politics** of the British interwar period I have found particularly useful John Carey, *The Intellectuals and the Masses* (London, 1992); Valentine Cunningham, *British Writers of the Thirties* (Oxford, 1988); Paul Fussell, *Abroad: British Literary Travelling Between the Wars* (Oxford, 1980); David Matless, *Landscape and Englishness* (London, 1998); David Mellor, ed., *A Paradise Lost: The Neo-Romantic Imagination in Britain 1935–55* (London, 1987); John Sheail, *Rural Conservation in Inter-War Britain* (Oxford, 1981) and Raphael Samuel, 'British Marxist Historians, 1880–1980: Part One', *New Left Review* (March–April 1980). Samuel's *New Left Review* articles on communism in Britain have been reprinted as *The Lost World of British Communism* (London, 2006).

There is, of course, a vast literature on the **Soviet experiment**. Among others, I found useful Martin Amis, *Koba the Dread* (London, 2002); Susan Buck-Morss, *Dreamworld and Catastrophe: The Passing of Mass Utopia in East and West* (Cambridge, Mass., and London, 2000); Robert Conquest, *The Harvest of Sorrow: Collectivization and the Terror Famine* (London, 1986); Stephen Kotkin, *Magnetic Mountain: Stalinism as a Civilization* (Berkeley, 1995); A. C. Sutton, *Western Technology and Soviet Economic Development,* vol. 2 1930–1945 (Stanford, 1971). The attractions of Russia for those in the West are described in David Caute, *The Fellow-Travellers: A Postscript to the Enlightenment* (London, 1973); Paul Hollander, *Political Pilgrims: Travels of Western Intellectuals to the Soviet Union, China and Cuba 1928–1978* (New York, 1981); Malcolm Muggeridge, *The Thirties* (London, 1940) and *Chronicles of Wasted Time* (London, 1972). For **Soviet museums** see Adam Jolles, 'Stalin's Talking Museums', *Oxford Art Journal* (October 2005); Wendy Salmond, 'Some Notes on the Experimental Marxist Exhibition', *X-Tra* 5:1 and Francine Hirsch, 'Getting to Know "The Peoples of the USSR": Ethnographic Exhibits as Soviet Virtual Tourism, 1923–1934', *Slavic Review* (Winter 2003), which is incorporated into her book *Empire of Nations: Ethnographic Knowledge and the Making of the Soviet Union* (Ithaca and London, 2005). Contemporary sources in English include Aleksei Fedorov-Davydov, 'The Soviet Art Museum' [1933], transl.

Wendy Salmond, *X-Tra* 5:1; and Howard Woolston, 'Propaganda in Soviet Russia', *The American Journal of Sociology* (July 1932) which mentions the images of bourgeois interiors shown in Leningrad's Ethnographic Museum. For **Soviet Science and its reception in the West** see Valery N. Soyfer, *Lysenko and the Tragedy of Soviet Science* (New Brunswick, 1994) and Gary Werskey, *The Visible College* (London, 1978). The proceedings of the 1931 Kensington congress, including Vavilov's paper, were published as *Science at the Crossroads* (London, 1931). The Lysenko affair was reported in Julian Huxley, *Soviet Genetics and World Science: Lysenko and the Meaning of Heredity* (London, 1949) and John Langdon-Davies, *Russia Puts the Clock Back: A Study of Soviet Science and Some British Scientists* (London, 1949).

The time spent in Britain by **Karl Marx** is described in Asa Briggs, *Marx in London* (London, 1982); A. E. Laurence and A. N. Insole, *Prometheus Bound: Karl Marx on the Isle of Wight* (Newport, Isle of Wight, undated); Wilhelm Liebknecht, *Karl Marx: Biographical Memoirs* [1901] (London, 1975); and Francis Wheen, *Karl Marx* (London, 1999). Franz Mehring's *Karl Marx: The Story of His Life* (London, 1936) describes how Marx wore out a strip of carpet in his study 'like a footpath over a meadow'. Lenin's time in London is documented in L. Muravyova and I. Sivolap-Kaftanova, *Lenin in London* (Moscow, 1983).

**Charles Babbage's** discussion of 'the Permanent Impression of our Words and Actions on the Globe we Inhabit' is to be found in his 1837 *Ninth Bridgewater Treatise: A Fragment* (London, 1967). Its possible impact on Dickens is suggested in John M. Picker, *Victorian Soundscapes* (New York, 2003).

**Harold and Olive Edwards** are remembered in Anna Horsbrugh-Porter and Marina Aidova, eds., *From Newbury with Love: Letters of Friendship across the Iron Curtain* (London, 2006).

# ACKNOWLEDGEMENTS

I would like to thank most sincerely the staff of the Institute of Archaeology in Oxford, particularly Ian Cartwright, Barry Cunliffe, Helena Hamerow, and Bob Wilkins, now retired; and the staff of Modern Papers at the Bodleian library, especially Colin Harris, for all of their help. Thanks too to the staff of the Hampshire Record Office; Southampton City Council; the Sackler Library in Oxford; English Heritage; the National Archives (UK); Cambridge University Library; Fisher Library and the Schaeffer Library at Sydney University; the Newbury Museum and the Keiller Museum in Avebury. Gould's Book Arcade in Sydney proved as good as any library for its stock of leftist literature of unlimited obscurity. A research fellowship at Clare Hall in Cambridge, and another one at the Power Institute at Sydney University have given me valuable time to think in, and colleagues to talk with. I am very grateful, too, to the Author's Foundation, which awarded me a grant in between those fellowships to write this book. At Granta I'd like to thank Christine Lo, Bella Shand and Sarah Wasley. I would also like to thank the typesetters at M Rules.

A huge number of people have contributed to this book in one way or another, some of them without realizing it. For their input, ideas, expert knowledge and conversation I'd like to thank Mick Carter, Peter Chasseaud, Chris Clark, Jane Garnett, Mina Gorji,

Amanda and Nick Gray, Ian Jeffrey, David Matless and Phil Willkinson; also Matthew Beaumont, Zach Beer, Stefan Collini, Stephen Foster, Chris Gosden, Deborah Harlan, Chris Hilliard, Adam Jolles, Martyn Jolly, Joe Kerr, Ewen McDonald, Arthur MacGregor, Peter Mandler, Susan Norrie, Sophy Rickett, Gervase Rosser, Pamela Jane Smith, Frances Spalding and Adam Stout. For answering my questions about Soviet ships I am grateful to the members of the online Axis History forum. I need hardly add that any mistakes I may have made are my own. I'd also like to thank my family, David Hauser, Margaret Hauser, and Andrew Hauser, and my grandfather, Jack Smethers, who, although he might bristle at the book's title (never mind its contents), was in some ways for me the prototype of its subject – he too sees world history in epic aspect. This book might never have appeared at all without the initial enthusiasm and support of Richard Wentworth, and then of Ian Jack and Liz Jobey at Granta. I was fortunate indeed to have the editorial guidance and sage advice of Ian, who had faith in the idea from the start. Last, and most of all, thanks to Peter Wilson.

All of the images except for those on pp 7, 19, 77, 83, 85, 87, 89, 152, 159, 162, 230, 240 and 243 come from the Crawford archive at the Institute of Archaeology in Oxford, and I am very grateful for permission to reproduce them here. The photograph of Woodhenge on p 83 is reproduced by permission of English Heritage. Major Allen's aerial photographs on pp 85 and 87 are reproduced courtesy of the Visitors of the Ashmolean Museum, Oxford. The photograph of the Cat Stane on p 152 is copyright of the photographer, Julie Howden, and is reproduced courtesy of the *Scotsman*. The photograph of the Donskoy Monastery on p 162 is reproduced courtesy of the Schusev State Museum of Architecture in Moscow. The photograph of Crawford in his office on p 230 is reproduced courtesy of the Bodleian Library (MS Crawford 75; 209). The still from *Things to Come* on p 243 is reproduced by permission of ITV plc (Granada International). For help with obtaining and reproducing images I am grateful to

Amber Dowell, Robert Fellowes, Tony Green and Wendy Salmond. For permission to quote from unpublished papers, thanks to the Bodleian Library, University of Oxford (MSS. Crawford); the National Archives (UK) (OS 10/4, KV2/2148); Amanda Gray; and the Rare Book and Manuscript Library at the University of Illinois (Crawford-Wells correspondence). Unpublished material by Gordon Childe (his correspondence with Crawford) is reproduced by permission of the Bodleian Library (MS Crawford 67) and the Institute of Archaeology, UCL. Quotation from *Mason & Dixon* copyright © 1997 by Thomas Pynchon. Every effort has been made to trace copyright holders where necessary for images and other material reproduced here; the publishers would be happy to hear from anyone who has not been properly acknowledged. This book's title, of course, should be credited as Crawford's.

# INDEX

Numbers in *italics* refer to illustrations.